MOHAMED SHEIKH

AN INDIAN IN THE HOUSE

THE LIVES AND TIMES OF THE FOUR TRAILBLAZERS WHO FIRST BROUGHT INDIA TO THE BRITISH PARLIAMENT

MOHAMED SHEIKH

AN INDIAN IN
THE HOUSE

THE LIVES AND TIMES OF THE FOUR
TRAILBLAZERS WHO FIRST BROUGHT INDIA
TO THE BRITISH PARLIAMENT

Mereo Books

1A The Wool Market Dyer Street Cirencester Gloucestershire GL7 2PR
An imprint of Memoirs Books Ltd. www.mereobooks.com

AN INDIAN IN THE HOUSE

978-1-86151-926-9

First published in Great Britain in 2019
by Mereo Books, an imprint of Memoirs Books Ltd.

Copyright ©2019

Mohamed Sheikh has asserted his right under the Copyright Designs and
Patents Act 1988 to be identified as the author of this work.

The address for Memoirs Books Ltd. can be
found at www.mereobooks.com

Memoirs Books Ltd. Reg. No. 7834348

Typeset in 11/17pt Century Schoolbook
by Wiltshire Associates Ltd.
Printed and bound in Great Britain by Biddles Books

This book is dedicated to my late father, Mohamed Abdullah Sheikh, and my late mother, Kalsum Ara Sheikh, who both immensely influenced my life.

CONTENTS

Acknowledgments
Introduction
About the author

◦❯❯◦ PART I ◦❯❯◦
DADABHAI NAOROJI - THE GRAND OLD MAN OF INDIA

◦❯❯◦ PART II ◦❯❯◦
SIR MANCHERJEE BHOWNAGGREE - THE FIRST INDIAN CONSERVATIVE

◦❯❯◦ PART III ◦❯❯◦
SHAPURJI SAKLATVALA - THE MIDDLE-CLASS COMMUNIST

◦❯❯◦ PART IV ◦❯❯◦
BARON SINHA OF RAIPUR - A BRILLIANT AND DEDICATED STATESMAN

The author with the paintings of Dadabhai Naoroji, Sir Mancherjee Bhownaggree and Shapurji Saklatvala which hang in the House of Commons

Acknowledgements

I would like to thank two former journalists, Ms Anusua Mukherjee and Mr Sunanda Datta-Ray, and two writers, Omar Ralph and Marc Wadsworth, for their assistance in researching and compiling material for this book. I should also like to thank Mr Jim Wadia for his kind help in providing additional information on Sir Mancherjee Bhownaggree. A list of the books and other sources which have provided most of the information in this book is given in the bibliography.

Introduction

For more than three centuries, from the East India Company's first trade missions to Asia until the long-awaited granting of independence in 1947, India was controlled and exploited by the British Empire. Indians were not considered fit to have a say in the running of their own country, let alone to be given any measure of political power. Over the final decades of the 19th century and the first decades of the 20th, four men helped to change that forever: Dadabhai Naoroji, Mancherjee Bhownaggree, Shapurji Saklatvala and Satyendra Sinha. These men were the first four Indians to achieve Parliamentary office in the United Kingdom, the first three as MPs, all for different parties, the last as a hereditary Peer who attained a ministerial office in Westminster.

While you could scarcely find four more contrasting personalities, they had several vital points in common: all four men loved and fought for their country, all four shared a passion for justice and equity, and all four were highly motivated and fiercely intelligent. Between them they earned India, and Indians, a long-overdue respect in the West, and opened the door for many of their countrymen to be welcomed into the ranks of government in their wake, including the author. This book tells their stories, and is a tribute by the author, Lord Sheikh, to the four trailblazers who first brought India to the British Parliament.

About the author

Mohamed Sheikh, Baron Sheikh of Cornhill in the City of London, was born in Kenya and brought up in Uganda, his parents originating from the sub-continent of India. He chairs businesses in the financial services and property sectors and has long been a leading figure in the insurance industry, and he also has an academic background. He and his company have received numerous awards and accolades and he is particularly involved in promoting inter-faith dialogue and undertaking humanitarian work. He has travelled widely overseas and has been awarded an Honorary Doctorate for his community work worldwide. He can best be described as a businessman, philanthropist, academic and a writer.

Lord Sheikh is a Conservative Member of the House of Lords and participates regularly in Parliamentary activities, holding senior positions in several All-Party Parliamentary Groups.

He was made a Life Baron in 2006 and is a Freeman of the City of London. He founded and funds a registered personal and family charity, the Sheikh Abdullah Foundation, in his father's memory.

This is Lord Sheikh's second book. His first, *Emperor of the Five Rivers* (2017), is an acclaimed account of the life of Maharajah Ranjit Singh, a 19th century leader of the Sikh Empire, who became a seminal figure in Indian history. The book was well received, and all proceeds were donated to a charity looking after orphans. Lord Sheikh is now working on his third book, a historical novel. All proceeds from *An Indian in the House* will be donated to St Christopher's Hospice.

About St Christopher's Hospice

St Christopher's was founded in 1967 as the world's first modern hospice in Sydenham, South East London, by Dame Cicely Saunders (whom the author has met). St Christopher's vision is of a world in which all dying people and those close to them have access to care and support, whenever and wherever they need it. Every year the hospice provides this care and support to over 6,500 people across south-east London, both in the community and at the hospice, meeting social, emotional and spiritual needs, as well as managing physical symptoms. The hospice provides specialised training for people working in end-of-life care and bereavement locally, nationally and internationally, to improve and develop hospice care. St Christopher's Hospice is a charity, and its continued work is only made possible by generous donations from everyone.

PART I

Dadabhai Naoroji
1825-1917
The Grand Old Man of India

Dadabhai Naoroji, the first Indian to win a seat in the House of Commons, rose from the humblest beginnings in a suburb of Bombay to become a tireless fighter for Indian independence and fair treatment by Britain and a towering figure in his country's history. His brilliant mind and dogged determination enabled him to unravel British claims of India's fair treatment and set the stage for an irresistible move towards independence. He is still remembered and revered, more than a century after his death, as the Grand Old Man of India.

CHAPTER 1

The boy who became 'the promise of India'

At the beginning of the 19th century, India was a land long divided and weakened by internal conflict, a country which had been largely controlled by a foreign business enterprise for the best part of two hundred years. There was still another century and a half to go before it would finally achieve throw off the shackles of the British Empire and achieve the status of sovereign nation.

In the wake of Aurangzeb, the last of the great Mughal emperors (1658-1707), the lack of a strong unifying force had left the country to flounder through a century of uncertainty and disunity, so much so that the historian and author Jadunath Sarkar remarked that India was 'truly spent' as a country. This weakness was handsomely exploited by the

British East India Company, which, during the 17th and 18th centuries, stepped in to take control ahead of rival European countries and to restore order and trade progressively as the old regimes collapsed. In the process it made many men rich, while mercilessly taking advantage of India and its people and stripping the country of countless irreplaceable assets. "The Company's servants plundered and oppressed the country's possessions without disguise or shame," as Penderel Moon put it in his 1945 book *Strangers in India*.

By the second half of the 18th century the company had become a military force as well as an economic one and was building an army which would eventually be 280,000 strong, although it could never entirely subdue, nor effectively manage, a country of 250 million people spread over several religions, more than 20 languages and over three million square kilometres. India was in truth being exploited on a scale which was more spectacular – and more shameless – than the world has seen before or since.

Fortunately, as the century wore on, a degree of enlightenment began to dawn among India's conquerors. Warren Hastings' governor-generalship (1772-85) was hardly unblemished – he was impeached for a number of alleged crimes, although eventually acquitted – but it was under his rule that the largely forgotten cultural heritage of ancient India began to re-emerge from the shadows. The Indian people themselves were largely unaware of the *Bhagavad Gita*, the celebrated work of Hindu religious philosophy which dates back to long before the birth of Christ. It was Hastings' decision to have its 700 verses translated from the original Sanskrit into English, and in the process the East, as well as the West, began to appreciate its huge significance. As Kusoom Vadgama put it in her book

India, the *Bhagavad Gita* "awakened the Indian people to the magnificence of their lost heritage... from this was to spring Indian self-awareness and cultural pride: seedbeds of an emerging political identity".

The British Government became increasingly uncomfortable with the East India Company's growing size and power and its almost entirely commercial motivation, and eventually it began to take control, bringing it into the ownership of the British Empire. Having lost its independence to a business, India was now under the rule of another country which initially did little more than continue the exploitation.

In 1813 the Government imposed an updated version of its original 1793 Charter which withdrew the East India Company's trade monopoly. At the next renewal in 1833, the Government would explicitly rule against discrimination, but in the meantime the 'natives' were considered, and treated, as inferior in every respect.

Such was the situation when Dadabhai Naoroji was born, on September 4 1825, in Khadak in the fishing village of Mandvi, a few miles south of Bombay (Mumbai). His father, Naoroji Palanji Dordi, a Parsi and a Zoroastrian priest, was a member of the Athornan line of the Dordis, a group within the Parsis. The word *dordi* literally means a rope made of twisted coir, and Dadabhai once said, "You may burn a dordi, but you can never take the twist out of it. So it is with me. When once I form a decision, nothing will dislodge me from it". Events were to bear out these words.

Little is known in detail about Dadabhai's early years, as sadly, a large quantity of papers relating to this period years have been lost. They became worm-eaten and were destroyed by the Bombay Improvement Trust when they acquired his house after his last move to England. According to *The Twist in The Rope*, a study of Naoroji by the Parsi author Farrokh Vajifdar, in accordance with a Hindu belief and an astrology chart, the name of Dadabhai was communicated to his parents by a fairy godmother who invisibly visited the household on the sixth day after he was born, the *chatthi*, and forecast that he would achieve fame. *Dada* means elder or father, while the suffix *bhai* implies a close comrade or brother.

Unfortunately Dadabhai's father died when he was four, and the boy was brought up, an only child, by his mother Manekbhai, described by Vajifdar as his "constant and devoted companion, nurse, teacher, guardian angel and good genius of his life for over fifty years". Dadabhai's biographer R P Masani[1] stated that she had remarkable natural intelligence, and was, according to Dadabhai, his "constant companion, nurse, teacher, guardian angel, all in one". He wrote about her later: "Widowed when I, her only child, was an infant, she voluntarily remained a widow, wrapped up in me, her everything in the world... Although illiterate, she was a wise mother. She kept a firm hand upon me. She was the wise counsellor of the neighbourhood. She helped me with all her heart in my work for female education and other social reforms, against prejudices of the day, she made me what I am."

Naoroji's family could trace their family tree through a line of priests all the way back to Zarthost Mobed (Mobed or Mobad means 'priest'), who settled in the port of Navsari, north of Bombay, in about 1200 AD. Navsari means 'New Sari'; Sari was the town in northern Iran where the family came from, because it had a similar climate. It became

---

1   Dadabhai Naoroji, Grand Old Man of India (see bibliography)

the main stronghold of the Parsi priesthood. If Dadabhai's father had lived, he would presumably have expected him to become the ninth priest in the family line, as passing on this rank was a duty rather than an option. As it was, while Dadabhai must have received some infant indoctrination in the Zoroastrian faith before he lost his father, it was left to his mother to continue her child's religious instruction, and the priesthood never claimed him.

The Parsis (the word originally meant 'Persians') are a cultured, fair-skinned people descended from Persian Zoroastrians who emigrated to India around the 9th century AD to avoid religious persecution. Having initially settled in Gujarat on the west coast, they were driven further south and most Indian Parsis settled in the area around Bombay (Mumbai), where their descendants live to this day, with some smaller groups in other cities. Here they tended to take up rural occupations, typically farming or fishing, for a living. Their skills enabled many of them to operate successful businesses when the British brought in new commercial ventures during the nineteenth century, and the area became relatively prosperous. In common with other coastal regions of southern India, it was and is fertile and productive, in contrast to vast swathes of the hot, arid interior. The Parsis continue to form a well-defined community in India.

Zoroastrianism, one of the world's oldest religions, embraces 'Humata, Hukhta, Huvarshta', or 'good thoughts, good words and good deeds'. Adherents worship a single deity, Ahura Mazda or Hormuzd. They pursue the path of truth and righteousness, respect the natural world and do not put pressure on others to adopt their faith. They are also devoted to the pursuit of knowledge and wisdom. In many respects Zoroastrianism is parallel to other faiths, including Christianity, with judgment and resurrection, angels and demons, heaven and hell, the purity of fire and the opportunity for salvation through good works.

Zoroastrian belief stems from a body of writing called the *Avesta* (which has its own exclusive language, Avestan) and in particular the 'Gathas' or sayings of the prophet Zoroaster, which are expressed in 17 hymns. No doubt Dadabhai was well tutored in the Gathas from an early age. Fire would have had a particular significance in his home, as with all Parsis, because its significance for purification meant that fires were kept in homes as well as in all Zoroastrian temples. He said later that tales of Persian folk heroes and readings of the *Shahnama* (Book of Kings – an epic poem about the history of Persia) in his early life retained their significance for him as he grew up, and he kept a list of the duties of the Zoroastrians beside him throughout his life.

Naoroji was among those Parsis who made it clear that they were Indians first and Parsis second, in contrast to adherents of some of the more fundamental faiths. He maintained this stance throughout his life, once stating: "Whether I am a Hindu, a Mohammedan, a Parsi, a Christian or of any other creed, I am above all an Indian. Our country is India; our nationality is Indian."

In 1824, Bombay having become a prosperous centre for maritime trade and commerce, an English school was set up for native children by a body called the Bombay Native Education Society; this was not without opposition from Britain, where many still felt that native Indians did not need education. Three years later a resolution was passed to set up a new centre of learning, to be called Elphinstone College, after the Hon. Mountstuart Elphinstone, the departing Governor of Bombay. Money was collected by public subscription to fund teaching professorships in the English language and the arts, science, and the literature of Europe. The classes began at the Town Hall in 1836, initially with just two professors, Arthur Bedford Orlebar (Natural Philosophy) and John Harkness (General Literature). In 1840, the professors' classes were amalgamated with the Society's High School to form the Elphinstone Native Education Institution. In 1845, the name was shortened to the Elphinstone Institution. Elphinstone College became a distinct body, separate from the high school, on 1 April 1856, and in 1860 it was affiliated to the University of Bombay.

Dadabhai's early years would have been typical of those of any Indian boy of his generation, simple and entirely lacking in luxury. The absence of a father no doubt made life all the harder, and it is unlikely that he or his mother would have been aware of or much concerned about the wider world

Elphinstone College

he was growing up into, or of India's troubled history, until later.

Dadabhai's education began at his local village school alongside other young children from the area. According to Vajifdar, his good fortune was to be talent-spotted by an assistant professor, Bal Gangadhar Shastri, who persuaded his mother to send him as an 'exhibition boy' to the new English school, paid for by the school. This was a life-changing opportunity for Dadabhai. For a boy from such a poor background, a good education was his only chance to earn a decent living so that he could look after himself and his mother, who could certainly not have paid for any kind of schooling.

Dadabhai, who described himself as a 'regular exhibition boy' at his school, was taught Mathematics and Natural Science by Professor Bell and English Literature and Philosophy by Professor Harkness, a Scot. "Eager of mind and willing of heart, the teenage Dadabhai learned to commune with the best minds of his day, and everything noble in him was kindled by the study of the lives and labours of the world's heroes," wrote Farrokh Vajifdar. "His fellow students recalled him with awe and affection. In appearance he was handsome, with singularly bright impish eyes, wide set, with calm yet penetrating gaze. A prominent, broad forehead, a fine aquiline Parsi nose and large ears complete the picture of a man of slim build, agile and alert in his movements. He sported the then customary moustache and neat beard which in later years proliferated... in character and demeanour he was upright and estimable. Early indications of a remarkable vigour of intellect, clarity of thought and quick judgement were discernible to his teachers, who thought him the perfect gentleman."

A note of amused vanity appears in an account of his life he wrote for a journal called M.A.P. in 1904. He wrote: "Owing to the fairness of my complexion, and I think I may say, the prettiness of my little limbs, I was always an object of show at weddings, processions, etc, generally appearing as an English general or admiral or in some gorgeous Indian Royal or Court dress brocade. Fond parents and friends of the child thus exhibited used to say of him: 'Oh, he is my dear *Jonglo* (Englishman)!' Little did I dream then that I should spend much of my manhood and older life in the country of the *Jonglos* and don their dress in reality".[2]

R P Masani describes him thus when in his teens: "In appearance he was handsome, with singularly bright eyes; in his movements agile and alert; in character and demeanour, upright and estimable. Academic honours crowned his career, giving unmistakeable indication of remarkable vigour of intellect and clearness of thought and judgment."

It seems that Dadabhai's story-telling ability and talent for leadership marked him out for success early on. These qualities made him 'a leader among the boys', and he 'acquired a self-confidence and reliance that come with such a position' as he put it later. He wrote that his teacher allowed the boys to do what they wanted for the first year at the new school (the classes had been divided between two teachers, the other being a strict disciplinarian – Dadabhai was lucky), but after that academic achievement was at the top of his agenda. He developed great determination and perseverance. Mrs Marianne Postans, in her book *Western India* (1858), has this to say about the people of Bombay at the time:

"The native society is elevating itself by means of newly-acquired intelligence to a point which must soon lead to the desirable object of mutual appreciation between European and native talent; and a desire on the part of the most intelligent among the people that their sons should obtain, by means of an English education, similar information to that which, through the medium of unreserved intercourse with us, they discover we possess. The groundwork for so desirable a superstructure as the perfect civilization of the native gentry is already laid by the college and schools which have lately been so warmly protected by the general society of Bombay... The work of improvement has been gradually, but surely, progressing, and the tone of society is changed. The native gentry now form a recognised and important part of the community; their sons are educated to fit them for any mercantile or political appointment to which they may be called; the English merchants are daily considered as forming a more valuable class."

On the subject of Elphinstone College and the native school, Mrs Postans wrote:

"These institutions are at present the great fountains from which it may be expected that the blessings of education will flow for the people of Western India... The Native Education Society's Schools are situated near the great bazaars, at the extreme end of the esplanade. Committees and examinations are held in the library, a splendid apartment fitted with a good collection of useful works, with globes, maps and papers, and adorned at either end with full-length portraits of the great benefactors of the institution."

Some 400 boys were admitted to the schools altogether, with a further 1500 in branch and infant schools connected with the institution, the only qualification for admission being a knowledge of the vernacular dialect. Eighteen scholarships were available, carrying with them a grant of ten rupees a month. There were strict rules regarding who was and was not allowed admission. The sons of tradesmen were inadmissible, or 'any below the caste of a *purvoe*, or writer'. Half castes were also excluded. This system seemed unavoidable, given that the 'wealthy and influential' would inevitably withdraw their sons if such boys were allowed admission.

Mrs Postans attended an examination of boys and young men from seven to 20 years old, and reported: "In accepting an invitation to attend a private examination of the scholars, I expected the display of some tolerable acquaintance with the English language, and the simple rudiments of education; I was wholly unprepared, therefore, for the scene which awaited me. The ancient learning for which India was once so celebrated, seemed about to be renewed; and the graceful and intelligent youths around us, destined to prove the restorers of arts and wisdom, such as in ancient days illumined the archives of this long-neglected land, which once shone amongst the nations of the world."

One of the students was Dadabhai Naoroji, and she gives us the first description of him:

"A little lad of seven years of age, with an overhanging forehead, and small sparkling eyes, peculiarly attracted our attention; the moment a question was proposed to the class, he quickly took a step before the rest, contracted his brows in deep and anxious thought, and with parted lips and finger eagerly uplifted towards the master, silently but rapidly worked his problem in a manner peculiar to himself, and blurted out the solution with a startling haste, half painful, half ludicrous. The little fellow seemed wholly animated with the desire of excelling, and his mental capabilities promised him a rich reward. By birth he was a Parsi, and it is remarked that even at an early age, lads of this class display a capacity for calculation, and mercantile pursuits, which accompany them through life... It was interesting to observe the good feeling which appeared to exist among the scholars. It was impossible to discover any jealous expression, when another took the highest position in a class; on the contrary, every eye beamed satisfaction when the truth had been discovered by any, and all seemed equally and sincerely gratified at the praises bestowed on the correct demonstration."

Dadabhai excelled at sport as well as in the classroom, and was often to be seen playing *pakardao*, or catch-as-catch-can, or *gillidanda*[3], Indian cricket, as it is otherwise known, a game which uses batons rather than balls and still survives today. He wrote that there was no enforcement of lessons, so he had often looked about for something to do. "I had a retentive memory and I could repeat any story I heard both spirit and in letter, and I was full of stories," he wrote in the M.A.P. article. "Most of my school hours were spent in spinning yarns to an admiring circle of school-fellows. So lax was discipline that often we would coolly march out of school and spend the whole day in games."

While he was no swot or teacher's pet, he seems to have made a clear decision early in boyhood not to descend to the level of some of the street urchins he played with. Vajifdar wrote: "He firmly set his mind against any temptation to follow suit; in fact through his life he abhorred the all-too-frequent use of obscenities among the lower strata." Dadabhai himself recalled that whenever a boy used bad language to him, he would reply, "Your bad words will

---

3   Gilli danda or gillidanda is thought to date back over 2500 years, but it is still popular today on the sub-continent – you can even play it on line.

remain in your mouth". He wrote: "I remember as if it were only yesterday how at a certain spot on a certain road I made a vow never to use low language. From that time forward, as my education advanced, other resolutions to do this and not to do that followed, and I think I may say that I faithfully adhered to them."

Clearly he found the time to study enthusiastically despite the demands on the family, and he certainly received the full support of his mother. In 1904 he wrote: "There is one whom if she comes last in this narrative, has ever been first of all, my mother. She voluntarily remained a widow (for almost 50 years), wrapped up in me, her everything in the world... Although illiterate and although all love for me, she was a wise woman. She was the wise counsellor of the neighbourhood. She helped me with all in her heart in her work for female education and other social reforms against prejudices of the day. She made me what I am."[4]

In keeping with custom, Dadabhai was betrothed at the age of eleven, to seven-year-old Gulbai, the daughter of a local man, Sorabjee Shroff. Ultimately this would prove far from a marriage made in heaven, as will emerge later.

It is clear that the death of Naoroji Palanji Dordi did not prevent his son from continuing to prepare for the priesthood, because we know that at 14 Dadabhai underwent the Navar ceremony, an initiation procedure which was a stage on the route to becoming a priest. However this appears to have been the closest he got to the priesthood.

In 1840 Dadabhai received the Clare Scholarship, and two years later he was admitted to the new 'class of normal scholars'. He soon became the shining light of the Elphinstone Institution. He went on to pass his exams with distinction in

4   Vajifdar/Ralph

1845, aged 19, making him part of the new intelligentsia of Bombay, and he now came to the attention of the outside community for the first time. Professor Orlebar at the Elphinstone Institution prophetically described him as "the promise of India". Sir Erskine Perry, the Chief Justice of Bombay and President of the Board of Education, noted his exceptional intelligence and fluent speech and suggested that he should be sent to Britain to study for the Bar. Sir Erskine even volunteered to pay half the costs of this if the Parsi community would pay the other half. However, the Parsi community was highly sceptical. Christian missionaries had been going to great lengths to convert Parsis in Bombay to their faith, and a few years before, by bribing the students with free teaching in return for their agreement to engage in Christian studies, they had suborned two young men, Dhunjiboy Naoroji and Hormusji Pestonji (the former was so successfully converted that he moved to Britain to study theology in Edinburgh and became a vicar in Staffordshire). The furore over this took years to abate. The Parsis were determined not to lose any more of their young students in this way, and accordingly they firmly vetoed Sir Erskine's proposal. This left Dadabhai with a conflict of loyalties, and he decided to stay in India; a sad loss to the legal profession no doubt, but a decision which would change history.

He had an avid appetite for reading, and according to Omar Ralph's detailed biography *Naoroji, The First Asian MP*, he was influenced at this time by two books in particular; one by Thomas Clarkson, the anti-slavery campaigner, on the slave trade and the other by John Howard, the 18th century philanthropist. In later years he wrote: "In reality [remaining in India] had been the best thing that could have happened. Otherwise I would have been bound to the narrow outlook of a subordinate Government Official Servant".

For the time being, Dadabhai decided to continue in education. He rejoined the Elphinstone Institution as Head Native Assistant Master in Mathematics and Natural Philosophy. By the age of 25 he was Assistant Professor, and by 1853, aged 28, he had become Professor of Mathematics and Natural Philosophy, the first 'native' to achieve the rank of professor. Professor Harkness, the Principal, called him 'an intelligent and zealous Native Professor'. His love of mathematical precision would mark his later work far from the classroom. Biographer Masani wrote later, "None who came under his spell could forget his winning simplicity, charm of manner and unfailing courtesy".

Outside the classroom Dadabhai was involved with the Parsi Gymnasium, one of a number that had been set up. He was also a member of the Widows' Marriage Association, founded to gain acceptance for the marriage of widows. Does this imply that he wanted his own mother to remarry? She certainly never did so.

It was at this time that Dadabhai first became involved in the social reform which would form the central thread of his life. Under a Professor Patton he set up a 'Students' Literary and Scientific Society' at the Elphinstone Institution. After hearing a college presentation in 1849 on the subject of female education, he became involved in a group which began to campaign for this revolutionary change. He visited local homes to offer to teach the 'three Rs' to the daughters of the household, with mixed responses. Pupils were conspicuous by their absence at first, but gradually the people of Bombay got the message and their young women began to present themselves for education. At first the Society arranged lessons in its members' own homes free of charge, but a school dedicated to female education opened in 1849 and four more soon followed, catering for a total of 371 pupils. Four Parsis in particular came forward to offer financial help; they were all members of the Cama family. The opposition rumbled on; *The Chabuk* ('whip') newspaper described it as an attempt to introduce 'English language and English manners' and to enable women to 'make slaves of their husbands'. Yet change was now afoot in Indian society, and no one could reverse the tide.

In August 1851, still only 25, Dadabhai, with Naoroji Fardoonji, founded a society called Rahnuma-e Mazdayasnan Sabha ('society for the guidance of true believers'), to expound the true tenets of the Zoroastrian creed and 'restore the Zarthosti religion to its pristine purity and simplicity'. More colourfully, they wanted to try to 'rout the hideous army of foreign godlings', according to Masani. Dadabhai and his friends were very conscious of how far their religion had departed from the original after centuries of being passed down through the oral tradition. The group was successful; "the religion of Zarathustra was weaned from most of the alien accretions", as Masani put it. Dadabhai himself recalled that the struggle had not been easy. "In the beginning, what vicissitudes did we go through!" he wrote in a thank-you letter to Kharshedji Cama. "What continuous struggles against opposition has the Society tried to make!" The society flourished, and Dadabhai would live to see its diamond jubilee in 1911.

By this time Dadabhai was making plans to harness the power of the press to help in the fight for the social and national causes he cared so deeply about. At that time there were five Parsi-owned Gujarati newspapers in Bombay, each with its own self-serving viewpoint and its own axe to grind. He felt the need for an independent title which would speak up for the people of Bombay. Helped behind the scenes by his friend Kharshedji Nasarwanji Cama, who provided both advice and money, the inaugural edition of *Rast Goftar* (truth teller) hit the streets on November 15 1851. The news at this time was filled with reports of a violent uprising by Moslems against Parsis because of what they perceived as insults against Muhammad in a local magazine. Accordingly the first three issues were devoted to discussion of the violence, which left many dead and wounded. *Rast Goftar* criticised the police for their hostility towards the Parsis, stating "...during the last two months justice has gone to rest and aggression has had its free innings". The paper quickly gained a reputation as a champion of truth and justice, and became increasingly influential. From January 1852 it became a weekly.

On a more peaceful note, Dadabhai continued to write prolifically on subjects such as natural philosophy and astronomy, mainly for *Dnyan Prasarak* magazine, which he edited, and *Samachar Darpan*, a Gujarati daily. His efforts were certainly appreciated by the *Hindustan Review* sixty years later: "If today the vernacular press of Bombay is the best conducted and most successful in the country, if today female education is more advanced in Bombay than even in Calcutta, Madras or Delhi, if today there is a richer literature in Gujarati than in any other Indian vernacular (other than perhaps Bengali), if today social reform and progress have made greater strides in the western presidency than in the rest of India, it is greatly due to the motivation, devotion and self-sacrificing labours and youthful energies of Dadabhai Naoroji."

Pride of place in Dadabhai's youthful library was the

Shahnameh (Book of Kings) mentioned earlier, an epic poem (50,000 couplets) by Firdausi (or Ferdowsi) around 1000 AD. This Islamic masterpiece relates the history of the Persian Empire and traces the origins of Zoroastrianism, and is one of the most valued, and valuable, ancient works of writing in existence[5]. The Shahnameh is of central importance in Persian culture and is accepted as defining the cultural identity of Iran, Afghanistan and Tajikistan. It traces the historical links between the beginnings of Zoroastrianism and its extinction in Persia following the Islamic conquest in the 7th century AD.

Dadabhai "was powerfully attracted and deeply impressed by the moral purpose, high idealism and timeless sense of justice which ran throughout the work" according to Vajifdar. Although the provisions of the Charter of 1833 appeared to open the way for much greater equality across India, in practice the East India Company was still run and controlled by the British in much the same old way: "There was an unwritten policy which excluded the natives" as Omar Ralph put it. Fears that the next Charter, due in 1853, would perpetuate the problem for yet another twenty years led to much debate, and specifically to the formation in 1852 of the Bombay Association. Indians were now increasingly resenting the control exerted over their country by a foreign power, particularly now that they were apparently being treated as a business subsidiary.

At the inauguration of the association in 1853, Dadabhai took his first step into the political arena by making a speech. He stated later: "When I made my first little speech at the inauguration of the Bombay Association in perfect

---

5   In 2006 a single sheet from one of the few extant copies of the
     Shahnameh sold for £904,000.

innocence of heart, influenced by my English education into great admiration for the character, instincts and struggles for liberty of the British people, I expressed my faith and confidence in the British rulers... such was my faith. It was the faith of the educated of the time." He complained that in their ignorance of India and its people, European officers tended to pass laws or regulations 'injurious to the nation' without realising it. He called for facts, and suggested that the Association should appoint people to tour the country and report on the status of the people.

Dadabhai appreciated from an early age the intrinsic British devotion to fairness and justice and refused to lose his faith in it throughout his life, despite many disappointments. His willingness to trust the British to play a positive rule in India's future made his protests about their misrule seem all the more reasonable. As Masani put it: "He believed... that the interests of the Indian people and the British people were essentially the same and that the continuance of the British connection could be made to conform to the best interests of India. It is necessary to hold these root principles of Dadabhai's political creed steadfastly before our eyes, if we would appreciate correctly the spirit of his agitation throughout his whole life".

In 1853 the India Reform Society was founded in London, with the aim of getting Indians admitted to the Indian Civil Service, which does not sound like an unreasonable expectation. The Government took little or no notice.

When Dadabhai heard about the oppression by the Islamic state of the 25,000 or so Zoroastrians remaining in Persia (modern-day Iran), he helped to set up a fund to provide education facilities, repair religious centres and provide help to old people.

Despite his public activities Dadabhai found time to devote himself to study, and he learned French, Persian, Hindustani, Gujarati and Marathi, the predominant language of Maharashtra, the state where Bombay is located. Later he said: "The six or seven years before I eventually came to England were full of all sorts of reforms, social, educational, political, religious etc... movements on foot and institution inaugurated by a band of young men fresh from college... Such were the first fruits of the English education given us at the Elphinstone College."

England was Dadabhai's next big adventure, and his decision to move there would have deep consequences for the rest of his life and for the future of the Indian people.

Naoroji in maturity

CHAPTER 2

A Parsi in England

By the 1830s a steady trickle of Indians had begun to settle in Britain, all driven by the desire for education, training or learning of some kind. In 1855 two brothers who were friends of Dadabhai, Kharshedji Rustomji and Muncherji or Mancherjee Hormusji Cama, issued an invitation to him which would change his life: the opportunity to accompany them to England to help them set up the first Indian-owned UK company, which would be involved in import and export. Apparently the link with the Cama family went back to Dadabhai's boyhood years, when a member of the family provided some of his schoolbooks.[6] The decision to move from mathematics to merchandise did not go down well with Dadabhai's beloved teacher Professor Harkness, who allegedly exclaimed "What a fall!"

6   Vajifdar

Dadabhai's decision to exchange his academic and political career back home for a commercial enterprise in England came as a shock to most who knew him. In his own words, he was "desirous of seeing an intimate connexion established between England and India and "to provide a home for young Indians so that they might freely go to England to compete for the Indian Civil Service and other services". It is clear that he never intended to spend long in a business career, and that the needs of his motherland were overwhelmingly the major force that drove him.

Travelling to England from India was a considerable undertaking at that time, involving a journey of several weeks over land and sea. On June 27 1855, at the age of 29, Dadabhai set sail from Bombay Docks on board the P&O ship *Madras*, travelling overland from Suez to Alexandria, where he boarded the *Sultan*, which finally docked in Southampton on August 22. He was accompanied by the two Cama brothers. The three men were to share a house in London, though it seems from his correspondence with Kharshedji Cama that Dadabhai spent much of his time in Liverpool, where most of the cotton business was based. The constitution of the company was very simple – no action was to be taken unless all three partners were in agreement, and any matter of dispute would be referred to the head office in Bombay. This sounds like a recipe for hopeless indecision, but they clearly got on well enough to run a successful business together, at least at first, despite inevitable conflicts of opinion from time to time (there is a saying that when three Parsis come together, you will get four different opinions).

Unfortunately there were some more fundamental differences between the three men. Mancherjee Cama was a more hard-headed businessman than either his brother or

Dadabhai, and he apparently complained to the head office in Bombay that they had given him a 'a pair of philosophers instead of traders' and that their principles of commercial morality were not beneficial to the firm's interests. For example, when Dadabhai checked the length of cotton on 100-yard reels, he found there was only 80 yards. Mancherjee apparently considered this normal practice, but his partners disagreed. However, head office sided with Mancherjee, to the distress of Dadabhai. So ultimately did Kharshedji, the man who had so generously sponsored Dadabhai in Bombay.

A bigger problem was the partnership's trade in opium, wines and spirits. Opium was still a legally trafficked substance, but Dadabhai would not agree to trading materials which led to the degradation of so many through hard drugs, or indeed wines and spirits. His biographer R P Masani described him as 'A philosopher-trader who startled his partners by his idealism in business, a patriot who was more concerned with the prestige and welfare of his company than with profits'.[7]

The trio certainly did not abandon their Zoroastrian way of life; they imported a Parsi cook and a waiter to look after them in the traditional manner. At first Dadabhai continued to wear his traditional Indian garb; he is reported to have customarily worn "a costume of his own devising: a long broadcloth coat buttoned all the way up, a white silk kerchief worn around the shirt collar and passed through a plain gold ring, black trousers and a black light velvet cap with a blue silk tassel" (Vajifdar). His staff and helpers dressed similarly. However as time went on he adopted the British style of dress while in Britain, and this set an example to other visiting Indians.

7   Masani

In 1856 Dadabhai was made Professor of Gujarati at University College, London, the first Indian to attain such a post in Britain. It seems unlikely that the position involved very much work during his early years of tenure, as he was kept occupied full-time with his business and social interests, but he continued in the post for the next ten years.[8]

Dadabhai continued to work with the Camas until 1858, when there finally came an amicable parting over their differences of principle, and he returned to India. Kharshedji left the partnership at the same time, or soon after. The men agreed to differ and shook hands on it, and Dadabhai's friendship with the family remained strong.

Dadabhai's time in Britain had opened his eyes to the way the West lived. He had seen England and its people and obtained an insight into their culture and political system which would never have been possible without the commercial venture the Cama brothers had involved him in. He had witnessed the speeches of Liberal reformers Richard Cobden and John Bright and a young William Gladstone and had the opportunity to read John Stuart Mill and Thomas Carlyle. In a time of great political change, England was the perfect place to learn about politics and parliaments. He admired the British sense of justice and fair play and felt sure he could take advantage of it to further his cause.

In 1857, during Dadabhai's first period in England, came the Indian Rebellion or Indian Mutiny, provoked by increasing resentment over several aspects of the East India Company's approach to government, including British social reforms, land taxes and the scornful treatment of landowners and princes. Dadabhai could only listen with disquiet to the news of the rebellion as it reached Britain, though he

8   Hinnells

was reassured by Queen Victoria's 1858 proclamation of equality for Indians and her promise to "respect the rights and dignity and honour of native princes" (He would have reason to remind Her Majesty of that promise later). In fact the rebellion, which "sent a thrill of horror from one end of the United Kingdom to the other",[9] was the crisis the British Government needed to finally accept that it could not run India like a business subsidiary. Though the rebellion was by no means universally backed by the Indian people and was ultimately suppressed, it finally led to the dissolution of the East India Company, after two and a half centuries, by means of the Government of India Act. Henceforth India would be controlled directly by the British Raj.

The Prime Minister at the time was Viscount Palmerston, one of the longest-serving statesmen in history and acclaimed for his skill in foreign affairs, serving three times as Foreign Secretary before he became Prime Minister. Palmerston headed the first Liberal government from 1859, when the party was formally created. Liberal in style as well as in politics, despite having originally been a Conservative, he presided over the transfer of the British East India Company to the Crown by means of the Government of India Act (1858).

On his return to India in 1858, Dadabhai began writing for *Shri Gyan Mala*, a journal published by one of his colleagues for a female readership with the aim of enhancing their knowledge of public affairs. He also proposed that a statue of Queen Victoria should be erected in Bombay in recognition of the loyalty of its citizens to their Empress. This reveals that in the wake of the Indian Mutiny he was anxious that his countrymen, or at least those in Bombay, should show a continued allegiance to Britain, which was now ruling

9   Masani

India directly instead of via the East India Company. In her proclamation after the mutiny Victoria had promised "equality among all Her Majesty's subjects and honesty with the Princes of India" and this statement was one which Dadabhai welcomed and would often repeat in later years.

The change in the administration of India was not at first as dramatic as might have been expected. Essentially, it was business as usual, with many of the same people running the country as had done so under the EIC, answering to a Viceroy who enjoyed a great deal of autonomy. One move which did open the way to greater change was the introduction of a Legislative Council, whose 12 members included representatives of the Indian aristocracy. The 565 Indian states continued to run their own affairs, with a new guarantee of independence, but ultimately all were answerable to Great Britain. The title of 'king' was proscribed and the rulers were now known by various Indian titles, the most senior being Maharaja (which ironically means 'great king'). In fact the British Government soon proved to be just as mercenary in most of its dealings as the East India Company had before it, so for all the maternalistic assurances of their Empress Dadabhai and his allies knew they still had a long fight ahead of them.

In January 1859 Dadabhai set off for Britain once more, accompanied by Pestonji Colah, Jamshedji Palanji Kapadia, a noted Persian scholar and historian, and three student protégés, who were his cousin Franji Rustamji Desai and two young members of the Cama family, Jamshedji Kharshedji and Hormusji Dorabji. With Colah and Kapadia he set up a company called Dadabhai Naoroji & Co and took up residence in Liverpool.[10] This new concern primarily dealt in

10   Masani p 78

cotton, and he made a resolve to trade more ethically than had proved possible with his last enterprise. This meant a promise never to indulge in short trading (selling on goods before you have paid for them yourself) or to accept payment from buyer and seller at the same time. It also meant staying out of the opium trade. It is clear that this business was not set up with the intention of making Dadabhai rich, but simply to enable him to pay his way in life and to care for his family as he continued his political and social campaigning.

Dadabhai's scrupulousness is demonstrated by an incident when he had invited tenders for a large contract, the supply of four vessels. Shown on one supplier's tender was the sum of 5 per cent as a commission to him personally. He furiously insisted that the item be deleted, and when it was he accepted the tender. His close supervision of the contract ended up costing the supplier far more than 5 per cent (which, no doubt, was why they had offered it).[11]

On his second sojourn in England, in his new role as a British-based businessman, Dadabhai became a director of the Queen Insurance Company. He joined or became involved with a number of bodies, including the Liverpool Literary and Philosophical Society, the Philomathic Society, the Council of the Liverpool Athenaeum, the Royal Institute of London, the Royal Asiatic Society of Great Britain and Ireland, the Anthropological Society, the Society of Arts, the National Indian Association and a masonic lodge. His business interests led to membership of the Manchester Cotton Supply Association, and he became an ally and lifelong friend of Samuel Smith, a cotton magnate and MP, who strongly supported the cause of Indian emancipation.

He gave many presentations about the Parsis and the

11   Masani

Zoroastrian faith, and about life in India under British rule, though his speeches were not purely polemical and he always sought to present a balanced and objective account. It was not long before he was being regarded as almost an unofficial ambassador to Britain.

Young, bright Indians were now trying to join the higher levels of the Indian Civil Service, but were being prevented from doing so by obstructive rules. Lord Lytton, the Viceroy, was quietly but determinedly against any increased role of Indians in government, as demonstrated by his attempts to create a two-tier civil service, with the senior tier, known as the covenanted branch, expressly designed to exclude almost all Indians. In one case, the Indian medical service blocked a young man's attempt to join with the paltry excuse that he would not be able to cope with the change of climate in England. Certainly the climate came as a shock to those who tried, at least as much as it did to the British in India (the main reason why in the Raj years, the British made their homes mainly in hill stations in cool, upland areas such as the Nilgiri Hills in western India). One young candidate, S C Cama, died in Britain at the age of 20 before he could sit the exam.

Another 20-year-old, Rustomjee Wadia, had arrived in Britain in June 1856 to begin his studies for the Civil Service entrance examination. He allowed himself until September 1858 to prepare for the exam, but while he was studying the Government spitefully reduced the age limit to 22 specifically to obstruct the attempts of Indians like him to enter the Service. Mr Wadia had to abandon his plan, because by the time he sat the exam he would have been 23. The first Indian to overcome these hurdles was C R Wadia, perhaps a relative, who in 1874 managed to pass the exam at

Lord Lytton, Viceroy from 1876-1880

the age of 18. He was followed by a trickle of successors, but it would be years before Indians could become fully accepted members of the Indian Civil Service.[12]

In 1861 Dadabhai, with Mancherjee Hormusjee Cama, formed a London-based association for Zoroastrians under the name 'Religious Society of Zarathushtrians in Europe'.

12   Masani p 83, Ralph p 38

The association's main function was to provide support for new immigrants from India. Dadabhai remained its president until 1908. Under Dadabhai's successor as president, another of the pioneers, Sir Mancherjee Bhownaggree, of whom more later, it became the Incorporated Parsi Association of Europe. Now known as the Zoroastrian Association, it continues to this day.

In the same year Dadabhai published a booklet about the Parsi faith, *The Parsee Religion*. His intention was clearly not to promote or even to defend it, but to clarify its principles and to point out, very candidly, its strengths and weaknesses. He explained that the priesthood, being a separate caste, took office by birthright and not by training, and delivered their ministrations by rote. Very few actually knew the *Avesta*. Accordingly, he commented on the priests: "From the state of their education and knowledge they are quite unfit for the pulpit; nor do they aspire to it, nor have any notion of the necessity of such teaching. Far from being the teachers of the true doctrines and duties of their religion, the priests are generally the most bigoted and superstitious, and exercise much injurious influence over the women especially."

The Parsi faith did have the benefits, he added, of avoiding idolatry (despite being a small community surrounded by people whose religion did indulge in it) and worshipping a single god. On the other hand, it had become somewhat degraded and contaminated over the years by contact with other religions which had vastly more adherents.

On the family front, life was not going so smoothly for Dadabhai. Immediately before leaving for England in 1859, he had become a father. His wife Gulbai had had to raise their child Ardeshir, known as Adi, alone, but his marital problems went beyond this. Although Dadabhai appears to have been devoted to Gulbai and 'cherished his wife dearly', spending time freely with her and never abandoning the attempt to broaden her outlook and her interests, she was not academically-minded like her husband and took little interest in the public life which was so important to him. Masani describes her as 'far from prepossessing and awkward in speech and manners' and says she showed 'not the least aptitude for study' and could not read or write, but states that this in no way diminished her husband's affection for her or prevented him from spending time with her.

Perhaps the arrival in 1861 of a second child, a daughter, Shirin, added to the pressure on Gulbai. It seems Dadabhai's mother Manekbhai – who was living with the family and must have been all too aware of her daughter-in-law's frustrations – regretted her earlier matchmaking far more than her son did. She insisted on looking for a second wife for him, one whose intellect would be a better match for his; although Zoroastrianism tradition did not sanction bigamy, the Parsi ruling body, the Panchayat, had allowed it, and many Parsis had taken advantage of this. However, Dadabhai would have none of it. Ironically, he himself had been campaigning against bigamy, and with others he was seeking to introduce a new Parsi matrimonial law which would outlaw it, whilst allowing widows to remarry. This duly passed into law in 1865. According to Masani, he said to his mother: "Put me in the place of my wife. Suppose I, your son, am suffering from the disabilities from which she suffers. Would you, in that case, ask my wife to marry a second husband?" This ended the debate.

It was a scurrilous rumour which brought about a settlement of the conflict. A Dr Archer who was living opposite Dadabhai's British home had three marriageable daughters, and it seems word flew back to India via Mancherjee Cama that Dadabhai was planning to convert to Christianity and take one of them as his bride. A distraught Manekbhai dictated a letter to him which wailed, "I tried to persuade you to take a second wife, but you would not listen to me! Now you think of marrying an Englishwoman, and bringing disgrace to our family!"

So concerned was Dadabhai that in September 1863 he sailed back to India without notice – his first return since 1859 – to confront his family and assure them that the story was nonsense. The visit led to family discussions which finally resolved one marital issue; Manekbhai dropped her plans to find him a second wife.

Dadabhai did not immediately return to England. While in India, he began to tackle another social convention which seemed blatantly sexist; the practice of banning women from the male dinner table. The Bombay Society of Parsees eventually succeeded in normalising the idea of mixed dining, even committing its members never to dine without women at the table (this must have depended on the availability of at least one female guest). The same group was also involved in teaching English to Indian girls, in collaboration with the female students of the Literary and Scientific Society's schools.

The return to England finally came in April 1865, and this time he took his mother, wife and two children with him. Whether this was because he now recognised England as his long-term home, or through pressure from his family to accompany him, is not recorded. They set up home in a rented property in Hornsey, North London, named by Dadabhai 'Parsi Lodge'. Here he could give his family the attention they had lacked for so long. His great friend and supporter Manockji Cursetji wrote later: "It was a sight at once charming and delightful to see him, when off work, unbend himself, squatted on the drawing-room carpet playing with his little boy and girl. His conversation was always interesting, informative and instructive, decked out with anecdotes and stories and flashes of friendly fun and ready wit. His voice had a singular charm; I still have it in my ears."[13]

The cotton trade was thriving at the time, helped by the American Civil War and the subsequent abolition of slavery, which had cut off supplies from that continent, creating a huge opportunity for Indian growers to make good the shortage by selling their own cotton to Europe. Dadabhai quickly 'amassed a fortune', as Vajifdar put it.

His new business, however, was somewhat handicapped by his own philanthropy. He bailed out several friends and associates who got into business difficulties, and at one point he gave £60,000 to a friend, Karsandas Madhavji. The result, in 1866, was his own bankruptcy. However his creditors were so impressed by his obvious integrity and his honourable attitude that they excused him his liabilities and allowed him to handle his own liquidation. Fresh loans from English friends enabled him to restart his business. As Serene Cursetji, the daughter of his business partner, wrote in her diary: "Poor Dadabhai has a great deal of patience and his troubles he bears marvellously. I learned from Papa that his affairs will have to be wound up in a day or two, this will be done more though the misconduct of his creditors, many of whom have behaved shabbily, very shamefully towards him, but I feel sure God will reward him for his righteousness." Later she added: "None could think from the unshaken

13   Serene Cursetji's diary, quoted by Masani p. 92

calmness and patience that reigned on Dadabhai's face that his affairs were in such a dreadfully painful condition… poor Dadabhai's mother was sad and kept crying for the whole day and speaking in more harsh terms to poor Mrs Dadabhai. All this was very painful."

In 1867 Dadabhai raised the question of admission of Indians to the Civil Service by sending a memo to the Secretary of State for India demanding that examinations be held in India as well as England. He also approached several MPs, and succeeded in getting Henry Fawcett, the Liberal MP for Brighton, to make this point in the House, arguing again that Indians were intrinsically just as intelligent and capable as Europeans. He also pointed out the absurdity of Indians not being allowed to work in the Indian Civil Service, saying that it was as ridiculous as keeping Englishmen out of the English Civil Service.

In 1868 Dadabhai's family returned without him to India, where later that year Gulbai had a second daughter. She was named Manekbhai after her grandmother, and known as Maki.

Dadabhai continued his quest for reform, always taking the attitude that the errors of British rule were down to ignorance rather than malice, a belief he maintained throughout his life. Much later, in 1904, he stated in a speech: "We Indian people believe in one thing, and that is that although John Bull is a little thick-headed, once we can penetrate through his head into his brain that a certain thing is right and proper to be done, you can be quite sure that it will be done."

He was strongly supported in his quest by a number of people. One was John Dickinson, the son of a papermaker, who had long counselled against forcibly annexing Indian states. He was a founder in, 1853, of the Indian Reform Society, set up by a group calling themselves the 'friends of India'. Another was Major Evans Bell, another reformer, who wrote several books about Indian matters. A third was John Bright, a prominent Liberal MP and one of the greatest orators of his generation, who put his finger on the Indian problem by writing: "It is my belief that if a country is found possessing a most fertile soil and capable of bearing every variety of productivity, and that, notwithstanding, the people are in a state of extreme destitution and suffering, the chances are that there is some fundamental error in the government of that country." In Parliament he pointed out that the taxes paid by Indian people were "more onerous and oppressive" than those of any other country in the world. Bright served as Chairman of the India Reform Society in 1856-61 and was instrumental in bringing its views to attention of Parliament.

When Dadabhai appeared before the Welby Commission many years later, he said: "The way of the Indian authorities is first to ignore any Act or resolution of Parliament or report of any Committee or Commission in favour of Indian interests. If that is not enough, then to delay replies. If that does not answer, then openly resist; and by their persistence carry their own point, unless a strong Secretary of State prevents it."

Though it may not at first have been apparent to Dadabhai, one of the major obstacles in the way of reform during those decades was the attitude of Lord Lytton, Viceroy from 1878-1880. His determination to operate a two-tier civil service, excluding Indians from the senior covenanted branch as far as possible, has already been mentioned. It was not until the 20th century that such barriers were finally removed and

Indian candidates had full access to posts in their own Civil Service. Lytton, who took his agenda almost entirely from the Anglo-Indian community, seems to have delighted in frustrating the efforts of the Indians to achieve reform. He received much support from the Anglo-Indian press; the *St James Gazette* stated, "Experienced Anglo-Indians assure us that the change proposed by Mr [Herbert] Paul might lead to consequences almost as disastrous as the Mutiny".

A major step forward was taken in 1865 with the founding of the London Indian Society, jointly by Dadabhai Naoroji and Womesh Chandra Bonnerjee, a barrister from Calcutta. At its first meeting, it was unanimously decided that the Society should be led by Indians, with Bonnerjee as Secretary and Naoroji as President. The LIS did not last long, however, before being reformed the following year as the East India Association, a wider body with a campaigning agenda. It was initially established in London by a group of Indians and retired British officials under the presidency of Lord Lyveden, a Liberal peer who had formerly been a Lord of the Treasury and Under-Secretary of State for the Colonies. The East India Association continued to function right up until 1966 (after a change of name in 1949 to the Britain, India and Pakistan Association), when it amalgamated with the India Society to become the Royal Society for India, Pakistan and Ceylon.[14]

Within two years the Association had 594 members, of whom 324 were Indians, many living in India. Its agenda focused on the economic development of India, and it

14   open.ac.uk

produced its own publication, the *Journal of the East India Association*, and put on lectures at Caxton Hall, its usual meeting place. Dadabhai gave one of the first of these, in May 1867.

A paper published in 1866 by John Crawford, President of the Ethnological Society of London, underlined the lingering insistence of many in Europe that the European races were morally and intellectually superior to the Asiatic peoples. Dadabhai retaliated with a paper in which he cited the academic attainments of Indian students at 18 when compared with British students, despite the latter being better taught and the former having first had to learn English. He itemised some of the many literary accomplishments of Asians, along with their achievements in the sciences, demonstrating the hypocrisy, racism and plain ignorance of the white view.

He now wanted to carry the campaign to India, and during a lecture tour in 1869 taking in Bombay, Calcutta and Madras he started the ball rolling with the creation of new 'local Indian associations' in those cities, calling for more middle-class Indians to become involved alongside the rich founder members. The tour met with great enthusiasm, and he was able to raise funding from several states where the rulers received his proposals favourably. Led by Pherozeshah Mehta, a protégé and lifelong supporter of Dadabhai, the public of Bombay, feeling that Dadabhai was neglecting his own interests, decided it was time to present a 'purse' to him in recognition of all that he was doing for India. A total of 30,000 rupees, the equivalent of around £2000, was collected for him. The first 5000 rupees was earmarked for a portrait of him, while the rest was offered to him in cash. He accepted this considerable sum with reluctance, feeling uneasy about taking payment for his mission but well aware that he could not afford to turn it down. In fact most of the money went straight to the East India Association, which was in a poor financial state. Dadabhai continued to appeal for support for the Association on subsequent visits home, helping it to equip and maintain a library and build up funds to ensure its stability.

Sir Pherozeshah Mehta, lifelong supporter of Naoroji

At a meeting on May 22 1869, the Bombay Association was reborn as the Bombay Branch of the East India Association, and further branches were formed in Calcutta, Madras and other cities. The Association now began to assess the true extent of India's economic situation, which had been severely weakened by the one-sided hegemony of Great Britain and the continuing unfairness of the British style of 'investment'. As Dadabhai put it, "English capitalists do not merely lend, but with their capital they invade the country". Certainly the British had provided India with a railway network, better roads and irrigation systems and better schools, but so far all this had been done over the Indians' heads and mainly at their own expense, with little thought to what they actually needed or could even make use of; a patronising "we know what's good for you" attitude. This was doubly frustrating, given that India was expected to pay the contractors unilaterally appointed by the British. No one worried too much if a project ran over budget or got into trouble, because the Indians could always be fleeced for a little more cash.

Over a few short weeks during the summer of 1870, the East India Association produced four papers on Indian economic and financial issues. Dadabhai outlined the basic 'wants' of Indians which were behind the papers: sufficient food, clothing and shelter, enough to 'provide for all social wants', sufficient individual saving, the improvement of public works and 'the means to pay for the high price of foreign rule'. He pointed out that if Britain would guarantee India's national debt, this would also guarantee the payment of interest on British capitalist investments. He felt the loans' main purpose should be to finance the rebuilding of India. "Blood cannot be got out of a stone," he pointed out.

"When prosperity is fairly served, revenue will take care of itself."

This was the birth of Dadabhai's 'Drain Theory' of the bleeding of India – his phrase. Exactly how severe the problem was could not be told from hard figures, because no single authority kept authoritative records of national income and expenditure. Dadabhai claimed that of £50m of revenue raised in India each year, some £12m or more was 'carried away to England' so that national capital was diminished year on year. These were example figures – he had yet to do his homework to discover the actual numbers. He also claimed that 'the proportion of the amount which the government of the country took for purposes of administration' appeared to be about 8 per cent in England, but 16 per cent in India, despite the fact that average income was about £30 per head in the UK and only £2 per head in India. "A ton might not be a burden to an elephant, but a few pounds could crush a child" as he put it.

Because so little reliable information was available, Dadabhai realised he would need to go to work himself to compile a truthful picture of the Indian economy. Later figures showed that from 1835 to 1882 India had imported goods valued at £943 million and made £1.5 billion on exports. However, when the cost of interest was taken into consideration, plus the cost of payments which should have been taken care of by Britain, and the fact that much of the money earned in India went into British pockets, it was clear that in truth India was languishing in perpetual debt, and it was growing deeper by the year. Dadabhai's conclusion in a paper of 1878 entitled 'Wants and Means of India' was that the average yearly income of the people was 40 shillings or 20 rupees, although they needed 34 rupees a year just to be able to live.

After Dadabhai's paper was presented, the President of the Bombay Association, Sir Charles Trevelyan, responded in detail. A man of considerable knowledge and experience – he had served at the highest level in government and become Finance Minister for India – he agreed that there was a genuine crisis, and although he would not agree that Britain was 'draining' India or that she was being impoverished, he did accept that there had been considerable extravagance, and called for a Select Committee of both Houses to examine the administration of India.

As Dadabhai's anger and frustration increased, his terminology grew stronger; at first he talked of 'material and moral drain', but it soon became 'deprivation of resources' and then 'the bleeding drain'. He realised that what the country desperately needed was capital investment, and that could, and should, only come from Britain.

Dadabhai's devotion to truth and fairness was becoming very clear. The rule of his life, according to his biographer Masani, was "never to accept a statement without verification, never to make a statement without being convinced of the truth of it".

The Association asked for a Select Committee of both Houses of Parliament to be set up to look into the problem. One was duly created, but it lasted only a year before being dissolved in the wake of a change of government. Henry Fawcett MP, whose continued efforts on behalf of the Indian reform movement had now earned him the sobriquet 'the Member for India', was proving to be a great ally and consistently fought for the admission of Indians to the Civil Service.

Although he was now in middle age, Dadabhai's vigour and determination were undiminished. A report by one of his three lieutenants in about 1873 reveals his daily routine. He started his day early and worked until lunchtime, when he would apparently eat nothing but three or four raw eggs. He continued to work until suppertime, working for an average 16 hours a day. This routine continued unchanged until he was in his seventies.

In the early 1870s he found himself dealing with a situation which must have distracted him considerably from his path in life. The new state of Baroda in Gujarat, which was oddly divided into four geographically-separated divisions, had a new Maharaja, Mulharro Gaekwar, who had been accused of misgovernment. Faced with the threat of a commission of inquiry, Gaekwar called in Dadabhai, whom he had met during the latter's fund-raising tour, and who had evidently impressed him. Dadabhai was reluctant to represent the Maharaja at the durbar (court) but agreed to advise him privately, and did so. The Maharaja offered him an 'honorarium' of 50,000 rupees, an enormous sum, which Dadabhai was most unwilling to accept. He explained that he could accept funds only for the East India Association and not for his own personal gain. Finally he agreed to take the money, but only on the basis that it would be kept in trust for his children.

In 1873, with the Maharaja's chaotic and corrupt administration collapsing around his ears, he appealed to Dadabhai to become his new Dewan (Prime Minister). This met with immediate opposition from the new British Resident, Colonel Phayre, who had been briefed against Dadabhai by the Maharaja's durbaris and mistrusted his reasons for considering a post with such a corrupt ruler.

Dadabhai consulted Sir Erskine Perry, who in turn spoke to Sir Bartle Frere, the Governor of Bombay. Frere warned him that he was taking on an extremely challenging task, but Perry advised him to take the job, on the basis that it would be for the benefit of Baroda. He was duly appointed, albeit on a temporary basis, despite determined lobbying by Colonel Phayre and a threat not to even allow Dadabhai to enter Baroda.

Dadabhai took up his new post unofficially that autumn, and immediately found himself drowning in a sea of official paperwork thrust at him by the Maharaja's courtiers, who were determined to keep their new boss from getting down to the serious business of reform. He had time for little else. According to Masani, "Sometimes he sacrificed an hour's sleep, sometimes he snatched an hour from work. He had his bath early in the morning; his toilet was quite a simple affair; he knew no breakfast, and even his luncheon (principally of raw eggs) did not take him more than three to four minutes."

Dadabhai showed great political shrewdness by the way he handled his new responsibilities. He had each of his three personal lieutenants appointed to a key post in the state. Homi Wadia was made Chief Magistrate and Head of the Criminal and Police Departments, Bal Mangesh became Chief Justice and Kazi Shahabudin was put in charge of revenues. Even so, it proved to be a rocky ride. When the Commission drew up a list of the Maharaja's malpractices, Dadabhai responded diplomatically that the best way to improve matters for the future was to draw a line under past misdeeds, as we might put it today. Colonel Phayre's view was that he should be defending the Maharaja's reputation instead of appearing to confirm his wrongdoings. This

Dadabhai refused to do, which did not please either Phayre or the Maharaja. Dadabhai found himself spending more time defending his reputation than running the principality, according to Omar Ralph.

Dadabhai was becoming increasingly unhappy about the level of corruption under the rule of the Maharaja. His insistence on demanding *nazarana*, or gifts and favours, from everyone in exchange for his assistance or indulgence had become blatant, and was proving a severe obstruction to justice and fairness in the courts. He refused to let go of this practice, and it finally resulted in Dadabhai threatening to resign before he was confirmed in the post. Masani wrote, "The perverse Maharaja... surrounded by men who were born enemies of the truth and righteousness, men who hated progress, men whose happiness depended on the misery and oppression of the multitude, continued to listen to those worthless durbaris who filled his mind with rubbish about his treaty right and instilled into his ears poisonous words calculated to antagonise him to the Minister. Dadabhai often exposed to his royal master the villainy of that crafty crowd, but he failed to break the magic spell they had woven around him."

In August 1874 the Maharaja received a letter from the Commission of Inquiry telling him he would be deposed if he did not put his administration in order by the following year. After that, the pressure on Dadabhai eased a little, and he felt able to continue. Dadabhai was invested as Dewan on September 23 1874, and immediately set about cleaning up the principality. A concession was made on land assessment to reduce the burden on the overtaxed peasants, and nazarana was outlawed. As a result, Dadabhai met with hostility from the Maharaja's durbaris as well as from Colonel Phayre. Dadabhai wrote through the Maharaja to the Viceroy, to Lord Northbrook and to the Government asking for Phayre to be removed. Lord Salisbury, Secretary of State for India, supported this request, and Phayre duly departed. Dadabhai now tried to have removed four courtiers who were in the pay of the Maharaja and were trying to defend his behaviour against all Dadabhai's efforts. He succeeded with three of them. As Vajifdar put it: "The old hangers-on… strove to forestall and countermand every move of the reformists. These pernicious beings, habituated to underhandedness and accustomed to lies, worked on the weak and vacillating Mulharro". Finally, after evidence was found that Mulharro had tried to poison Colonel Phayre, he was deposed and deported.

By then Dadabhai had had enough of the Maharaja and his entourage and had already decided to depart. He left the post in January 1875, just a few weeks before his successor, Sir Sayajirao Gaekwar, took office. Sir Sayajirao proved to be a huge improvement, soon instituting much-needed social reform.

Though Dadabhai managed to struggle through these longest 13 months of his life, his greatest test to date, with his principles and reputation intact, indeed enhanced, his health clearly suffered; for a time he was confined to bed with a fever. On medical advice he spent four months recuperating at Tithal on the coast of Gujarat, although even there he was still receiving and writing letters about the Drain Theory and other matters. The stress of the Baroda episode left its mark on him, and he was probably never again quite as strong and well as he had been before. In 1887 he stated in a letter: "To lead a right life is in our power; with that we can meet all troubles and surmount and survive them".

On his return in the summer of 1875, he was elected a

member of the Municipal Corporation of Bombay, for the same district where he had been born. Shortly after he was also elected to the Town Council. He returned to the public eye with his energy and determination little diminished, but this phase of his life did not last long; the following year he made the decision to return to England, to attend to his business. Correspondence from the time indicates that it was not doing well, and in 1881 Dadabhai wound up the firm, transferring the remaining business to the Camas.

During Dadabhai's long absences from home his family's care was watched over by Muncherji Mirani Dadina, a friend and former pupil who was now a teacher. Households were considered to need male supervision even in the absence of the father, so Gulbai must have continued to accept a subordinate role. Muncherji was already bound to the family and would become more so, because Dadabhai's son Adi was now betrothed to his daughter Virbai. Later further ties were formed when Dadabhai's elder daughter Shirin was engaged to Muncherji's son Fram, while his second daughter, Manekbhai or Maki, was engaged to Muncherji's other son, Hormusji, or Homi.

Adi in youth had a rebellious, free-spirited nature, which brought him into conflict with Muncherji, a strict Parsi. It seems Dadabhai tended to side with his son, because he acceded to Adi's request for a seven-rupee allowance after Muncherji had limited him to only three. Shirin called him, affectionately no doubt, a *'chokha Marwadi'*, a 'proper Marwadi'[15] – a reference to an ethnic group in India and Nepal, successful business people originating from the Marwar region of Rajasthan who were regarded in rather the same way that some cultures have viewed Jews. A furious

15   Masani p 184

dispute ensued over discipline after Adi managed to shoot himself not once but twice in the same leg and then damaged some furniture, again with a firearm.

Adi was clearly bright and successful; he won a scholarship for proficiency in surgery and joined the Grant Medical College in Bombay. When he married Virbai at Diwali in 1880, Dadabhai did not even know about it; he first learned of the marriage some time later. He was thrilled, however, to learn of the birth of his first grandchild a year later.

When Muncherji's son Homi wanted to spend some time in Britain before marrying, his father was against the idea, fearing he would bring an English wife back. Dadabhai however supported the plan, and Homi was allowed to go. He married Maki in 1897. Maki went on to achieve a first among Asian women by qualifying in medicine in the UK, with an LRCP and FSPG at Edinburgh and an LM in Dublin.

Dadabhai's mother Manekbhai died in 1875, a great blow to him. No doubt he took comfort from his growing extended family. Dadabhai was a devoted and attentive father and he seems to have become an equally dedicated grandfather. Adi eventually had eight children, three sons, Jal, Kershasp and Sarosh, and five daughters, Meher, Gosi, Nargiz, Perin and Khorshed. Dadabhai wrote to them all regularly, and in their replies they addressed him as 'Dad'. His attitude is revealed in one letter in which he wrote, "Now, my dear children, I shall be satisfied if you only say, "we are well". You may write to me what you have done at school during the week – just as you told me a lot of things when I was in Bombay and saw you all in the evening." Kershasp graduated from Christ's College, Cambridge, before signing up for the Middlesex Regiment and seeing action in the First World War. He was awarded a temporary commission, and was one of the first Indian soldiers to command British troops.

Dadabhai was one of the first Indians to be appointed members of Bombay Town Council, in 1875 on his 50th birthday. He turned his attention to the profligacy of British management, and focused in particular on the Vehar loan, a loan for water services on which exceptionally high interest was being charged. It turned out that £60,000 in excess charges was being imposed.

Back in Britain, Dadabhai started to examine the finances of India under British rule. In 1878 he produced his famous booklet *The Poverty of India*, which showed, among other things, that India was producing only half as much as it was supposed to be. India was in perpetual debt to Britain, an artificial debt which existed only because of the way the British chose to exploit India, and it had been that way for centuries. The country was still being ruthlessly milked dry. Dadabhai compared it to the wealth once squeezed from the European nobility by the Catholic Church under Pope Innocent III during the Crusades of the 12th century, which created a severe economic drain on England and other European countries. India needed the balance restored through new capital from Britain, unencumbered by the usual punitive interest rates. The problem certainly wasn't showing any signs of going away by itself – as late as 1879 Lord Lytton removed import duties on cotton to help protect the British cotton industry at the expense of the Indian one.

In *The Poverty of India* Dadabhai went to an immense amount of trouble to collate and, in effect, audit the official figures for production and receipts for every part of India, supporting his argument with hundreds of pages of meticulously-collated columns of figures. It is the work of a skilled book-keeper, and certainly not holiday reading. He concluded: "It will be seen that... there is hardly enough of production even in a good season, leaving alone all little luxuries, all social and religious wants, all expenses of occasions of joy and sorrow, and any provision for bad seasons... The high and middle classes get a much larger share, the poor classes much less. Such appears to be the condition of the masses of India. They do not get enough to provide the bare necessaries of life". In a later passage he states: "There is an enormous transfer of the wealth of this country to England, and the remedy is the employment of natives only, beyond the exigencies of British rule." He goes on to say, "The chief cause of India's poverty, misery, and all material evils, is the exhaustion of its previous wealth... The obvious remedy is to allow India to keep what it produces." This meant to limit (cap, as we would say today) all forms of expenditure. "Under some judicious arrangement of the kind I propose, the people of India, being allowed to keep what they produce, will rise in material prosperity... blessing the hand that gave such prosperity, and increasing the benefit to the English people manyfold, by the extensive commercial relations that must then necessarily be developed between England and India: and all fears of any danger to the British rule will be dispelled."

Over the next few years Dadabhai's main concern continued to be the East India Company and trying to sort out the economic mess it had got his country into. He did take time out to attack Lord Lytton's Vernacular Press Act of 1878, introduced to curtail the freedom of the Indian native-language press and prevent it from criticising British policies, such as making India pay for the Second Afghan War which broke out that same year.

He was still running his business, albeit in a hands-off style. It was trading in much else besides cotton, even machinery, watches and bracelets, but apparently making little money. Dady Cama, who was in control whenever Dadabhai was away, even advised him at one point to wind up the business because of the threat posed by a large bad debt. In the end Dadabhai did so, leaving his associates to take over, but he continued to trade autonomously from Bombay in collaboration with them, probably just to keep the wolf from the door. His main preoccupation now was researching India's economic situation in the hope of trying to help repair his country's finances. Certainly his former associates continued to support him in this.

Now Dadabhai was beginning to assemble the information he needed to start pressing for reform. He was constantly ordering more official 'blue books' (financial records), as well as budget details and other financial records. He began a correspondence on his findings with Lord Hartington, Secretary of State for India from 1880-82. In one typical letter (November 1880), he wrote: "Europeans occupy almost all the higher places in every department of government either directly or indirectly under its control. While in India they acquire India's money, experience and wisdom, and when they go, they carry both away with them. Thus India is left without, and cannot have, those elders in wisdom and experience who, in every country, are the natural guides of the rising generations in their national and social conduct and of the destinies of their country; and a sad, sad, loss this is! There may be very few social institutions started by Europeans in which natives, however fit and desirous to join, are not deliberately and insultingly excluded."[16]

16   Masani p 204

Over the years that followed Dadabhai found himself constantly stonewalled, yet he never for a moment gave up his mission, nor did he lose faith in the inherent decency of the British.

Henry Hyndman (1842-1921), founder of the Social Democratic Federation

One person who encouraged him in his efforts was Henry Mayers Hyndman, a prominent British socialist and the founder of the Social Democratic Federation. Hyndman too was studying what the British had been up to in India and he wrote to Dadabhai for information. Though more militant in his approach than Dadabhai, he became an invaluable supporter and a lifelong ally and correspondent.

There came a welcome change in 1881 with the replacement of Lord Lytton as Viceroy by Lord Ripon. This must have come as a major relief to Dadabhai. Ripon proved to be far more sympathetic to the Indian cause and took the attitude that, as he put it, Britain should be "making the educated natives the friends and not the enemies of our rule". He favoured a free press – one of his first actions was to repeal the hated Vernacular Press Act – ample education, the admission of Indians to the public services and an increase in self-government. Many Anglo-Indians opposed this new liberalism, and Ripon was widely condemned and criticised by them for his reforms. Nevertheless he brought India a small but important step closer to autonomy, and when he left office in 1884 Dadabhai was among those who celebrated his contribution at a public meeting. History has judged Ripon the most popular of all India's viceroys.

In 1883 Dadabhai founded *Voice of India*, launched to provide a platform for those demanding justice and fair treatment for his country. It had the effect of making the British in India more aware of the concerns and problems of Indians. Dadabhai paid for its production himself, and although it did not have a large circulation it was very widely read, even being read out by the literate to those who were not. In 1890 it was incorporated with the *Indian Spectator*.

In the same year Dadabhai was one of a small group of reformers to be elected to Bombay Corporation. He was now beginning to suffer poor health, and at this stage he had to take a six-month rest. Fortunately, by 1884 he had recovered, and in January 1885, in his 60th year, he became Vice-President of the Bombay Presidency Association, a development of the Bombay Association and the local branch of the East India Association. Later that year he was invited by Lord Reay, the Governor of Bombay, to join the Bombay Legislative Council, a move in part intended to satisfy Indian demands for more representation on public bodies.

In 1885 the Indian National Congress was created, and Dadabhai was one of the key figures behind it, speaking at the first meeting and becoming President the following year. The Bombay Presidency Association, described by the *Times of India* at the time as 'the leading political association of India', set this body up as a nationalist socialist and democratic movement, and it quickly became, and remained, the flagship of Indian independence. When *swaraj* finally came in 1947, the INC formed the first Indian government, and it remains the dominant party of India today.

The INC was actually the brainchild of a white British man, Allan Octavian Hume, a retired Civil Service officer who suggested the idea in an open letter to graduates of the University of Calcutta. The first meeting received the approval of the Viceroy, Lord Dufferin, perhaps reassured by the prominent role of an Englishman, and the first president was Womesh Chandra Bonnerjee, the man who had founded the London Indian Society with Dadabhai 20 years earlier. Bonnerjee became, alongside Naoroji, one of the first two

Allan Octavian Hume, political reformer and co-founder of the Indian National Congress

Indians to stand for Parliament in the UK, unsuccessfully contesting the Barrow in Furness seat for the Liberals in 1892.

At the INC's first meeting on December 28 1885, 18 of the 72 delegates were from Bombay. Dadabhai spoke on his drain theory and the cost to India of British policies, as well as the difficulty Indian candidates experienced in being appointed to senior posts in the Indian Civil Service, thanks to the two-tier structure designed to discriminate against Indians. At that time 95 per cent of the lowliest posts in the service (those paying no more than 75 rupees a month) were held by Indians, while at the other extreme, only a handful of natives held any of the posts paying more than 1000 rupees. Recruiting more Indians to the Service was, said Dadabhai, "the most important key to our material and moral advancement". The INC put forward the view that entry examinations should be held simultaneously in England and India and that successful candidates in both countries should undergo the necessary further studies together in England. The minimum age for entry should be raised to 23. The INC's reasoned, and reasonable, arguments made it hard to dismiss its gently-put demands. When fears were raised that it would press for home rule, in the same way Ireland was doing so at the time, Dadabhai stated (1888): "I am a warm Home Ruler for Ireland, but neither I nor any other Indian is asking for any such Home Rule for India... our demands are far more moderate".

In fact, during its few years in operation the INC limited its demands to reform of the Legislative Councils, increasing the number of members. Nevertheless the hard core of conservative opposition back in Britain was not happy. In 1900 the Secretary of State for India, Lord Hamilton, wrote to Lord Curzon, the Viceroy: "Naoroji has been bombarding me with letters written in high-faluting sentimental style... I thought it just as well to give him a piece of my mind in very courteous language, which I have done... as it is very desirable to bring home to the educated natives the absurdity of nourishing these dreams and hallucinations in connection with India".

The campaign for fairer treatment of India still had a long way to go.

CHAPTER 3

Into the lion's den

Unsurprisingly, Dadabhai Naoroji was growing increasingly frustrated by the failure of India and his fellow Indians to influence such entrenched British attitudes. He must have followed with the interest the progress of Lalmohun Ghosh, the first full-blooded Indian to stand for election to the British Parliament[17]. Ghosh was a generation younger than Dadabhai, having been born into an upper middle-class family in Krishnanagar in 1849. The son of a member of the judiciary, he left for England in 1869 and subsequently qualified as a barrister at the Calcutta bar. He soon became involved in the civil service entry issue which had concerned Dadabhai, and on returning to England in 1879 he made a

---

17   He was preceded by an Anglo-Indian, David Ochterlony Dyce Sombre (1808-1851), the eccentric and wealthy descendant of a British mercenary and one of his two Indian Muslim wives. Dyce Sombre became the Whig MP for Sudbury in 1841, but was removed the following year after allegations of bribery and corruption during the election, which led to the disenfranchisement of the constituency in 1844 and its incorporation into Western Suffolk.

presentation on 'the duty of England to India' which met with such a warm reception that a set of rules for admission of Indians to the service, drawn up seven years previously but never acted on, were immediately implemented.

Ghosh went on to plead for the repeal of the Vernacular Press Act (as mentioned earlier, it was duly repealed in 1881 after Lord Ripon took over as Viceroy). He moved to England in 1879, and in 1885 he became the first Indian to stand for Parliament. He was adopted as the Liberal candidate for Deptford in south-east London, standing on a moderate Indian nationalist platform of greater self-rule for India and home rule for Ireland. Deptford, a largely working-class area and the home of many dock workers, was selected because it was thought to have a particularly radical electorate. Ghosh met the Prime Minister, William Gladstone, as part of an Indian delegation, and campaigned energetically with his brother, son and daughter, becoming a prominent political figure. He won many supporters, include Florence Nightingale. Like Dadabhai later, however, he came in for plenty of racist sneering. The *Kentish Mercury* called him an "Indian Baboo, who comes to the locality a total stranger, without a single tie of sympathy with the people of whose political, social and religious interests he aspires to be the guardian and representative".

In the event Ghosh lost to the Conservative candidate, William Evelyn, by 367 votes. The Liberal Party won power, but failed to secure an overall majority, and accordingly another election was held the following July. Ghosh contested the seat again and was again beaten by Evelyn, with a slightly more decisive 627 votes; there was a clear swing to the Conservatives across the country. Had he been successful in either year and become the first Indian in Parliament,

Ghosh would be taking a more prominent role in this story. In the event he returned to India, where he combined his practice at the bar with continuing to campaign for Indian rights. In 1903 he was elected president of the nineteenth Indian National Congress, where he made a plea for the introduction of compulsory primary education. He died at the age of 60 in 1909.

The Graphic reported after the first result was declared: "The peculiarity about the Deptford election, as witnessed by our artist, was that Mr Evelyn was apparently less popular than his Asiatic rival, the former, though a winner, being pelted; the latter, though a loser, being cheered. Perhaps it was a case of the classes against the masses".

Having witnessed Ghosh's attempt at election, so nearly successful, Dadabhai realised that it was time for him to try the same route towards effective political influence in Britain. The considerable work he had done from India over the past three decades had met with only slow and grudging progress towards reform. Perhaps a seat in the House of Commons would finally change things.

In March 1886 *The Hindu* of Madras announced that Dadabhai Naoroji was to stand in the Woolwich constituency in the forthcoming election. It stated: "As an authority of Indian economic questions there is none equal to him in all India. He has devoted over a quarter of a century of his life to the study of India's subjects, and by pressing his views on the Secretary of State and upon influential Englishmen in England he has turned his knowledge to the best account possible. Old as he is, Mr Dadabhai is a man of remarkable energy, and his great patriotism has won for him the confidence of his contemporaries of the Hindus and Mohammedans as well as Parsis in every part of the country."

Dadabhai had made this decision following a tip-off from a contact, Martin Wood, former editor of *The Times of India*, that Ghosh had decided against standing for the Woolwich constituency that year. Initially with Woolwich in mind, Dadabhai spent much of the first half of 1886 canvassing support, while continuing to pursue the issues that were dear to him, such as the overpriced Vehar loan.

He knew he would have an uphill struggle. The cultural racism which was prevalent at the time is well displayed by these words from a local newspaper: "We retain all the objections we have ever expressed to the intrusion of this Oriental gentleman into our home politics and we know that his birth and religion form a strong and natural objection in the minds of a large number of intelligent Christians in this country to his assuming the position of a parliamentary representative". It was less than 30 years since the first professing Jew, Lionel de Rothschild, had been allowed to sit in the House of Commons. Even the Oxford colleges would then admit no more than two Indians at a time. Having said that, there was generally less prejudice against Parsis in Europe than against other Indians, thanks to their typically fair skin and their professional and educational achievements.

At that time the Woolwich seat encompassed the parishes of Woolwich, Eltham and Plumstead. Perhaps Ghosh decided against contesting it because of the strength of the Conservative candidate; Edwin Hughes had held the seat with a comfortable majority in 1885 and he would go on to retain it by 1836 votes the following year. The constituency's boundaries have been changed three times since then, and it now forms part of the Greenwich and Woolwich seat.

During the spring months of 1886, Dadabhai approached many prominent statesmen and others whose advice he felt would be useful. Generally their replies were evasive and unhelpful. He was advised by Mr Hodgson Pratt to stand for a Scottish constituency, because the Scots Liberals were more liberal than their English counterparts, and by William Digby, a former secretary of the National Liberal Club, founder of the Indian Political Agency and the editor of *India,* to get an English hat, in order to appear 'altogether like an Englishman'. Most of those he consulted felt he had little or no chance of success, but he remained undeterred.

In the end the seat Dadabhai targeted was not Woolwich but Holborn, as he received an invitation it seemed foolish to refuse. The Liberal Association there invited his nomination, which he duly submitted, and it was accepted on June 18 1886.

In a letter to Dadabhai a few days later, Florence Nightingale wrote: "My warmest good wishes... so important is it that the millions of India should in the British Parliament be represented by one who, like yourself, has devoted his life to them in such a high fashion – to the difficult and delicate task of unravelling and explaining what stands at the bottom of India's poverty, what are Indians' rights, and what is the right for India... rights which we are all seeking after for those great multitudes."[18]

It is clear however that Dadabhai knew what a long shot it would be to get himself elected in Holborn, and the best he could say that it was 'not utterly hopeless'. Dadabhai's campaign attracted the sympathy of much of the press, including the *Pall Mall Gazette* and *The Times*, which stated:

18 Ralph p 89

"By returning him to the House of Commons, Holborn would prove itself one of the grandest constituencies in Great Britain".

Perhaps it was a little too grand for a Liberal candidate. Colonel Francis Duncan, his Conservative opponent, was a Scottish-born Royal Artillery officer, a lawyer and a military historian with solid support in the constituency. Despite his military background he was a deeply religious man. He had taken the seat the previous year with a 24 per cent majority over the Liberal candidate, Charles Harrison. Holborn, close to central London and not long previously the home of Charles Dickens, has long been closely linked with the legal profession, which will not have done Duncan any harm.

Then as now, political campaigning required money, and Colonel Duncan had plenty, in addition to great personal influence. Dadabhai had very little, thanks to the scant attention he had paid to his business affairs and his tendency to give away what he had to those in need. In the ballot on July 7 he did better than most observers expected by notching up 1950 votes against Duncan's 3651, a healthy total for a first attempt, if a long way short of success. He had greatly raised his profile, however, and made many friends in London and across Britain. Recognising this, Dadabhai was far from disheartened. He remained in Britain, preparing to fight again at the next opportunity, and to raise the funds he would need to do so. He was not helped by a Parsi friend and business associate in England who for years refused to repay £2000 he owed him. Dadabhai's desperation may be gathered from the tone of a letter to the man: "Do pray, pay me my money... I have a large payment to make and I need all the money you owe me to meet this requirement and other current expenses... what a trouble you have proved to me!"

Despite these obvious financial concerns, we have one clue that in fact Dadabhai had a long-term sponsor whose name he was loath to divulge. In a letter during his time in office to one of his allies, Narendranath Sen, he wrote: "I do not need any money help. I cannot tell you how that is – beyond that there is some silent patriot in India who appreciates the future result of my work and with full knowledge of my position and expenditure has supplied me with all I needed before and would need for some time to come. Had I not found such a friend of India, I should not have been able to do what I have done, however much or little it may be."

Maharaja Shri Bhagvat Sinhji, Thakore of Gondal, the 'silent patriot' said to have funded Naoroji during his attempts to become an MP

According to biographer Masani, the 'silent patriot' was Maharaja Shri Bhagvat Sinhji, Thakore of Gondal in Gujarat, a lifelong friend and admirer.

In 1887 Dadabhai suffered a setback in his campaign for simultaneous exams for the Indian Civil Service; he lost the support of the Muslim faction, who feared the change would lead to the dominance of Hindus in the Service.

By then he had the Finsbury Central seat in his sights for the next election, due in

1892. At the time this was a new seat, defined as covering the parish of St James and St John in Clerkenwell and created for the 1885 General Election in the Redistribution of Seats Act of the same year, one of seven single-member constituencies moulded from the former two-member Finsbury Constituency. As this suggests, constituencies were far smaller at that time than they have since become; the total votes cast for the two leading candidates for Finsbury Central in the coming election would total less than 6000. In 1918 it would be merged once again with the rest of Finsbury to provide the single-member seat of Finsbury, covering Finsbury Metropolitan Borough. Today it is part of the Islington South and Finsbury constituency.

Finsbury's lack of any natural boundaries or obvious landmarks has not helped it to gain or keep an identity separate from Islington or Clerkenwell. Primarily a working-class area, it was known in the 19th century for traditional crafts such as brewing, watchmaking and jewellery making.

Finsbury Town Hall today

It has since been gentrified to some extent by the expansion of business and industry from central London.

It took 8-10 ballots before the committee could whittle the choice of candidate down to four names. When the final ballot was held on August 15 1888, Dadabhai achieved a winning 49% of the votes. However there were those who were reluctant to accept his victory. They claimed that the vote was not valid, on the slender excuse that many of Dadabhai's supporters had rushed out of the room in triumph as soon as the vote was cast and failed to wait for a further, final vote. A fresh vote was held – even though the Secretary had already confirmed Dadabhai's victory in a letter to him – and this time Mr Richard Eve, previously the second-placed contestant with 45%, was declared the winner.

This must have severely tested Dadabhai's faith in British decency and fair play. It did not deter him from his course, however; he announced his decision to stand for the seat regardless of the vote. "Both money and mind have a hard pull upon them, but one must do one's duty, or life is hardly worth living," he wrote to his family.

It is hard to imagine a British Prime Minister in a public address calling an Indian a 'black man' and stating that the British electorate was not ready to elect such a person. That is what happened in 1889, and it did its perpetrator, Lord Salisbury, a great deal of harm and the subject of the comment, Dadabhai Naoroji, a great deal of good.

The Prime Minister, trying to explain the reduced Conservative majority in Holborn, told a gathering in Edinburgh: "It was undoubtedly a smaller majority than Colonel Duncan obtained, but Colonel Duncan was opposed by a black man, and however far we have advanced in overcoming prejudice, I doubt if we have yet got to that point of view where a British constituency would elect a black man... I imagine the colour was not exactly black, but at all events, he was a man of another race."

Many ordinary British people were shocked by this, and the press had some fun at Salisbury's expense, given the factual inaccuracy of his remark; one commentator had written earlier, "If Mr Naoroji had changed his name to Mr Brown or Mr Jones, no one would know him to be a Parsee". *The Star* observed that in truth the Prime Minister's own skin was darker than Dadabhai's, and a cartoon in *Hindu Punch* portrayed a black-faced Prime Minister alongside a white-faced Naoroji and quoted Herbert Gladstone (son of the previous Prime Minister) as saying "I know Mr Naoroji very well, and I know Lord Salisbury by sight, and I am bound to say that of the two Lord Salisbury is the blackest". The *Christian Million* in 1886 had commented that Dadabhai looked so English that "his name might be Brown or Jones, did it not happen to be Dadabhai Naoroji".

Dadabhai was not personally offended – he was rarely offended by anything – but plenty of other people in both India and Britain took offence on his behalf, not least because of his reputation as a man of unquestioned honesty and decency. It was said that Salisbury earned a rebuke from Queen Victoria, and the press rallied behind Dadabhai from that point on. The *Weekly Dispatch* stated: "The mischief done by Lord Salisbury is irreparable. That sneer will be quoted in every paper and pass from mouth to mouth in every bazaar in India. There is indeed only one way in which its fatal poison may be counteracted. If some British constituency were to send Mr Naoroji to Parliament by acclamation, then the Indian people would see that Lord Salisbury spoke not the voice of England, but merely expressed his own caddish contempt".

Sir Lepel Griffin, Chairman of the East India Association, made a vicious and explicitly racist attack at this point in a letter to *The Times*, calling Dadabhai 'destitute of local sympathy or local knowledge' and labelling the Parsis 'the Jews of India'. He went on that Naoroji was "an alien in race, in custom, in religion, no more unsuitable a representative could be imagined or suggested. As to the people of India, Mr Naoroji no more represents them than a Polish Jew settled in Whitechapel represents the people of England." The *Bengal Times* of Calcutta expressed the view that "a Hindu, Mussulman or Parsi representative of a British constituency is a contradiction in terms. It would be as absurd as an English President of an Indian Congress." In London, *The Star* was equally discouraging: "The experiences of good Mr Lal Mohun Ghose in Deptford should be a standing warning against Baboo candidatures among English working men. Home Rule for India may give these gentlemen a chance, but they must bide their time, for English electors will [have] none of them."

The effect of this opprobrium, as far as Dadabhai was concerned, was almost entirely positive. According to Sumita Mukherjee, writing in the Journal of the Oxford University History Society (2004): "This notoriety helped Naoroji in his campaign for Central Finsbury and, in private correspondence with Dinshaw Wacha, the secretary of the INC, he was reassured that he would 'now draw greater sympathy than before from the British electors'". And so it was. Right-thinking people flocked to his support, condemning Salisbury, Griffin and others whose racism had been exposed. The National Liberal Club held a banquet to advertise its disapproval. Lord Ripon loudly encouraged the people to support Dadabhai's campaign for election.

It may also be that at this time, working-class voters wanted leaders who would support them and were less concerned about their race or colour. Sumita Mukherjee further commented in her 2004 paper: "Although Imperial sentiment was running very high during the Golden Jubilee in 1887, especially in the capital, working men may have been relatively unconcerned about the ethnic origin of their MP as long as their interests were served."

Then, in June 1890, Mr Eve found himself another seat to contest. This appeared to leave the field clear to Dadabhai, but then a new association put up Mr Ford, who had come third behind Eve in the original battle. Though spurned once again, Dadabhai continued his fight, receiving valuable moral and practical support from William Digby, the man who had told him to get an English hat (unsurprisingly, he did not adopt this suggestion). In July 1891 Dadabhai wrote to several newspapers outlining the duplicitous and obstructive behaviour of the bulk of the Liberal Party. After much discussion and internal manoeuvring, Mr Ford withdrew his candidacy, leaving the field clear to Dadabhai at last.

Among the key points of Dadabhai's manifesto were home rule for Ireland, the endowment of London County Council, allowing women to stand for seats on London County Council, rating to apply to vacant properties, direct popular veto of the liquor traffic and graduated income tax rates on higher incomes; and of course agreement to the Indian reforms for which he had been campaigning so long. Racial prejudice contained to colour the campaign against him, and he was branded a 'fire worshipper' by the Conservatives in an attempt to make his faith sound a good deal less civilised than it actually was.

Yet he received support from high places. Lord Ripon, Lord Reay, Lord Rosebery and Herbert Gladstone all sent their best wishes, as did Josephine Butler, a leading women's rights campaigner. Messrs Eve and Ford, who had nothing against Dadabhai personally, also weighed in behind him, as did the Liberal party machine, putting the dispute over his selection firmly behind them. Lord Salisbury had supplied Dadabhai's Conservative rival, Captain Penton, with coaches for use on election day, and on hearing this the Maharaja of Baroda provided carriages of his own for Dadabhai's use.

The feminist and social reformer Josephine Butler wrote assuring him he was 'one of the most uncompromising friends of womanhood' and praising his 'clear insight into all that is false and unequal in our British laws regarding women'. "Your standard of moral excellence for men and women alike, and of the integrity of marriage and the purity of the home, are all that the most convinced Christian could desire in accordance with the ethical teaching of Christ" she wrote. "You may be sure of our prayers for your success."

It was during this election campaign that Dadabhai first came into contact with Mancherjee Bhownaggree, another Bombay-born Parsi. That was about all they had in common, as Bhownaggree's life had been much more illustrious than Dadabhai's. He had come to Britain in 1882, aged 31, and had been called to the bar three years later. Since then he had been a practising barrister and had been appointed judicial councillor to a maharaja. In Europe, he was head of the European Parsis. Bhownaggree too had a parliamentary seat in his sights, although there was no secret about the fact that it would be on the other side of the political spectrum.

Despite the differences in their politics, however, he volunteered to help Dadabhai in the 1891 poll; in return he gained valuable insight into what was involved in contesting a British election. He may have been motivated by his stated belief that Indians should regard their nationality as more important than their religion or their politics. It would be another three years before Bhownaggree would get his chance to follow Dadabhai into Parliament. Diametrically opposed as they were in the political arena, the two men were never enemies and even became allies in later life, over matters concerning their nation and their faith.

The election on July 6, when it came, was a cliffhanger. Dadabhai won by 2959 votes against Captain Penton's 2956. The first Indian ever to be elected to the British Parliament had scraped in by just three votes. "The sky was rent with cheers which resounded from St Paul's to Chelsea," wrote Masani.

CHAPTER 4

An Indian in Parliament

Dadabhai's election to Parliament in 1892 was celebrated around the globe, and the electors of Finsbury were as widely congratulated as he was. Pherozeshah Mehta commented: "Many people profess to be sceptical as to the patriotism and political sagacity of the electors of Central Finsbury in choosing an Indian for their representative. But they have rendered a service of incalculable value by proving... that the instincts of English political wisdom are capable of triumphing over the direct prejudices of caste, colour and creed".

However, the election result itself hung in the balance for a time. Captain Penton, the defeated candidate, demanded a recount, which served only to increase Dadabhai's majority from three to five. There was another worry – those coaches so generously funded by the Maharaja of Baroda to enable

Dadabhai's supporters to get to the polling booths. Homi Dadina, one of Dadabhai's helpers and soon to be his son in law, ignorant of the Corrupt Practices Act, had used cash at his disposal to play host to some of the supporters. Those working for Captain Penton cunningly asked him for coaches for their supporters, without making clear whose side they were on. Dadina fell for this and even gave them cash for drink. At a court hearing that December, each side challenged the others' votes. To the great relief of Dadabhai and his supporters, the petition was finally withdrawn, but not before he had run up a very large legal bill.

'Dadabhai Narrow Majority' (to quote a play on words popular at the time) had been left almost penniless by the cost of fighting the election, and he began to think of returning to India. Fortunately, when word of this got out he received vital support in the form of a gift of £1000 from the state of Baroda for which he had done so much, and other states followed suit.

Dadabhai refused to take the oath on the Bible as he was not a Christian, but he was allowed to take the oath of office in the name of God on his copy of the *Avesta*. When he made his first visit to the House on February 28 1893, he gave an effusively grateful maiden speech and was called by the *Daily Telegraph* 'an eloquent and fervent recruit to opposition ranks'. The topic was the gold standard, in which he took a keen interest, because India's currency was based on the value of silver and the Government's proposals for the gold standard threatened to devalue it, piling hardship upon hardship. This debate opened up the whole question of India's economic position and provided a valuable opportunity for Dadabhai to argue his country's cause.

Part of his speech was reported in Hansard as follows:

"They should consider India in two aspects—both as a self-governing country, like China independent of outside political influences, and as a country under foreign domination, with many important forces influencing her for evil and for good... As far as trade and commerce between two independent countries were concerned it made no difference what currency existed in those countries... As exchange fell, prices fell with it proportionately in England, and all the talk about India getting immense quantities of silver when there was a fall in exchange was simply absurd. The Manchester manufacturer was not such a fool as to pay 6d. per pound for cotton in England when by sending a telegram to Bombay he would be able to get the same cotton for 3d. per pound.

"He was exceedingly thankful to those hon. Members who had shown so much sympathy towards India, but somehow or other the argument was always on the side for which it served its purpose. India was at one time exceedingly poor, and at another time exceedingly prosperous. But whatever the state of India might be, the system of exchange had nothing to do with it.

"Then take India, as it was, under foreign domination. It was true that India, under her peculiar circumstances, felt the pinch. India had to remit £16,000,000 sterling to this country every year. This year, or perhaps next year, it would unfortunately be £19,000,000, because for several years the India Office had got capital paid by Railway Companies in England, and did not require to draw their bills in India to that extent...

"The position was, therefore, this: India had to send from her "scanty subsistence" a quantity of produce to this country equal to the value of £19,000,000 in gold. As gold had risen, India had to send more produce in proportion to the rise in gold, no matter what the currency was — silver, or copper, or anything. The sympathies of those who wished well to India in the course of the Debate were therefore a little misdirected. The remedy for the evils from which India was suffering did not lie in introducing bimetallism, or changing the currency into gold or restricting the silver currency, but in reducing the expenses of the excessive European Services to reasonable limits.

"After a hundred years of British administration—an administration that had been highly paid and praised— an administration consisting of the same class of men as occupied the two Front Benches, India had not progressed, and while England had progressed in wealth by leaps and bounds— from about £10 in the beginning of the century to £40 per head—India produced now only the wretched amount of £2 per head per annum. He appealed to the House, therefore, to carefully consider the case of India. He knew that Britain did not want India to suffer – he was sure that if the House knew how to remedy the evil they would do justice to India, but he wished to point out that bimetallism and the other artificial devices that had been put forward were simply useless, and that India would get no relief from them whatever. On the contrary, much mischief would be the result. With regard to the meeting of the Conference again, he thought it would be useless...

"He was of opinion that England must stick to the sound scientific principle of currency that she had adopted. Nor should she allow the currency of India to be tampered with. He thanked the House for the favourable hearing accorded to him, and hoped that before any step was taken to change the currency system either of this country or of India they would think once, twice, and three times."

Dadabhai failed to push through an amendment designed to address this problem, but his eloquent and well-evidenced arguments for it earned him great respect in the House. In the long run the gold standard would prove to give India a stronger economic future because of an international flight from the use of silver for that purpose, but that would not become clear for many years.[19]

One of those listening to that speech from the gallery was 15-year-old Muhammad Ali Jinnah, who would go on, more than half a century later, to found Pakistan in order to give Indian Muslims their own country; he had arrived in England shortly after the election to take up an apprenticeship in shipping (he soon decided to study law instead, becoming the youngest Indian yet to be called to the English Bar). Jinnah became a devotee of Liberalism and a great supporter of Dadabhai.

Dadabhai soon turned out to be a capable speaker who kept his message plain and focused and his arguments fair and balanced. His only weakness was that at times he could be long-winded, not a recipe for success in the House of Commons. He proved an active Parliamentarian who soon found himself both fielding and facing many questions, and repeatedly filled over a page of the Order Book with notices of motions calling for information on India. The Indian press began to call him, as they had Henry Fawcett, 'the 'Member for India', a label which he did not welcome, although he had little choice but to accept it.

Dadabhai's position as an MP gave him access to figures which enabled him to strengthen his argument about the drain theory. For example, he was able to show that revenue and expenditure figures did not balance as the Government

19   Masani p 333

claimed, because they did not allow for the charges India had to pay on its debts. He suggested that if British investment went into Indian manufacturing, the wealth created would develop a very large consumer market for British exports.

Hostility in the right-wing press did not cease after the election. Reports stated that Dadabhai had received pledges from no fewer than 13 maharajas amounting to gifts totalling £38,000, an absurd claim. He was forced to send a statement to the London dailies firmly denying the existence of any such gifts.

The old issue of favouritism for Anglo-Indian candidates entering the Indian Civil Service re-emerged, and in March 1893 Dadabhai won a significant battle. He had been forced to withdraw a Bill aimed at rectifying this problem by providing for examinations to be held simultaneously in India and the UK; it was blocked by the front bench of his own party. But then Herbert Paul MP, whose turn it was next to present a Bill, agreed to use that opportunity to table a resolution to the same effect. After a long debate, Paul's Bill was passed in the House by 84 votes to 76, an acclaimed and unexpected victory for Dadabhai, the Parliamentary Committee and India, although the proposed change was still some way short of coming into law, let alone into practice.

In 1893 he led the establishment of an Indian Parliamentary Committee which would form a caucus in Parliament to pursue India's claims. Most members were Liberal, with some Labour members joining in. From an additional membership of about 20 it quickly grew to more than 100 members, wielding considerable power in the House. This was a most uncomfortable development for the Anglo-Indian community, who set up an 'Anglo-Indian Defence Association' to counter the new body. Directly out of this would come the decision to support a Conservative Asian candidate for the next election – Mancherjee Bhownaggree.

Dadabhai was a member of Gladstone's last Liberal administration, and he strongly supported Gladstone's determination to achieve home rule for Ireland. For this purpose the Government had introduced the Government of Ireland Bill 1886, which had failed by 30 votes to pass into law. At this time the Irish issue had a much higher profile in the House than the Indian question, so Dadabhai's own agenda suffered somewhat.

Dadabhai's record in the House of Commons was exemplary, and matched only by that of the Chief Whip. He attended 654 out of 704 divisions in the House and found someone to 'pair' for him (vote in his place) for all the other 50. In his three years in Parliament he raised ten questions on matters concerning India, from the treatment of Indians in Madagascar to speed limits for petrol-powered vehicles.

Outside the House of Commons, Dadabhai involved himself with many different groups around his constituency and became an Odd Fellow, a Forester, a Druid and a Good Templar. He also supported or attended meetings of the Band of Hope Society, the London Municipal Reform League, the Working Men's Club, the Women's Liberal Federation, the Women's Franchise League and later the National Union of Women's Suffrage Societies. He gave a vote of thanks when the New Vestry Hall was opened in Finsbury (it later became Finsbury Town Hall). He spoke to the London Chamber of Commerce, the Clerkenwell United Rate Payers' Society, the Central Finsbury Radical Association, the Temperance Movement, the Institute of Bankers, the Goldsmiths' and Foresters' Union and the Stone and Zinc Preparers' Association, to name but a sample.

He campaigned for fairer ground rents, and his first motion concerning the constituency related to the use of Lincoln Inn Fields for leisure use; he won the motion in the Commons but it was rejected by the Lords.

Dadabhai was made President of the Local Government Board, and he used his influence there to try to prevent the detached Muswell Hill portion of his constituency from being transferred to neighbouring Hornsey – this despite the fact that Muswell Hill represented a Tory enclave, and his seat would have been safer without it.

The opium trade was one major issue Dadabhai tackled without achieving success, at least at the time. For many years the Government had been reluctant to give up the profits it was making from both India and China in the opium trade, despite the obvious harm to users. In a letter of 1881 he wrote: "What a spectacle to the world! In England no statesman dares to propose that opium may be allowed to be sold in public houses at the corner of every street... and yet at the other end of the world this Christian, highly civilised and humane England forces a 'heathen' and 'barbarous' power to take this poison and tempts a vast human race to use it, and to degenerate and demoralise themselves with this 'poison'! And why? Because India cannot fill up the remorseless drain... the opium trade is a sin on England's head and a curse on India for her share in being the instrument."

Moves to control the trade were abandoned as the Gladstone Government ran out of steam towards the end of its term. Public opinion against opium was growing, but it would not be until the early 20th century that it would finally be consigned to history.

The curse of alcohol was another social issue which Dadabhai worked hard to remedy, and he was a founder member of the Anglo-Indian Temperance Association, set up in 1888.

In October 1893 Dadabhai received the shocking news that his only son Adi had died after a heart attack, aged only 34. He and Virbai had seven young children, with an eighth on the way, and suddenly Dadabhai's family needed him. In fact he was about to return to India anyway to address

Lord Harris, cricket-mad Governor of Bombay (1890-95)

the Indian National Congress. When he stepped off the ship in Bombay on December 3, dressed in his national costume of black coat and turban with red silk trousers, he was overwhelmed by the crowds. Lord Elgin and the Governor of Bombay, Lord Harris, were there to greet him, along with council representatives from all over the presidency. Only later, once he had braved the tumultuous crowds, met the official reception committee, led by the Governor, Lord Harris, and finally been taken to his home in a carriage pulled by four grey horses, was he able to have some private time with his family to deal with the tragedy of losing Adi. His first priority was the grief-stricken Virbai; he urged her to remain in Cutch, where the family were living, and secured the support of the Maharaja of Gondal to support her and her now fatherless children. Later Virbai became tutor to the heir to the throne of Cutch.

Two weeks later Dadabhai boarded a train for the 800-mile journey to Lahore for the Indian National Congress meeting, and was greeted all along the way by crowds who had come to show their appreciation for the Grand Old Man of India. At the Sikhs' Golden Temple at Amritsar, he was invested with a robe of honour. Even the Muslims celebrated his arrival when he reached Lahore. "His reception at Lahore has perhaps not been surpassed since the days of Ranjit Singh" (a great leader of the Sikh Empire), wrote William Hunter in *The Times*.

In a speech to the crowds, Dadabhai urged them to rise above sectarian feelings and remember that they were Indians first and foremost. He also urged them to remain loyal to the Crown and have faith in the British sense of justice. As President of the Congress, he stated the urgent need to seek direct and permanent representation for India with the British Government. When he left for Britain again on January 22 1894, he left his people with a new vision of their future.

In 1895 Dadabhai won a major victory with the appointment of a Royal Commission to look into the financial inequity between Britain and India. He spent many weeks preparing for the hearing. However Gladstone (the 'Grand Old Man' of British politics, as some called him) stood down in March 1894, and the Earl of Rosebery, who succeeded him as Prime Minister and Liberal leader, followed suit barely a year later. The now beleaguered Liberal Party had little choice but to call an election, set for July 16 1895.

The party had no qualms about Dadabhai standing for re-election, but the Liberals had fallen from favour, and the Conservative candidate, W F B Massey Mainwaring, won by a decisive 805 votes. This same election was the occasion on which Mancherjee Bhownaggree took office for the first time, having won Bethnal Green for the Conservatives by a majority of 160.

Dadabhai must have half-expected his defeat, given the changed political climate; he told the *Sunday Times*: "I have just been carried away by the wave of Conservatism that has for the time being wrecked British Liberalism. No doubt a good many who are less well informed will regard it as a matter of racial prejudice." Undoubtedly his supporters back in India were more shocked and disappointed than he was. Even the pro-Establishment *Times of India* remarked: "We cannot record without regret the widespread disappointment which Dadabhai's defeat has caused in this country. We do not think he ever seemed to his most resolute opponents as other than a straightforward, sincere and disinterested champion of the views he adopted".

Dadabhai was not too disheartened by the loss of his seat, as a political career had never been an ambition in its own right; he saw it as merely one way of achieving his vision for India. His three years in Parliament had raised his profile enormously and enable him to advance the Indian cause in many ways, despite the lack of decisive new legislation in his favour. Nor did he feel the need to return to his native country. Now close to his 70th birthday, he acquired a permanent home, 72 Amberley Road London SE (south of the river, to the east of Woolwich), and soon had three of his grandchildren staying with him for long enough to attend a private school in Forest Hill.

72 Amberley Rd, Maida Hill London SE, once the home of Dadabhai Naoroji.

There were now moves to have Dadabhai knighted, but he resisted them, saying he wanted to keep away from honours and 'personal decoration'. He maintained this stance for the rest of his life, always saying that his popular recognition as the 'Grand Old Man of India' meant far more to him than a knighthood. "Is it vanity that I should take a great pleasure in being hailed as the Grand Old Man of India?" he wrote. "No, that title, which speaks volumes for the warm, grateful and generous hearts of my countrymen, is to me, whether I deserve it to not, the highest reward of my life".

Freedom from his duties as an MP left him more time to devote to the impending Royal Commission under the chairmanship of Lord Welby, which was to consider the question of whether India was better or worse off under the British Crown. Specifically it looked into cases where excessive or unjust payments had been made by the Indian Government; one of the most blatant was a case where a telegraph company continued to be paid a fixed return on capital for 50 years after the service it provided had collapsed. The principal was that British expenditure should not be subsidised by milking India.

As one of only three members (out of 14) who could be counted on to argue for India (the others were his allies William Wedderburn and W C Caine), Dadabhai knew he would have his work cut out. Three of the members were Anglo-Indians who regarded the job in hand as simply tweaking the existing system, while Dadabhai and his supporters were seeking much more far-reaching reforms. However, he had been investigating the problem and gathering evidence for the past quarter of a century, and he was far better briefed on the facts and figures than any of the other participants. Among many facts and figures he present to the Commission, he showed how in ten years his 'drain' had amounted to a total of 359 million rupees

William Wedderburn, Scottish-born Bombay judge and political ally of Naoroji. Wedderburn co-founded the Indian National Congress with A O Hume.

lost to India. His remedies were more representation by Indians and fairer distribution of costs, with no more one-sided contributions to the Imperial system in which India had no say.

Clearly he still felt his work so important that nothing could be allowed to interrupt it. When his daughter Maki pressed him to travel home to attend her wedding to Homi Dadina, he refused. She put off the plan, hoping to persuade him, but finally he wrote to her in November 1896: "Nothing can delight me more than to be present at your wedding. But I am helpless. I have undertaken a duty, which, I have no doubt you will agree with me, I *must* perform. This is nearly the last work of my life, and its fruition as far as it can go. Unless you wish me to throw away the whole work of my life, it is impossible for me to stir... The manner in which the people of India received me and for which we were all so glad shows what I owe to them. No, dear, give up the idea of my presence... it is useless, my dear child, to wait."

Finally the Welby Commission came to some positive conclusions, although they were limited in scope. It agreed that the expenditure expected from India did exceed tax revenue, and that the tax system should be overhauled. Dadabhai and his allies responded by preparing a separate report which covered some of the ground deliberately omitted from the Commission enquiry, notably how various departments were taxing the Indians without reference to one another, leading to intolerably high burdens. They also suggested that Indians should be appointed to the relevant councils of the Secretary of State and the Viceroy. They asked for a Select Committee of the House of Commons to be set up to enquire into the 'overall financial condition of India'.

Dadabhai wrote in 1897 that Indian views had now been given free expression at last. The Commission was a small but important step forward in achieving fairer treatment for India.

CHAPTER 5

The later years

In February 1897, Dadabhai took the opportunity provided by Queen Victoria's Golden Jubilee to write congratulating Her Majesty, while pointing out that her promise of 1858 to ensure equality for Indians had hardly been kept. No reply is recorded. His campaigning never ceased, and in 1897 and 1898 he took his message around the country, concentrating particularly on Lancashire, where at a series of public meetings he tried to explain how the Government's manipulation of export regulations, although ostensibly benefiting the Lancashire cotton trade, was in truth economically damaging on both sides, because India's government-inflicted poverty was making it impossible for Indians to afford the products of the Lancashire-based cotton industry. "Make it possible for the 250 or 300 millions of India to take £1 per head of British products, and it would be out of the power of England to supply the demand," he said. Prominent Indians were brought over to help him argue his case.

In 1898, the gold standard once again became a bone of contention. Dadabhai pointed out that applying it to the rupee would artificially inflate the value of the Indian currency and therefore the taxes payable to Britain. In the end a somewhat unsatisfactory compromise was struck.

Throughout this period Dadabhai received unstinting support and encouragement from his friend Henry Hyndman, who (having begun his political life as a Conservative) had in 1881 founded Britain's first socialist party, the Democratic Federation, and promoted the ideas of Karl Marx. The autocratic Hyndman claimed rather immodestly that he had 'done more for India than any man living', but certainly he gave Dadabhai great encouragement in his mission. He advised him of the growing fears among the Anglo-Indian community that there would be another uprising.

In 1888 a shy young law student had been given a letter of introduction to Dadabhai Naoroji. The student was Mohandas Kharamchand Gandhi, later to become better known as Mahatma Gandhi. Gandhi later wrote: "Indian students in London had free access to the Grand Old Man at all hours of the day. Indeed he was in the place of father to every one of them, no matter to which province or religion they belonged... whenever an address by [Dadabhai] was announced, I would attend it, listen to him from a corner of the hall, and go away having feasted my eyes and ears." To Dadabhai he wrote early in their friendship: "You will... oblige me greatly if you will kindly direct and guide me and make necessary suggestions, which shall be received as from a father to his child".

Gandhi as a young man

Dadabhai was described by Gandhi as his constant advisor and inspiration. The two corresponded regularly, all their letters handwritten. They also met on many occasions. In his foreword to R P Masani's book on Dadabhai, Gandhi described Dadabhai's office as "a garret perhaps eight feet by six feet. His desk, his chair and a pile of papers filled the room. I saw that he wrote his letters in copying ink and press-copied them himself."

In 1893 Gandhi moved out to South Africa, which had begun importing Indian labour in 1860, and it was there that he met with the racist attitudes that fired his great fight against racism and for Indian independence. He began what he later termed his 'satyagraha' campaign (an invented composite word meaning 'insistence on truth'). The problem was that after serving their terms, the Indians quite understandably wanted to set up as legitimate farmers and traders in their own right, which was not what the white colonists had in mind. They did all they could to get rid of the people they had imported to serve as little better than slaves. Dadabhai, appalled by this turn of events, took the matter up with Lord Ripon, but was advised that as South Africa was independent, the only course was one of persuasion.

In 1894 Gandhi wrote to Dadabhai for advice, saying "You will oblige me very greatly if you will kindly direct and guide me and make necessary suggestions, which shall be received as from a father to a child". He continued to correspond regularly with Dadabhai, seeking advice on ways to achieve his aims. The older man was able to advise him on the constitutional aspects, and Gandhi also received support from Mancherjee (now Sir Mancherjee) Bhownaggree. They were unable to stop the Asiatic Registration Act from coming into law in 1908, but the resistance continued undiminished, until finally South Africa gave way. In 1914 the government passed the Indian Relief Act, which made some significant concessions, recognising the validity of Hindu and Muslim marriages and allowing free entry for educated Indians.

In 1900 the worst famine for 25 years hit India, and Dadabhai campaigned around the UK for relief from his people's suffering, helping to set up a famine relief fund. His patience was clearly beginning to run out and his tone was hardening, as can be seen from a speech he made in July that year, quoted in *India*: "Great Britain, during the whole period of her connection with India, never spent a single farthing of British money on the Eastern Empire... from the time when Great Britain first obtained jurisdiction over India down to the present day it has drawn millions upon millions sterling from that Empire; Great Britain had appropriated this Indian wealth, thereby reducing the population to extreme poverty... The Indians have not the slightest voice. British rule was supposed to confer great blessings on the Indian race. But what has been the result? Millions of the people dying from famine and disease." In a letter to a journalist, Dadabhai wrote: "I am afraid the Race Question will become in time a burning one... the Indian Question will be a terrible matter for England, if she does not look out."

Dadabhai's days as a British MP had appeared to be over, but in 1900, after considerable wrangling, he was selected as the Liberal and Radical Association's candidate for North Lambeth. This constituency had been created when Lambeth was divided by the Redistribution of Seats Act 1885 for that year's General Election. Dadabhai was invited to stand for the seat by the Liberal and Radical Association in North Lambeth, but his selection was complicated by some who preferred another candidate, a Mr W Wightman,[20] and then by allegations against Dadabhai that he had given money to certain people in the party. There followed nearly six years of internal skirmishing, with all manner of slander and misrepresentation aimed at Naoroji, before the next General Election finally came round in 1906. Somehow Dadabhai managed to maintain his position as the

20   Ralph pp168-169

Liberal and Radical candidate for most of this time despite backstage machinations designed to deter him, usually in favour of Wightman. "Compared to the machinations with the party, [the election] must have seemed a small affair," wrote Ralph. Finally Mr Wightman helpfully resolved the matter by dying.

In the months leading up to the election, Dadabhai managed to canvass some six thousand homes and address the electorate many times. He wrote letters, spoke to the press and made himself ceaselessly available for interview. Despite the racist sneers, most of the papers rallied behind him. When polling day came, this did not prevent Dadabhai from coming third behind the Liberal and Conservative candidates with a modest 733 votes.

By now he was 80 years old, so it says something for his reputation that he was called upon to stand, and a great deal for his stamina and determination that he was able to campaign as effectively as he did. As Masani put it, "Advancing age made no difference to him. If anything, he appeared to get more virile and more militant as he grew older."

Despite this, he was now growing increasingly conscious of his years and how far away he still was from seeing fair treatment for his country. After the election his attention turned increasingly to the younger generation, urging educated young men to become missionaries for India. And yet he still devoted most of every day to campaigning in one form or another, according to a report in the *Reading Standard* in March 1901.

The establishment of the Commonwealth of Australian Colonies on the first day of the new century gave Dadabhai pause for reflection. Here was a country which in little more than a century had risen from nothing but a penal colony to become a flourishing and wealthy new nation, while all the while India had languished in enforced poverty.

In 1901 he published another book, *Poverty and Un-British Rule in India*, a much more comprehensive account of his case that India was being unfairly treated. Again it was far from light reading, being packed with statistics, but it became, and has remained, an authoritative reference book for those seeking to investigate the true economic position of India in the late 19th century.

That was also the year when Naoroji joined the National Democratic League and contributed to a fund set up for the Labour leader, Keir Hardie, a move which suggested a growing sympathy for the socialist movement. George Lansbury MP wrote some years later that if Dadabhai had been of a later generation, he would undoubtedly have been a member of a socialist party. He was still fit and active at 75, and a letter in the *Reading Standard* describes how on a visit to the town to talk on 'The Condition of India' he rose at 7 am, addressed a school for 45 minutes in the morning, then spoke to a crowd of a thousand people in the afternoon before making a one-hour speech at the Assembly Rooms in the evening: "The famous Indian orator unsparingly criticised the government of India, showing how they had failed in their duty." At a later meeting in Camberwell he told a public gathering: "It is for you as electors of your country, you who have the sovereign power in your hands, to see why there has been a loss of thousands of Indians in famines. You have not spent a shilling in the formation of the Empire. The blood that was shed was also Indian blood. You have been regularly draining and bleeding us of millions... These millions do not go to make you any better off, they go into the pockets of the capitalists. Britain claims that Britons never shall be slaves. Is it her intention that she should make others slaves? You must insist that your representatives in Parliament do India justice."

On September 4 1903, his 78th birthday, 'Dadabhai Day' was inaugurated, and it would be celebrated for the rest of his life and beyond.

In his later years Dadabhai spent more of his time writing and less addressing meetings. He continued to write almost daily to the press and to influential bodies of various kinds to set out his views on various topics related to the Indian cause. One of the individuals he corresponded with was Jamsetji Tata, India's great industrial pioneer, who had founded the Tata group in 1868 and was now trying to develop an autonomous Indian business without dependence on British finance; after his death in 1904 the Tata Iron and Steel Works was established, and Tata remains a major industrial force today, owning some 150 companies including Jaguar Land Rover and Tetley. Tata, like Dadabhai, was a Parsi born in Navsari, and had followed his footsteps in travelling to England (a decade or so after Dadabhai) and setting up a textile business initially. He also shared Dadabhai's dedication to education for his people, and sponsored many young Indians to study for the Indian Civil Service.

At a Conference of Democrats in 1905, in his 80th year, Dadabhai moved a resolution demanding the establishment of a universal system of old age pension, based entirely on citizens' rights. In the same year Lord Curzon, the Viceroy, instigated the Partition of Bengal, separating the mainly Hindu west from the mainly Muslim east, supposedly in the interests of administration, but really with the aim of dividing the population in the hope of weakening the independence movement. The Bengalis were not fooled, and the partition provoked outrage; six years later it had to be rescinded. Indirectly, however, it helped Dadabhai and his supporters, because it so inflamed political opinion in India that opposition to British rule was once again at the forefront of the political agenda. As Dadabhai's biographer

Lord Curzon, Viceroy from 1899-1905

Masani put it: "When Lord Curzon attempted to put back the clock and when New India was in open revolt against the autocratic Viceroy, the hero of our story was past four score years, still carrying on a country-wide platform campaign in the United Kingdom, demanding redress of India's wrongs and proclaiming self-government as the only remedy".

Masani, commenting that year after year Dadabhai's criticism of the defects of British rule was growing more bitter, wrote that he was 'being driven gradually to extremism', the result of his 'dire disappointment'. Even so, he never lost his faith in British justice.

Also in 1905, Dadabhai was invited to be President for the 22nd Indian National Congress in Calcutta the following year, and accordingly he sailed for India at the end of November 1905. The Congress took place at a time of growing division between the conservative wing and the younger radicals. Dadabhai's invitation to preside was a useful compromise, as his reputation was great enough to satisfy the conservatives, while the more revolutionary members recognised that he could never be accused of upholding traditional attitudes. Indeed, his fight for self-government to stop the 'draining' and 'bleeding' of India was intensifying. He told Congress that in his fight for *swaraj* (independence) he had "felt so many disappointments as would be sufficient to break any heart and lead one to despair, and even, I am afraid, to rebel", but he had never despaired and never would. Perseverance, he said was, the only way forward. This was not entirely what the radicals wanted to hear; they felt they had all been 'persevering' for quite long enough already.

Dadabhai left India after the Congress in good shape, telling a journalist in September 1906 that he was in 'the best of health' and was enjoying the late summer heat. Asked to what he attributed this, he replied, "To life-long abstinence, to avoiding tobacco, to eschewing spices and condiments and to working hard". But his youthful vigour had inevitably faded by now. He suffered an attack of bronchitis, coupled with severe back pain, while a fluid retention condition prevented him from taking his regular walking exercise. His granddaughters Gosi and Nergis went to London to nurse him, and finally in April 1907 he felt well enough to resume his normal activities. However, he was not well enough to attend a farewell gathering of the London Indian Society, and had to spend a period in a nursing home before he was fit enough to travel.

Dadabhai said his final farewell to Britain on October 11 1907, telling the London Indian Society on the dockside that should it ever sanction any form of violence to continue the struggle for independence, his name must be removed from the roll. The *Daily News* wrote of his departure: "Last Friday, at the age of eighty-three, Mr Dadabhai Naoroji said goodbye to England for the last time, and sailed for India, the sands of life running very low, his heart worn out with many wars and his eyes grown dim with gazing on the pilot stars. What his feelings may be I know not, but for half a century he has kept alive among Indians the belief that in the end England will be true to her own best traditions; that she will make of India a trusted partner, instead of a bond slave."

His health continued to be uncertain on the voyage, and a reception committee in Bombay had to be abandoned. He was taken to his home at Versova, where his granddaughter Meher looked after him, followed by his daughter Maki, who gave up her medical post to care for him. It must have seemed the end was near, but in fact he made a good recovery, and was quickly back to dealing with an 'enormous' quantity of correspondence, both in connection with his mission, from the many people wanting to seek his help or advice and from his children, his grandparents and even their teachers. He continued to take a particular interest in the education of all Indians. Condemned prisoners wrote asking him to appeal for mercy on their behalf; students asked for financial help to continue their studies; businessmen who had been swindled wanted him to seek redress; hopeful authors sent him their manuscripts. Few of them seem to have worried that a man in his mid-eighties might struggle to help.

Dadabhai expressed his fury when in London on July 1 1909 – Dadabhai Day – an Indian revolutionary activist, Madan Lal Dingra, shot dead Sir William Curzon Wyllie, the Assistant District Commissioner, as well as a doctor who tried to save him. Lal Dingra was hanged a few weeks later.

When the Transvaal Asiatic Registration Act came into force in July 1909, requiring all Asians to register and apply for a certificate of identity, Gandhi was in the forefront of the protests (it was then that his 'satyagraha' concept was developed), and Dadabhai made representations to the British Government. Five years later the Act's effects were effectively nullified by the India Relief Act, which abolished a £3 poll tax on Asians and recognised marriages of faiths other than Christian.

With advancing age Dadabhai travelled less, and Versova became a place of pilgrimage, for poor Indians and prominent citizens alike. The correspondence, if anything, grew. A letter to the Viceroy in 1909 extended to 80 typed sheets and went through the entire history of British rule in India. In April 1910 he compiled a lengthy summary of India's financial situation, followed in July by a similar paper on trade, a brief update to Poverty and Un-British Rule in India.

Gulbai died in the same year, after more than 60 years of a somewhat distant marriage, literally and metaphorically. Excluded from so much of her husband's life by his devotion to the great cause of India, and not helped by her illiteracy – one wonders how many letters he would have written to her if it had been otherwise – she would have been entitled to feel a little neglected, yet she was clearly as loyal to him as he was to her.

One of Dadabhai's last public acts was to welcome Queen Victoria's grandson, King George V, to the shores of India for the latter's visit in 1911. When the 'Great War' began in 1914, he did not hesitate to urge his countrymen to fight for the British Empire. He wrote, "Fighting as the British people are at present in a righteous cause to the good and glory of human dignity and civilisation... our duty is clear – to do, everyone, our best to support the British fight with our life and property." In the event, 50,000 Indians died fighting for Britain in the war. One who survived was Dadabhai's grandson Kershasp, who as previously mentioned joined the Middlesex Regiment after graduating from Christ's College, Cambridge, and distinguished himself in action in France. Kershasp proved to be a chip off the old block, bearing 'all Dadabhai's traits of chivalry, intrepidity and spirit of service and sacrifice', according to Farrokh Vajifdar in *The Twist in the Rope*. He was one of the first Indian soldiers to be promoted to officer rank.

Dadabhai startled his followers in 1915 by agreeing to become President of a new Home Rule League for India, set up by a Mrs Annie Besant. Not only was he now 90 years old, but the new League, admirable as its aims were, was more radical in its approach than the Indian National Congress and appeared to be in direct competition with it. Sir Dinshaw Wacha warned him: "By allowing your name to be associated with the League as its President you are in reality assisting those why by indirect and tortuous means are trying to wreck the Congress which you and other founders have built up with such care, wisdom and foresight during the last thirty years". Dadabhai replied that he did not agree that the new organisation posed any danger to the INC; Mrs Besant had promised him that. In the event, through various delays, the League did not get under way until it was too late for Dadabhai to take an active part.

By 1916 Dadabhai was becoming much less active, and the one event of that year that stands out is the conferring upon him in January, alongside Pherozeshah Mehta, an Honorary Degree of Doctor of Law by Bombay University. Sadly, Mehta died the day before the ceremony.

Dadabhai's health was now beginning to fail in earnest, and in the spring of 1917 arrangements were made to move him to a house in Cumballa Hill, Bombay, where he would be more comfortable during his last days. On June 30, shortly after that move, he died, surrounded by his family. He was 93 years old. His body was consigned to a Tower of Silence, in keeping with Zoroastrian tradition, and his funeral was attended by 15,000 people. An editorial in *India* commented: "His pre-eminence among [Indians] was undisputed, and his popularity was immense. It is over twenty years since Sir Pherozeshah Mehta voiced the universal opinion by describing him as the only man Indians recognise as having the right to make a representative claim for all India."

Sir Narayan Chandavarkar, an INC stalwart and a prominent Hindu reformer, summed up Naoroji's unique contribution to the life of India as follows: "If we take stock of his life and his example, may I not say with perfect justice and trust that in his career, in all he did, in all he suffered, and in all he taught, he was the Prophet Zoroaster's religion personified, because he was the man more than anybody else of pure thought, of pure speech and of pure deeds.... The sun that rose ninety-three years ago, over India is set, but I say it is set to rise again in the form of regenerated India, for Dadabhai lived and worked for us with a devotion which must remain for all of us an inspiring example".

Unlike his great admirer and disciple Gandhi, Dadabhai Naoroji was born too soon for the modern media, so there are no moving images of him and very few photographs to facilitate the documentary maker. If this had not been the case, perhaps he would have been as iconic and famous a figure around the world as the great Mahatma, having also achieved great and extraordinary things for his nation and for the cause of fairness and equality around the world. In India, however, he is much more prominent in people's memories. There are at least two Dadabhai Naoroji Roads, one in Mumbai and the other in Karachi, Pakistan. The one in Mumbai features a much-visited marble statue to him, overlooking the Flora Fountain. The Finsbury area of London has a Naoroji Street. Dadabhai Day, introduced on September 4th 1903, is still marked annually by Indians. In the UK in 2014, the then Deputy Prime Minister, Nick Clegg, inaugurated the Dadabhai Naoroji Awards for services to UK-India relations.

Dadabhai Naoroji's statue in Naoroji Road, Bombay, overlooking the
Flora Fountain

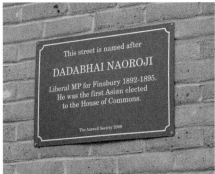

Dadabhai Naoroji Street, London, a
new street named after the Grand Old
Man of India

A caricature of Sir Mancherjee Bhownaggree published in *Vanity Fair* in 1897,
soon after he became an MP

PART II

Sir Mancherjee Bhownaggree
1851-1933
The first Indian Conservative

Sir Mancherjee Bhownaggree has never been viewed in the same heroic light as Dadabhai Naoroji. He certainly did not achieve the older man's near sainthood as a champion of India abroad; as a staunch Conservative and a devotee of the Crown, he supported British rule in India and campaigned for his Commons seat on an anti-immigration platform. Yet at the age of 44 he became his party's first ethnic minority British MP, and although his reputation was sullied by enemies who persistently attacked him for being, as they saw it, pompous and self-serving, he was a man of passion and conviction who went on to fight for his countrymen's interests, particularly for the Parsis, consistently and effectively for much of the rest of his life.

CHAPTER 6

A precocious talent

In August 1851 in Bombay, Dadabhai Naoroji was busy launching Rahnuma-e Mazdayasnan Sabha (his 'society for the guidance of true believers'), part of his mission to restore the original Zoroastrian creed. On the 15th of that month in the same city was born the man who would become the first Conservative Indian member of the British Parliament and a leading light of the Zoroastrian movement in Europe – Mancherjee Merwanjee Bhownaggree.

Bhownaggree was born to well-to-do parents, Merwanjee Bhownaggree and his wife Cooverbai. Merwanjee (1824-72) was a Parsi merchant, the postmaster for the town of Gozo and also the head of the Bombay State Agency for the state of Bhavnagar in south-east Gujarat, a couple of hundred miles north of Bombay and extending to about 3000 square miles; there were close links between the Bhownaggree family and the state, and the name Bhownaggree derives from Bhavnagar, also rendered variously as Bhaonagar, Bhaunagar or Bharnagar. According to Encyclopaedia Iranica, Merwanjee was also a newspaper proprietor and a banker.

Like Naoroji, Mancherjee was educated at Elphinstone College and Bombay University, where a dissertation he wrote on the East India Company was awarded a prize. Clearly young Mancherjee was fond of writing and good at it, as his first career was in journalism; when he was 20, Robert Knight, the editor of the English language daily journal *The Bombay Statesman*, took him on as a sub-editor. According to *Famous Parsis, Biographical and Critical Sketches*, published by G A Natesan in Madras in 1930, "while a student he showed considerable literary ability, and was led to adopt the profession of journalism, for which he showed brilliant capacity".

Bhownaggree's writing, even at this early age, went well beyond the subs' desk on a newspaper. In April 1872, when he was not yet 21, his school thesis was developed into a book, *The Constitution of the East India Company*. Its thesis was that it was in India's interest to be ruled by Britain, as long as the rule was fair. It opened with an ornately-worded introduction which gives an early indication of his love of using a dozen words where three would have done: "Sensible as the writer of the following few pages is of their imperfectness as regards both their literary workmanship and the information he has endeavoured to embody in them, he thinks it due to himself to acquaint the reader of the circumstances which induced him to allow their appearing in this form".

The book, which extends to 330 pages and around 60,000 words, is high-flown and hard to follow in parts, but it constitutes a detailed and astonishingly literate and mature account of the EIC story, from its earliest beginnings to the present date. Bhownaggree is open about the many errors the company made over its centuries of rule, but he defends the company in some respects. For example, he stated that the grievances expressed at the time when the Government of India Act of 1833 was being considered for renewal 20 years later had in fact been made by the company's own employees, or had come from 'that class of natives which was then pretty generally known as young India, whose superficial education had instilled in their minds a misguided notion of freedom and good government'. He agreed that complaints about the failure of the justice system in India, and the failure of the Government to employ Indians in senior positions as promised by the 1833 Act, were justified, stating (p. 206): "…the Company had intentionally failed to comply with the letter and spirit of the clause in the Act of 1833 which ordained no distinction of caste or colour to be observed in the distribution of offices in the Indian administrative service. It was hard to conceive anything that could go so far to cast reflection upon the Company's intention as the bare assertion that they had not given a single office of emolument or trust to a native. Scanty and superficial as the knowledge of most of the members of Parliament in 1853 regarding India was, it must have made their very blood boil to hear that the Company had adjudged 180,000,000 of God's creatures so depressed below the level of their own civilisation that no two of them were fit to hold situations of importance in their own land."

In 1877 Bhownaggree turned to a less contentious topic by

publishing a Gujarati translation of Queen Victoria's *Leaves from the Journal of Our Life in the Highlands*, dedicating it to the Prince of Wales. Along with the subject he chose for his dissertation, this reveals an early affinity for Britain and the British. Like many Parsis, including of course Dadabhai Naoroji, he took a great interest in English culture.

Bhownaggree married Motibhai in 1872, aged 20. They went on to have two sons, Merwanjee and Nussarwanjee, and one daughter, Perin. However, Motibhai plays little part in the rest of his story, because she could not tolerate the cold British climate and very quickly returned home for good. Like Gulbai Naoroji, she continued to live in India while her husband rose to prominence in England, and saw him again only on his periodic visits to Bombay. Perin spent time in both countries; not long before her father died she had a portrait of him painted in London by a Mrs Radcliffe Beresford, and the picture is still held by the family in Bombay.

In 1873, when Bhownaggree was only 22, he succeeded his father as the head of the Bombay Agency for Bhavnagar. This presumably necessitated a move to that state, and certainly it reduced his opportunities for writing and journalism. Because Bhownaggree was fluent in English, he was often asked to entertain European visitors and political luminaries. There was much entertaining, with fine parties to attend. He was soon living comfortably, mixing in high-class circles and becoming part of public life. Pictures of him from the time show an affluent, well-dressed Indian who had already adopted the Western style of dress.

As part of his service for the Thakore of Bhavnagar, Bhownaggree made his first visit to Britain, to promote the state there informally (formal lobbying was not allowed). In the wake of the Indian Mutiny, the British had imposed rules controlling the number of guns that could be fired as a salute for the various Indian leaders, all the way up to 21 guns for the maharajas of the three biggest states, while the smallest were entitled to only nine. The Thakore was not happy with his allocation. According to John Hinnells and Omar Ralph in their 1995 profile of Bhownaggree (see bibliography), a gift of 100,000 rupees (one *lakh*) was sent to the Liberal Party's Northbrook Club, and the Thakore was shortly after awarded the Order of the Star of India, 'a suitable increase in his standing'. Soon after this, Bhownaggree was made a Commissioner of the Indian Colonial Exhibition in South Kensington.

In 1881, still barely 30 years old, Bhownaggree was made both a Fellow of Bombay University and a Justice of the Peace. He was active in various social organisations, including the first Girls' English Academy in Bombay, for which he acted as Secretary for a period of more than seven years, according to the Natesan profile. He served on the governing bodies of various establishments, including the Mechanics and Gymnastics Institutes.

At about the same time he became the joint secretary of the Bombay branch of the East India Association, the body set up by Dadabhai Naoroji to influence public opinion in Britain. The Association did not last much longer and became defunct in the 1880s.

By 1882, India could hold him no longer. That was when he made the long journey to England to study law; his studies were funded by the state of Bhavnagar, generously enough to enable him to live in some style. *The Champion* of September 27 1896 stated that Bhavnagar had paid him a pension of 30-35,000 rupees, equal to roughly £1500, or six times the normal pension of an Indian in the British

Government, in order to retain his services, suggesting he was still in the pay of his old masters when he became an MP. This does not seem to have infringed any moral codes; Naoroji too had benefited from the patronage of a prince. In fact Bhownaggree does not appear to have ever used his position in Parliament to pursue the interests of Bhavnagar.

As Bhownaggree's career and reputation developed he began to argue for the rights of Indians, while holding to his pro-Britishness, and he continued to take a great interest in female education in his homeland, writing a paper on the subject which won him a silver medal from the Royal Society of Arts. He was also appointed Secretary and principal organiser for the Rukhmabai Committee, set up in honour of the physician and pioneering feminist Rukhmabai (she did not use a surname) to uphold the rights of Indian girls and women. One of its first campaigns succeeded in raising the age of consent for Hindu girls from 10 to 12.

In or about 1885 Bhownaggree gave a presentation to the Society of Arts in London on female education in India, under the chairmanship of the great poet and cultural critic Matthew Arnold, and was awarded the Silver Medal of the Society for a written report on the same subject.

In 1885, after just three years' law study in London, Bhownaggree was called to the Bar at Lincoln's Inn. He lectured to the Society of Arts and was the first Asian to be elected to its Council. He also chaired several meetings of the East India Association, set up by Naoroji twenty years previously. In 1886 he was appointed to the Commissioners of the Colonial Exhibition held at South Kensington, work for which he was made a Companion of the Indian Empire (CIE), along with his involvement in the Imperial (later Commonwealth) Institute. Bhownaggree had clearly made a deep and favourable impression on British society within a very short time of leaving India, although at this stage there is no indication that he was contemplating a political career.

Shortly after being called to the bar he reported to the Society of Arts a criticism of 'Female Education in India', under the chairmanship of Matthew Arnold, who worked as an inspector of schools when he was not engaged in poetry or literary criticism. According to Natesan, his treatment of the subject was so warmly appreciated that the Silver Medal of the Society was awarded to the writer. After that he continued to be an active member of the Society, which led in 1902 to his being elected a member of the Council, the first Indian to be so honoured. He was one of the Commissioners of the Indian and Colonial Exhibition held at South Kensington in 1886, when he was created a Companion of the Indian Empire (CIE). The Exhibition in due course led to the founding of the Imperial Institute, which in turn became the Commonwealth Institute. Bhownaggree later provided funds for a corridor within the Institute.

Bhownaggree was devoted to his sister Awabhai, known as Ave, and had acted as her surrogate father since the death of their father Merwanjee. In 1888 Ave died, still a young woman, and the depth of his grief at her loss is clearly expressed in a letter in which he wrote: "I have lost the zest in life; certainly I do not wish to improve my prospects or aspire to honours. I regard the volume of life in that respect closed to me." He also wrote that he was considering joining a religious community, but that his faith in Zoroastrianism stood in the way. According to his family, he prayed daily from the *Avesta*, the sacred book, and throughout his life he never discarded the sacred Zoroastrian shirt and cord, the *sudre* and the *kusti*. In memory of his sister he founded the Bhownaggree Home for Nurses in Bombay, and with his mother he set aside 25,000 rupees for its construction. He donated money in her memory for the eastern colonnade leading to the Indian section of the Imperial Institute building, part of Imperial College, and paid for a stained-glass window in her memory to be installed at his Anglican parish church, St Luke's. He also provided a medal for the pupil graduating with the highest marks from the Alexandra Girls' English Institution in Bombay.

In the late 1880s and early 1890s Bhownaggree maintained a steady correspondence with Sir George Birdwood, an official Government commentator and acknowledged expert on India, and a man regarded as an important champion for India in Britain. In 1888 he intimated to Sir George that he was ready to give up not just his responsibilities in Bhavnagar but his life in India. He wrote: "I feel like a counsellor to Bhavnagar State, as there is nobody in the Maharaja's confidence to whom the work could be transferred. But I am bent upon having some arrangement made before many months are over which would relieve me of the work. This would not interfere with the plan I have formed of being here in India for some time to see the completion of the Memorial Hall for which my mother and I have set apart Rs 25,000 in memory of my sister. Then my work in this life will be over, and I shall be free to leave this land to settle down in some quiet place in England."

Bhownaggree had 'nearly a thousand acres of land' in Gujarat, he told Sir George, but clearly spent very little time there. He even thought at one time of acquiring a farm in England[21], but as there is no subsequent record of any such thing we must assume that nothing came of the idea.

21 Letter to Sir George Birdwood, 8.5.1891 (British Library)

Four years later his desolation at the loss of Ave is made clear in another letter to Sir George, written on November 22 1892 in Bombay:

"Today, the fourth anniversary of my Ave's passing away to the realms of everlasting happiness, I am passing the time in pious thoughts, doing as little of mundane work as I can… It has been a great comfort to be with my dear saintly mother today, who has all along borne her grief most bravely and sacredly, and she has been to me both a solace and an example." His letter goes on to draw parallels between the Catholic Church and the Zoroastrian faith, saying how similar their observances are, but how much more positive the former is in dealing with bereavement ("they do it with much pleasure and rejoicing"). Then he refers to an engraved case Sir George had sent to him "containing the braids of [Ave's] hair which you, my kind and dear friend, have with such delicate and loving thoughts & care placed in that richly-wrought case… I am almost afraid to open the case or outer box, for I do not know where to enshrine it." He was still puzzling over that several months later.

THE OPENING CEREMONY OF THE

FRAMJEE DINSHAW PETIT
Laboratory of Scientific Medical Research

AND THAT OF THE

AVABAI BHOWNAGGREE HOME FOR NURSES

On Tuesday the 17th February 1891.

Their Excellencies Lord and Lady Harris will be received at the entrance by the Surgeon General with the Government of Bombay, the Principal and Professors of the Grant Medical College and the Medical Staff of the Jamsetjee Jejeebhoy Hospital.

On Their Excellencies taking their seats Mr. Bhownaggree will invite Lady Harris to open the Bhownaggree Home and Mr. Framjee Dinshaw Petit will invite His Excellency the Governor to open the Laboratory.

Their Excellencies followed by the assembly will proceed to the main entrance of the Bhownaggree Home.

A key will be presented to Lady Harris who will then enter the building and declare it open.

Their Excellencies and the assembly will then proceed to the Framjee Dinshaw Petit Laboratory where a key will be presented to His Excellency who will then enter the building and declare it open.

Their Excellencies and the assembly will take their seats in the upper Hall of the building and His Excellency will address the assembly.

A vote of thanks will be proposed to Their Excellencies by Surgeon General Pinkerton and seconded by Brigade Surgeon Gray.

Notice announcing the opening of the Avabai Bhownaggree Home for
Nurses and the Framjee Dinshaw Petit Laboratory of Scientific Medical
Research on February 17 1891.

An essay by John McLeod entitled 'Mourning, Philanthropy, and M. M. Bhownaggree's Road To Parliament', quoted in *Parsis in India and the Diaspora* by John R Hinnells and

Alan Williams, examines these commemorative projects and comments as follows: "By the late nineteenth century, anglicized Parsis like Bhownaggree could integrate this British practice of mourning through statues and buildings with an overlapping one from their own tradition... Bhownaggree's memorial projects represent a coming together of the Victorian British practice of preserving the memory of the deceased, the Parsi custom of commemorating the dead with charitable gifts, the Parsi culture of benevolence, and nineteenth-century Parsi notions of progress (which was often associated with such causes as female education, Western medicine and the British Empire). The memorial projects helped pave the way for Bhownaggree's election to Parliament in 1895. They cemented his ties with important people in India and Britain. They showed that he could practise the sort of open-handed generosity then expected of MPs."

In Bombay, Bhownaggree carried out a more public project in memory of Ave, a new home for the Alexandra Native Girls' English Institution (now the Alexandra Girls' English Institution). Most of the school's early administrators and students were Parsis, and Bhownaggree himself served as school secretary from 1873 to 1882. He, his parents, his wife and Awabhai all appear on lists of donors to the school. Following the demolition of Bombay's city walls in the 1860s, a row of imposing buildings had been constructed on an open area west of the old city walls.

According to John McLeod: "Bhownaggree had his eye on a vacant corner plot on Esplanade Road [now Mahatma Gandhi Road], across Napier Road from the Alexandra Institution.

In March 1889 he met with the Governor of Bombay, Lord Reay. He wanted Reay's government to provide the land for the hall, and to match the trust's contribution to construction. Reay agreed to grant a site, though not necessarily the prime location that Bhownaggree desired. Government funding, however, would only be possible if the hall were more than a mere private memorial. Bhownaggree therefore told Reay that he intended the hall to be devoted to a series of lectures on the basis of the university extension scheme in England, but specifically for women."

Hard on the heels of the school came a nurses' home, paid for by the Dufferin Fund, which had been set up to bring British women physicians to India. This too would be a memorial to Awabhai. Completed in 1891, it accommodated 20 nurses, and Bhownaggree's Christmas cards that year bore images of his late sister and the new home. He topped up the now-depleted fund from his own money.

Unfortunately the death of Ave was not the last tragedy to strike the family; Bhownaggree's elder son, Merwanjee junior, died in 1900, when still only 26. It appears his younger son Nussarwanjee followed his father into the law profession, because Bhownaggree wrote to Sir George Birdwood in 1894 that the young man had passed his exams and he intended him to go to Oxford to read for the bar, apparently with a view to a lucrative position back home ("It will be a good course for him to take up one family connection with Bhavnagar.")

By now daughter Perin had married a distinguished physician, Dr J N Bahadurji. They had a daughter, Piloo, who married into the Wadia family of Bombay Parsis and went on to live in London and Bombay.

In 1887, after qualifying as a barrister, Bhownaggree

returned to India at the invitation of the new Maharaja of Bhavnagar, to take on the role of Judicial Counsellor and help draw up a new state constitution.[22]

The Maharaja sought reforms in the areas of revenue collection, the judiciary, post and telegraph services and economic policy. Six years younger than Bhownaggree, he appears to have been a kindred spirit, and certainly he made Bhownaggree a close ally. His father, Bhownaggree's earlier sponsor, had died when he was very young, bequeathing him (upon his majority) the impressive title His Highness Maharaj Raol Shri Takhtsinhji Jaswantsinhji Sahib, Maharaj Raol Thakore Sahib of Bhavnagar. Takhtsinhji was clearly a reformer, and his first official act upon reaching his majority in 1878 was to give the green light to a railway connecting Bhavnagar to the main railway network, such as it was. The railway brought a great deal of trade and development to the states and firmly positioned the state in the vanguard of Indian modernisation.

The new Maharaja's reform programme "provoked a virulent attack upon the chief, who brought his defamers to trial in the High Court of Bombay" (from an entry credited to Bhownaggree in *Encyclopaedia Britannica*). It was Bhownaggree's duty to defend his master's plans in court (something for which he was clearly well equipped). Bhownaggree's account goes on: "The punishment of the ringleaders broke up a system of blackmailing to which rajas used to be regularly exposed, and the public spirit of Takhtsinhji in freeing his brother chiefs from this evil was widely acknowledged throughout India, as well as by the British authorities".

The new constitution was duly adopted, and it became

---

22 From 'Zoroastrian & Parsee Studies', Hinnells

a model for other states seeking reform. The English legal and administrative practices introduced by Bhownaggree represented radical change and led to criticism in the Indian media. He responded by challenging his opponents' libellous activities and exposed corrupt practices by his opponents, such as reliance on personal favours. This success in playing a pivotal role in reforming the administration of Indian states established a reputation that would long outlive him. The reforms brought Takhtsinhji an Empress of India Gold Medal in 1877, and a knighthood four years later. According to the Natesan profile: "So successful was the experiment and so effectively founded was the new constitution in its judicial organisation that it was reproduced by other States. It struck a blow at the absolute exercise of individual authority, and put an end to the strife of rival factions which is so fruitful a source of mischief in the India of the Princes".

This episode in Bhownaggree's life recalls Naoroji's experience some 15 years earlier, when he had done so much to fight the old ways in Baroda and bring about valuable and long-lasting reforms at the expense of the old system of *nazarana* (gifts and favours used to buy favourable treatment). At least Bhownaggree had the Maharaja and his Prime Minister (the Dewan) on his side, whereas Naoroji's foes had been led from the top. In 1890 Bhownaggree, the Maharaja and the state councillors brought a defamation action against their opponents and won the case. This further helped to cement his triumph and build his reputation as a man who was not to be opposed lightly.

A grateful Maharaja offered Bhownaggree a generous reward – a large area of land containing several villages. He accepted it, but only on the basis that it would be returned to the state after one generation, a provision which he confirmed in his will. This sounds surprisingly socialist in spirit for a 19th century Conservative, evidence for Bhownaggree's far from traditional political attitude.

In 1893 Bhownaggree arranged for the Maharaja to visit England to attend the opening by Queen Victoria of the Imperial Institute, for which he had provided funds for a corridor in memory of Awabhai.

Bhavnagar is no longer a royal state, but the once-royal first family continues to take an active role in the public eye as well as in business, with hotels, real estate, agriculture and ship-breaking) and is still held in high regard by the population.

CHAPTER 7

The Conservative candidate from Bombay

The depression which seems to have afflicted Bhownaggree following the death of his sister did not fully abate until 1891, when he began preparation for a return to Europe. His letters to Sir George Birdwood reveal a great appetite for Continental touring, particularly Germany ("I dearly love once again to be on the Rhine") and are variously postmarked in Bonn, Berlin, Dresden, Frankfurt, Vienna and Brussels. In one letter he confided to Sir George: "I always arrange my room wherever I go with a sacred corner or sanctum in it, and when I do it to my liking, I am in the best of moods with myself."

Bhownaggree's great attachment to, if not dependence on, Sir George is demonstrated in a letter from Bombay of March 1991, confirming an arrangement between the two of them to meet up during the former's forthcoming tour of Europe:

"I trust, fully trust, the pleasure which I have promised myself of having you for just a fortnight, if not more, on the continent will hold good. You know what an utter disappointment it will be to me if you fail in this. It will be to me like a dinner without the principal, or rather the only, guest." A shame that Sir George's replies are not to hand.

Another letter from this period reveals that Bhownaggree was happier in small and intimate social and family get-togethers than at large and glamorous gatherings. He wrote to Sir George in May 1991: "I must bring myself to go into large assemblages – meeting distinguished people & royalty on small occasions is quite another thing, and so I must thoroughly argue it out with you whether after all it's worthwhile again launching on the glossy gleaming waves of active ornamental life." However he was already aiming high, because in the same letter he states: "…your suggestion to see the King, if you send me a letter to His Majesty, is most tempting. So if you can do it, kindly send it."

As he approached his 40th birthday in August 1891, Bhownaggree must have been surveying his expanding figure with chagrin. He wrote to Sir George, letter undated but probably early 1891: "The stoutness troubles me, but perhaps you will find it not yet grown to detestable proportions. Well, how can I keep thin?… Only the day before yesterday I came to Proverbs XXVIII v. 25: 'He that putteth his trust in the Lord shall be made fat'. This at least is comforting!"

In June 1894 his view of his own health was more positive: "I take regular exercise. I keep out of doors all the time I can spare… I am keeping my good health, and the cold has almost left me."

Bhownaggree clearly became close friends with Lord Harris, the cricket-mad Governor of Bombay from 1890-95, and valued his support highly (though their relationship certainly had nothing to do with cricket). In February 1891 he wrote to Sir George Birdwood: "Last Wednesday I was lunching with Lord and Lady Harris at her special invitation. The party was *en famille*, and we were very familiar, Lady Harris & the baby with other ladies & myself being a party. They were all very nice to me, and I have evidence and proof that that Lord Harris is personally getting more and more kind and sympathetic towards me as he gets to know me better. More about this when we meet, as I can scarcely write it on paper."

The following month another letter related how he went shopping and to see the 'Japanese depot' with Lady Harris, who was 'affability itself'. He wrote: "I don't think even such Indophiles as the Freres[23] or Reays[24] had ever given a chance to any Indians during their regimes of dining with them unofficially, and this gracious act of Lady Harris' last Wednesday has made a grand impression about her simple ways of friendly nature." This and other references in Bhownaggree's letters indicate that Lady Harris must have been fond of him and enjoyed his company.

In September 1891 Bhownaggree was elected as a member of the Managing Committee of Charitable (Religious) Funds of Europe, his first new commitment for some time. He settled permanently in England in 1891 and actively associated himself with public bodies connected with India; he became head of the Parsi organisation in Europe and chair of the Indian Social Club. His political affinities were now becoming clear, and he believed that although many Indians in public life expressed support for the Liberals, there were many others who would support the Conservative point of view, given the chance.

23 Presumably the family of the late Sir Bartle Frere, who had been the first Governor of Bombay, 1862-1867

24 11th Lord Reay preceded Lord Harris, having been Governor of Bombay 1885-90

In 1891 Bhownaggree volunteered to help Naoroji to campaign in Finsbury, an offer which was gratefully accepted. The experience gave the younger man valuable insight into what was involved in fighting an election. It must have been very obvious to Naoroji how diametrically opposed to his own politics the newcomer was, but he did not pass judgment on his fellow Indian, simply accepting his offer to help at face value.

Letters to Lord Harris confirm that by the spring of 1894 Bhownaggree was planning to get into Parliament himself. In March that year he laid bare his feelings in a long letter to Sir George Birdwood, based on a recent conversation he had had with Lord and Lady Harris:

"One of the most interesting [topics] was the fact that Mr Naoroji's election, and the tactics of the India party in Parliament, and their interviews with newspapers and suchlike dodges, by which they palm off on the British public… the notion that all India is en bloc liberal and radical. That the people of India love the liberals and hate the conservatives. That they mope and moan when the latter are in power and expect nothing from them. How untrue all this is! India is solid conservative, and by her traditions, institutions, customs, religions and the very atmosphere which she lives in cannot be otherwise. These views however were held back from the British public, and Indian committee folk and others of Wedderburn's ilk not only spread mistaken ideas about political India but actually misrepresent people's wishes, as witness what they say about people here being athirst for simultaneous examinations and suchlike. Now how to remedy this growing evil, which threatens to become serious and make the Conservative Party unnecessarily odious in people's estimation here. Why will not the Conservative party start me as their candidate for some constituency? I may never succeed in being returned. But the very fact of there being someone from India who is Conservative would break the Radical theory like a house of cards. Then it will make me free, or rather justify me in declaring the opinions of conservative India from platforms, which will further dispel the Radical conspiracy. Lord Harris took in all this and said the idea was a very good one & workable, but said he could do very little to forward it from his present position...

"Everyone of note or wealth & influence, & most of all Parsees, who have seen me, wonder why I haven't yet stood for a Conservative constituency. They all think it was time the Congress fad of Radicalism was laid bare, & the nonsense talked to the English public unchallenged in the name of the people of India was exposed. Of course my idea is but a dream, and it is to be kept private until I have had Captain Middleton's opinion of the advice of friends like yourself, & I hope therefore you will treat all this as a confidential idea to be broached to anyone in confidence who you think might advise me when I am in London again, which I hope may be in May."

That claim that India was 'solid conservative' would no doubt have startled Dadabhai Naoroji and his supporters, if they had heard it.

Bhownaggree's first open declaration that he planned to enter Parliament himself came at a function to honour Naoroji on his election. According to the *Indian Spectator* of August 21 1892, Naoroji said: "And let me venture on your behalf that the day is not far distant when our friends on the Conservative side may find a fellow subject from India of their own way of thinking, and see fit to elect him as representative of their own constituencies in the British Parliament".

Naoroji may have smiled upon Bhownaggree's rise to political prominence, but the feeling was not shared by all his fellow Indians. One man in particular developed a very public detestation of Bhownaggree, and continued to

Sir Dinshaw Wacha, Bhownaggree's lifelong opponent
(courtesy George Howell Archive, Bishopsgate Institute)

express it freely throughout his life. This was Sir Dinshaw (or Dinshah) Edulji Wacha, a member for 40 years of the Bombay Municipality, one of the founders of the Indian National Congress and its secretary from its inception in 1885 until it was absorbed by a more radical group in 1907. Wacha was a great ally and supporter of Dadabhai Naoroji, sharing his keen interest in economic affairs and his discontent with India's economic plight (both men were involved in the cotton industry), but he loathed and despised Bhownaggree from first to last, and never relented from making vicious attacks on him, the effect of which was to stain Bhownaggree's reputation and image long after his lifetime.

Wacha wrote: "Our contention... is not that he is a Conservative but that he is a tool of the Anglo-Indians and does harm to India's cause by his abject slavery to them. If as a Conservative he could do real service to India, India would not care from which side of the house he served their interests". In a letter to Naoroji in 1891, he reported a speech by Bhownaggree at the *Pateti* (New Year) celebration, in which Bhownaggree had praised Lord Harris, the Governor of Bombay, who was highly unpopular among the Indians, partly because he had a reputation for sacrificing his public responsibilities to an obsession with cricket. Wacha wrote: "It is a shame therefore for Bhownaggree to pose as an exponent of the community (which he is not)... The general opinion is that he made the Pateti occasion an opportunity to promote his own selfish ends. This is the view I take too. I am really disgusted. Everybody knows that Bhownuggree *(sic)* is playing a high diplomatic game all for himself. I only hope you as a shrewd veteran will not be swayed by his sweet tongue."

Hinnells comments on this: "It is ironic that Wacha of all people should complain about a lack of concern for the community. Even the hagiographic biographer responsible for the 1930 Natesan publication *Famous Parsis* cannot find any contribution Wacha made to the Parsi community, but Bhownaggree laboured for nearly three years for the Zoroastrians in Britain". Hinnells described Wacha as "a rather testy, self-opinionated individual who could not tolerate any views different from his own. He seems to have been effective in ensuring Bhownaggree is not remembered as the committed supporter of India and her development that this research has shown him to be".

Despite the stark contrast in their politics, the man he canvassed to help him was Naoroji himself, who despite being well aware of his fellow Indian's politics was very willing to do so, no doubt because of the help he had received from the younger man three years earlier, and perhaps also because of his lifelong belief that Indians should regard their nationality as more important than their creed or political inclination.

The seat Bhownaggree was chosen to fight was Bethnal Green North East, which had been created for the 1885 election (it would be abolished in 1950). Consisting of the north and east wards of Bethnal Green, it had been held since its creation by George Howell (1833-1910), a self-educated trade unionist leader. Traditionally Liberal and very working class (the Labour Party did not yet exist, though its birth was just around the corner), this part of Bethnal Green was typical of districts where the plague had flourished, and it was teeming with the problems of the mass underclass of London. Disease, prostitution, corruption, poverty and decay were rife. The western end of Bethnal Green and neighbouring Whitechapel had recently been the scene of the most notorious series of unsolved murders in British history, those carried out by Jack the Ripper in 1888. It was one of the worst slum areas of London, mainly characterised by tumbledown old buildings with many families living in

Two views of Bethnal Green around the turn of the 19th century

each house. The chief occupations of the more respectable residents were market gardening and weaving. Help was at hand, though not just yet; a few years later, Bethnal Green's Boundary Estate would be the location of the world's first council housing scheme.

George Howell (courtesy George Howell Archive, Bishopsgate Institute)

Although there had been four candidates in 1892, an Independent and a Social Democratic Federation candidate, in 1895 Bhownaggree had only one opponent, the Liberal incumbent George Howell, who was 18 years older than him. Howell was a builder's son from rural Somerset who had begun to take an interest in left-wing politics as a teenager, joining the chartists and becoming a lay preacher. He moved to London at the age of 21 and met many radical thinkers of the day, including Karl Marx, and played a leading part in the London Builder's Strike of 1859, in support of a shorter (nine-hour) working day. He was elected to the London Trades Council and became a forceful campaigner for women's suffrage. In 1871, Howell was appointed secretary of the Trades Union Congress. He won the Bethnal Green North East seat on a Lib-Lab ticket in 1885, the year of its creation, and held it successfully in 1886 and 1892.

The idea of an Indian standing for the Conservatives was entirely novel at the time. According to the Natesan profile: "It seems [Bhownaggree's] residence in England had taught him that as far as India was concerned, her people had to appeal to both the great parties when in power, and that instead of relying upon the Radical party alone, as was the fashion at the time, it was equally to the interest of his country to remind the Conservatives of their duty and responsibility towards her."

Thanks to Howell's stature, the first two men to be offered the chance to stand for the Conservatives in Bethnal Green North East both declined, believing the seat to be unwinnable against him. Bhownaggree was the party's third choice, and the first to accept. Presumably he calculated that his insight into the political climate and his shrewd understanding of the electorate would help him to win. He was not helped by a claim in *The Times* that he too was likely to withdraw at the last minute, but he soon disproved it by standing his ground.

According to Rozina Visram in her book *Ayahs, Lascars and Princes, The Story of Indians in Britain 1700-1947*, the Tories finally selected Bhownaggree in part because of Tory unease at the growth of the Congress lobby, in both India and England. "Bhownaggree was put up by the Tories as a 'counterpoise' to Naoroji, the Congress spokesman," she wrote. "He was a man dear to the Conservative ideal, with 'nothing quixotic or crusading' in his temperament. Bhownaggree represented a different Indian voice and was a convenient weapon for the Tories against the Congress and the 'Indian Opposition' in Parliament. Bhownaggree deeply admired the work the British were doing in India, for he believed this work to be 'in the interest of India' – India as represented by the 'powerful Rajah and contented sepoy, the landholder, the shroff [banker or moneylender], the merchant and the trader'... Is it any wonder then that the Tories were eager to make this 'sound imperialist' the voice of India? The Conservatives lauded Bhownaggree as a mediator, who with his background and education was 'peculiarly suited' to represent India. They felt confident that his views would be successful in the House of Commons as he did not associate himself with those who wished to destroy and revolutionise the organic institutions of this country'. Bhownaggree, in short, was an ardent upholder of British rule in India."

Visram states that Bhownaggree received the support of the entire Tory machine – "the senior Tory establishment, the Tory ladies and the Tory press all swung behind him". This spared him from long battles with the party association of the kind Naoroji had had to fight. He was described as having a ready wit and it was stated that 'in repartee on a platform he always held his own'.[25] His wealth enabled him to invest personally in his campaign, and his promises to give a helping hand to local charities cannot have done any harm.

However grateful Bhownaggree might have been for this backing, and however wedded he was to Conservative values, he was much too shrewd to trumpet them during his campaign. He stood on a platform of British worker's rights,

25 Obituary in the Bethnal Green News

Two posters from Bhownaggree's 1895 election campaign (Wikipedia) promising to support Lord Salisbury's Aliens Bill to restrict immigration (in direct opposition to Dadabhai Naoroji) and the prohibition of imported goods made by convicts. A Bhownaggree leaflet blamed 'foreign pauper aliens' for putting up local house rents, causing overcrowding and insanitary dwellings, and competing unfairly with local tradesmen.

A flyer (bottom, previous page) focused on the danger to wages and employment of allowing 'alien' immigration to continue unchecked, together with the economic dangers of adopting a Liberal approach to free trade between nations, as the Conservatives saw it. The reverse side explicitly stated the threat to local people of allowing these policies to continue. A campaign jingle ran:

In this cause of Liberty
And your bread and beer,
Come, vote for Bhownaggree – And unity.

Ralph and Hinnells wrote: "Here we have an unknown and highly-educated Asian man standing against the self-educated trade unionist leader George Howell in an impoverished and overcrowded area of inner east London that represented home to a mainly artisan population. Howell had comfortably held Bethnal Green North East as a Liberal-Labour candidate since 1885. It barely requires stating that this was viewed as an 'unwinnable' seat, but with Conservative Party guidance and support, Bhownaggree set about an energetic campaign to secure local votes."[26]

Bhownaggree's campaign was largely concerned with playing on workers' anxieties over his 'foreign pauper aliens',

26 https://mjohansenblog.wordpress.com/2014/09/15/the-bethnal-green-humpty-dumpty/

who had become a hotly-contested topic in the East End because of the relatively large Eastern European population which had settled around Whitechapel and Stepney, in particular, since the 1880s. The aliens also included Jewish refugees fleeing pogroms in Russia and Poland. At their peak they numbered around 150,000 people. This was why anti-semitic, anti-migrant organisations such the British Brothers League, led by Major Evans-Gordon MP, and the British Industries, Trade and Labour Defence League, won such massive support. Bhownaggree addressed both organisations in a builder's yard, and assured them he would back any anti-alien legislation proposed by Major Evans-Gordon. Nobody seems to have commented on the irony of an Indian immigrant campaigning to tackle immigration, presumably because his obvious affluence and high level of education put him in a very different class from the 'pauper aliens'.

Bhownaggree stressed his opposition to Home Rule for Ireland and moves to disestablish the Church of England (separate it from the state). A Liberal movement had developed towards disestablishment which was opposed (and still is today) by the Conservative Party. He headed off concerns that he would devote his energies to his own country after election rather than to constituency interest by saying he would not advocate any claim for India, but would 'take up matters as they were'[27] (as will be explained, he later saw a need to change direction on this and devoted most of his Parliamentary time to India, though he did not neglect Bethnal Green). He was endorsed by the Licensed Victuallers, the City Goldsmiths and Fishmongers and the Green Street Costermongers. The *Eastern Argus* called him "a true British citizen in more senses than one." A good

27 *Eastern Argus*

oratory style undoubtedly helped, according to Hinnells, as did a national swing to the Tories.

Bhownaggree may have seen the wisdom at this stage in his career of softening the pompous manner which had alienated people in the past. He still had "a rather imperious manner" according to Hinnells, and "did not take criticisms easily or extend much courtesy to those who opposed him personally. However he was willing to change his mind and act decisively, and worked tirelessly for what he considered to be a good cause."

Voting took place between July 13 and August 7 and the result was announced on August 12. Lord Salisbury led an alliance between the Conservatives and the Liberal Unionist Party, while his opposition was the Liberal Party, led by Lord Rosebery. There was a 2 per cent swing to the Conservatives and the LUP, who won 411 seats of the total of 670 and controlled practically the whole of southern England, Salisbury continuing as Prime Minister. Naoroji lost his seat in Finsbury, but in Bethnal Green North East, no doubt helped by the national swing, Mancherjee Bhownaggree astonished the populace, and the country, by defeating George Howell. He had clearly won a remarkable popularity among the poor voters of Bethnal Green, despite his air of wealth and privilege and his right-wing politics. Bhownaggree won by a small but clear majority of 160, securing 2591 votes to Howell's 2431.

His victory came as a shock to many, not least to his defeated opponent, who bitterly complained in a letter that "after ten years' hard labour in Parliament" he had been "kicked out by a black man, a stranger from India, one not known in the constituency or in public life". According to Hinnells and Ralph, it was voters' concerns about immigration "plus a good oratory style, an arduous and effective campaign, some Liberal complacency and a national swing towards the Tories, [that] provided the combination of factors which yielded the surprising success".

Bhownaggree's victory for the Tories was looked upon with 'serious apprehension' by Indian National Congress members, according to Rozina Visram's book. R P Masani, in his biography of Naoroji, wrote: "His political creed differed from Dadabhai's so radically that his election gave rise in India to serious apprehensions. Indeed Bhownaggree's attitude was then spoken of in Congress circles as Anglo-Indianism gone mad... It might have been a matter of some consolation for India if instead of one so distrusted, another Indian, W C Bonnerjee, who had been attempting to wrest Barrow-in-Furness from the Unionists, had been elected. But while the Liberals were routed in almost every contested election, the famous Bengalee lawyer was also among the wounded."[28]

Womesh Chandra Bonnerjee (1844-1906), who like Bhownaggree was a barrister, has already been referred to as the first secretary of the London Indian Society and the first president of the Indian National Congress. His foray into British politics was less successful and at the 1895 election he was defeated in Barrow in Furness by Charles Cayzer for the Tories, securing 2355 votes against Cayzer's 3192. He did not stand for Parliament again.

Mike Harris, writing recently in *Little Atoms* magazine,[29] agrees: "It was immigration that got the Unionist candidate from India over the line. Bhownaggree went on the attack, telling local newspapers he opposed 'competition from pauper

28 Masani

29 http://littleatoms.com/hidden-history-conservatives-first-ethnic-minority-mp

aliens, and the rates from being burdened by them'."

Sir Dinshaw Wacha remained 'implacably opposed' to him, according to Hinnells, and commented in a letter to Naoroji: "On this side people have not much faith in his assurances, which, it is observed, will only be kept so long as they suit his purpose. He will then throw up his allegiance and show his teeth… there is deep distrust for him in matters affecting our county's welfare. He and Malabari are known to be self-seekers. They pursue their personal objects and in doing so, do not care whether they betray the county`s interests or not, so long as they are patted on the back by the Anglo-Indians here and the ignorant and credulous Englishmen on your side."

In early 1893 Wacha had attacked Bhownaggree with the phrase 'that pomposity of Bow and agree', a term which was readily borrowed by other opponents. According to John Hinnells: "Bhownaggree's distaste for the Indian National Movement and unquestioning support for British rule in India brought him the nickname 'Bow-and-agree', the displeasure of Dadabhoy [Naoroji] and the hostility of Pherozeshah Mehta, the Indian politician who was one of Naoroji's closest allies… He is largely ignored in many books written by Parsis about Parsis, even when they seek to collect as many positive accounts of their co-religionists as possible" (Hinnells cites as examples Katrak, 1958, and Nanavutty, 1980).

Sir Pherozeshah Mehta was, like Bhownaggree, a lawyer from Bombay who had studied Law at Lincoln's Inn. He was called to the Bar there in 1868, the first Parsi to achieve this, returning to Bombay to practise. When the Bombay Presidency Association was established in 1885, Mehta became its president, and remained in the post for the rest of his active life. He was a great supporter of Naoroji in working for wider educational opportunities for Indians, as well as for better sanitation and health care. He is remembered today as the 'Lion of Bombay'.

Hinnells continues, questioning whether historians and Parsis alike have been fair to Bhownaggree: "It has not only been outsiders who have played down Bhownaggree's importance. He is ignored in almost all books on Indian politics, save for a brief discussion in Visram 1986. What is particularly surprising is his eclipse from Parsi publications... There appears to be a community wish to be distanced from someone who has the image of having been disloyal to India." Hinnells also quotes Sir Dinshaw Wacha as writing to Naoroji in 1895 as follows: "Mehta laughs Bhownaggree to scorn for his presumption to pose as India's representative when he represents absolutely nobody... I give the sentence in his own words: 'The pretensions of Mr Bhownaggree to depose Mr Dadabhai [Naoroji] in the hearts of his countrymen of all classes and degrees could only be received in India, as they actually were received, with amused shouts and roars of laughter.'"

An article entitled "The Bethnal Green Humpty Dumpty" on Michelle Johnson's London Historitage website[30] suggests: "The awkward fact that Britain's first ever Asian Conservative MP gained electoral success by running an outspoken campaign against 'foreign pauper aliens' may explain why the early story of minority representation in Britain has never been sufficiently analysed or celebrated in wider historical narratives. It goes on: "Few people today are aware that London had two Asian MPs in the 1890s. This is surely partly because the case of Mancherjee Bhownaggree

30 https://mjohansenblog.wordpress.com/2014/09/15/the-bethnal-green-humpty-dumpty/

cannot be at all comfortably accommodated within the most immediately relevant or obvious existing thematic frameworks, such as empire, colonialism, post-colonialism or multiculturalism. [He was] also and frequently subjected him to personal insults – including the title of this piece, taken from the *Madras Standard* of 1897. Other sources suggest that a more positive interpretation is possible. Sensitively handled, the career of the 'Bethnal Green Humpty Dumpty' has much to tell us about such topics as: Anglo-Indian relations and networks; working men's voting patterns in east London; grass roots responses to immigration in the East End; and minority representation in Britain since the end of the nineteenth century."

Although he had become something of a hero in Great Britain, Bhownaggree's compatriots back home in India were much less impressed by his achievement. According to Natesan: "While he was thus lionised by the British public and the British press, it must be owned that he failed to enlist the sympathy and appreciation of his own countrymen in his doings in England. It was unfortunate that the only Indian member of the House of Commons should have stood aloof from the patriotic movements in this country and found himself in opposition to such stalwarts as Dadabhai and Mehta. Bhownaggree was then hob-nobbing with Anglo-Indian reactionaries and was wont to speak of the Nationalist aspirations in India, in a strain which was resented by the leaders of progressive thought in this country".

In fairness, once he was in Parliament, Bhownaggree focused mainly, and later almost exclusively, on Indian affairs, particularly the economy. He impressed the House by the vigour and eloquence of his speeches, and conducted a long battle in support of Indians in South Africa and other overseas dominions of the Crown. Later he objected to a proposed increase in pay for the British Army in India, as the Indian taxpayer would as usual have to pay for it – a 'flagrant act of injustice', according to Bhownaggree. His detailed statement of the case for Indians in the Transvaal after annexation was the basis of a Blue Book (Blue Books are annual accounts of key national statistics), and was sent to Lord Milner by the Colonial Secretary, Alfred Lyttelton, who commented that he felt much sympathy for the views expressed, and that it would be difficult to give a fully satisfactory answer. As a result, some key aspects of the proposals were dropped.

Bhownaggree made more than 200 interventions or contributions to debates in the House of Commons during his Parliamentary career. According to Hinnells in *Zoroastrians In Britain* (1996) he 'spent twice as long in Parliament as Dadabhai Naoroji and intervened more frequently on a wider range of subjects'. He made his maiden speech in the House on September 3 1895 on the topic of Indian taxation, seconding a motion by J M Maclean (Cardiff) that: "This house views with apprehension the continual increase in the burdens of Indian taxpayers caused by the annexation or military occupation of large areas of unproductive territory on the land frontier of British India [in Chitral]." Bhownaggree's response was very short. Hansard: "He said he [seconded the Motion] unhesitatingly, because the burden on the Indian taxpayer had grown in recent years to an enormous extent. But he should disclaim any connection between the Motion and recent events in Chitral. The word "annexation" had been used in connection with Chitral in the course of the Debate; and it was well to point out that it was not very applicable. It was only recently that Sir George Robertson put upon the throne of Chitral its own proper Mehtar, which showed that Chitral was not completely annexed, in the same sense as Burma was annexed. But, at the same time, it could not be denied that recent events in Chitral, the glorious achievements of our Army, British and Indian, and the prudent resolution of the Government to retain its hold on Chitral, were capable of being read by ambitious military officers in a somewhat different light from that in which they were regarded on the floor of the House of Commons. Many of the difficulties of the Government of India could be traced to this cause. Ambitious officers had before now embroiled themselves in matters which had made it impossible for the Government to escape being brought into conflict with tribes on the frontier. In order, therefore, that the resolution of the Government to retain Chitral, and the approval of the feats of our Army in that region, might not mislead such officers to follow the same course in the future, and also for the reason that there might not be aroused in India an apprehension that the policy of the present Government was annexation, and that they were determined to advance the frontier of India to the furthest limits, and thereby make the burden of the taxpayer so intolerable that India would be plunged into bankruptcy, he begged to second the Motion."

Hansard shows that while this was Bhownaggree's only performance in 1895, he made 23 speeches the following year. On February 14 he asked the Secretary of State for the Colonies (Joseph Chamberlain) about the treatment of British Indian subjects in South Africa, a topic to which he would return frequently. On April 10 he challenged him about new rules forbidding British Indians from purchasing land there. Three days later he was asking the Secretary of State for India (Lord Hamilton) about the Government's contributions to the Imperial Institute, seeking an assurance that they would be devoted to Indian interests. On June 2 he urged the Secretary of State for India to consider allowing sugar refineries to sell rum, in order to help them to develop, as had been promised in a Resolution of 1882. Later that month, on the 19th, he asked the Secretary of State about the response to a scheme designed to encourage the construction of railways in India by private enterprise. On July 6 he made a lengthy contribution to a debate on the use and funding of Indian troops abroad, opposing a resolution to continue leaving India to foot the bill.

On July 21 he returned to matters closer to home, asking the Secretary of State for the Home Department if there were any plans to fence off a stretch of the Regent's Canal in his constituency where 31 people had drowned in eight months (he returned to the topic several times). On other occasions during his time in the House he raised the issue of an 'imbecile

Joseph Chamberlain, Secretary of State for the Colonies 1895-1903

child' aged eight who had had to be accommodated in an adult lunatic asylum, and complained that 21 of his constituents had been made homeless by a school development scheme. In 1900, after hearing that there was no longer enough space for the Buckland Museum of Fish Culture at South Kensington Museum, he suggested that it might be found a home in Bethnal Green. Another constituency concern he raised in the House was the local incidence of smallpox. Not all the matters he raised were of life-changing import; in March 1903 he asked the Postmaster-General if two-word district names like Bethnal Green could be counted as one word for the purpose of sending telegrams (predictably, the answer was no). In his later years in the House, however, he seems to have lost interest in constituency matters, and almost all his later comments and interventions concerned international issues, ranging from coolie labour in Natal and anti-Indian racism in South Africa to the damage done by earthquakes and the number of children in education in the Presidency of Madras.

On the subject of a tragedy further from home, he asked the Under Secretary of State for Foreign Affairs on August 6 "whether a petition has been received by the Foreign Office from the widow of Dr. S. R. Boyce, a Parsee medical officer lately employed under Her Majesty's Commissioner and Consul General in British Central Africa, who lost his life in a slave expedition near Lake Nyassa, for a maintenance allowance for herself and her two infant children; and whether, in view of the fact that in attacking the slave dhows, the commander of the expedition having been killed and the second officer severely wounded, Dr. Boyce led the men, and fell a victim to treachery on the part of the Native Chief Makinjira, the Foreign Office will take such petition into favourable consideration, and grant a maintenance allowance to Dr. Boyce's widow and children, who have been left utterly destitute by his death?" The answer was yes.

In October 1896, a year after his election to Parliament and still riding high on his victory, Bhownaggree headed back to India. According to Ralph and Hinnells, "Bhownaggree saw himself returning as a son of the land who had won his position for Conservative ideals, not the radical ones he had opposed, which had hitherto dominated Indian political debate."

Bhownaggree would not have expected the kind of adulation Naoroji had received after his victory three years earlier, but he certainly did not expect the reception he actually encountered, which was one of overwhelming hostility; it seems Wacha and his allies had made a good job of undermining any reputation he might have hoped to gain in his home city so far. *The Gujarati* of October 25, reporting that a mere 15 Parsis and five or six people from Bhavnagar were there to receive him as his ship docked, stated: "The truth is that Bombay distinctly and flatly refuses to honour Mr Bhavnagri." The Parsi-owned *Jam-e Jamshed* stated: "... we deem it our duty to warn beforehand Mr Bhownaggree's friends against any attempt at giving undue importance to his return to this country". Wacha wrote, in a letter intended to persuade influential people not to attend a dinner given in Bhownaggree's honour: "As to this busybody Bhownaggree, he is determined to play the grand role. Possibly a Jubilee Knighthood is in store for him next year. So the more actively he falls in with the views of the rabid Anglo-Indians the greater will be the advancement of his personal ambition. I am glad to say that our agitation so far has had the desired effect".[31]

---

31 Patwardhan, 1977

Ralph and Hinnells report that a collection of press articles entitled *The Indian Political Estimate of Mr Bhavnagari, or the Bhavnagari Boom Exposed* was published in Bombay in 1897. It contained 148 articles from 31 newspapers and was edited anonymously, though it is presumed to be Wacha's work. It was clearly published to counter Bhownaggree's claim to represent the Indian people, and was loaded with hostile and often personal comments. Wacha's hatred of Bhownaggree appears to have amounted almost to an obsession. Sadly, much of the mud he slung stuck, and it continued to colour public opinion of Bhownaggree for the rest of his life, only partially alleviated by his increasingly pro-Indian performances in the House and his considerable efforts for the Parsi community.

Other papers reported that Bhownaggree stated he had come to mourn following the deaths of his mother and his friend the young Maharaja of Bhavnagar, who had died at the age of only 38. This may suggest that he quickly abandoned any attempt at presenting himself as a returning hero.

On December 7, Sir Dinshah M Petit hosted an entertainment for 250 guests, mostly anti-Congress people like Bhownaggree. But it was becoming clear, to Bhownaggree and everyone else, that the Indian Congress had far more supporters than it did opponents, while the Conservative Party in India had far fewer. As the *Madras Standard* of January 3 1897 put it: "…nothing can save the Bethnal Green Humpty Dumpty, not all the heaven-sent fatuities in which the *Times of India* and *The Pioneer* have swathed him".

The hostility of his reception clearly came as something of a shock to Bhownaggree, who began to moderate his criticism of the Indian National Congress from that time on. It must also have affected his supporters back in England, who must have realised that he was not half so popular in India as he, and they, had believed. Over the years that followed his return from India, he became more questioning in his support of the Government, and more energetic in his pursuit of Indian causes. During his second term of office, according to Ralph and Hinnells, he asked more questions about Indian economics than Naoroji had in his Parliamentary career. His attacks on William Wedderburn, Naoroji's key ally in Parliament, softened, although he opposed Wedderburn's proposal for a Parliamentary Inquiry Commission for India. However he increasingly raised other issues from the general to the particular, such as the plight of Indians in South Africa. For example, in February 1900 he reported that 82 British Indian settlers in Natal had been forcibly deported to India, and that while in detention they had been subjected to 'brutal treatment' by Portuguese soldiers, who had robbed them of all their money and 'outraged the modesty of their women', without intervention by the British representative.

Back in the House after his Indian excursion in January 1897, he contributed to a debate on a plan for an independent enquiry into 'the condition of the masses of the Indian people' during the Indian famine of 1896-97. The gist of his stance was to accuse the opposition of blaming the Government in part for the famine. He stated that the amendment, and the manner in which it was proposed, were 'simply calculated to advertise a certain class of agitators, who were never tired of impressing upon the people of India the inadequacy of British rule and the want of sympathy between the rulers and the ruled'. He rejected a claim that Indian public opinion had called for the enquiry, stating: "Had not that opinion been manufactured in a small room, not far from the House of Commons; sent out thence to India; brought back in the form of newspaper articles; and passed off on the House of Commons as the public opinion of three hundred millions of people?"

On March 4 he queried the appointment of a German to a key position at the Imperial Museum, Calcutta, asking if there had been any attempt to find an Indian candidate (he later raised a similar concern about a European engineer being sent to Bombay at a high salary to train Indians). On August 2 he tabled a Notice of Motion stating: "That this House views with concern the fact that the old industries of India are fast disappearing without being replaced by new ones to any appreciable extent, with the result that its vast population has to largely depend on the imports of foreign manufactures for even the most ordinary articles of everyday use, a circumstance to which is mainly due the condition of poverty under which large sections of the people of India still labour; and that, inasmuch as the present system of education, among other causes, has had a tendency to divert the energies of the people from the preservation and development of industrial pursuits, this House is of opinion that an inquiry should be held, by such means as the Government of India consider advisable, with a view to ascertaining and suggesting measures for remedying the evils indicated." The Motion was not debated.

Bhownaggree's more sceptical attitude to Government policies did not prevent him from being made, during the Diamond Jubilee of Queen Victoria in 1897, a Knight Commander of the Most Eminent Order of the Indian Empire. He was now Sir Mancherjee.

Bhownaggree got to his feet 16 times between March and August 1898, addressing issues both at home and abroad.

Sir Mancherjee Bhownaggree wearing the insignia of the Most Eminent Order of the
Indian Empire, which he received in 1897
(courtesy George Howell Archive, Bishopsgate Institute)

He made his unwavering support of British rule clear in a speech in the House on June 7 1898:

"British rule has not contributed to the causes of the poverty of India. British domination is a blessing compared with the dominations which have prevailed from the beginning of the recorded history of the country; and luckily it is a domination not within the power of the people to get free from. In brief, the people of India ought not to be made discontented; they ought rather to be made to realise their position, and to recognise that, with all its drawbacks, the present regime is a period of peace wherein they have leisure, and opportunities to think out the more effectual ways and means of developing the material resources which Nature has endowed their country with. Tell them that this result can be achieved, not merely by book education – by only turning her sons into barristers, doctors, and professional men, platform orators, and newspaper leader writers. That is a state of things which has kept the country poor so far. I am as much in favour of giving the people book education as anyone else, but the education they receive should not end in turning them into mere spouters and writers, but should be directed into the channels which lead to a healthy national growth. I may say that both those who affect to be in active sympathy with them on the one hand, and the Government of India on the other, have failed to point out these lessons to them." The dig about 'spouters and writers' may have been aimed at the INC; Bhownaggree saw it as dominated by intellectuals, and knew that many of its leaders were arts graduates. In a later speech (26 July 1900) he called for an amendment to the effect '…that the Government of India should adopt measures for the elementary industrial and technical instruction of the poorer communities, so as to fit them for more profitable manual labour in other directions besides agriculture'.

During the same debate, on the Indian Budget, he called attention to the poor attendance of the Opposition despite its claim to support Indian interests, pointing out that its benches were 'practically empty' on the occasion of this important debate. He stated: "I notice this fact to prove to the people of India how the interest of the two political parties in their welfare is misrepresented to them by some of their so-called friends".

A hint that Dadabhai Naoroji's earlier cordiality towards Bhownaggree had moderated comes in a letter from Dadabhai to his daughter in 1897, in which he explained why his work in England was so pressing that he could not attend her wedding. "To the difficulty of my work, Mr Bhownaggree has made a great addition" he wrote.

Although he remained a practising Zoroastrian, Bhownaggree began attending the Sunday services at the local Anglican parish church, St Luke's.[32] He placed two further memorials to his sister Ave in the church. The first was a white marble tablet showing her in profile and bearing the inscription 'To the glory of God and in loving memory of Ave Merwanjee Bhownaggree'. In the north wall of the church, Bhownaggree installed a stained-glass window with three panels. Ave is at the centre, with an angel above her, flanked by the figures of Zoroaster on the left and Christ on the right.

At the 1900 election Lord Salisbury continued to head a dominant Conservative government, while the Labour Party, in its initial guise as the Labour Representation Committee, appeared for the first time, winning two seats, and Winston

32 Parsis in India and the Diaspora, Hinnells

The stained-glass window which Bhownaggree had installed in his sister Ave's memory at St Luke's Church, Redcliffe Square, Kensington.

Churchill began his 64-year political career, winning Oldham for the Conservative Party. Mancherjee Bhownaggree again stood for Bethnal Green North East, this time against a new Liberal opponent, Harry Levy-Lawson, Viscount Burnham, who had inherited both the *Daily Telegraph* and a seat in the House of Lords from his father, the 1st Baron Burnham. Despite Burnham's influential position, Bhownaggree was re-elected with 53.4 per cent of the vote and an increased majority of 379 votes, largely because, according to Hinnells and Ralph, he was seen as 'a good constituency MP who supported local causes'. It is clear that the Conservatives saw him as a powerful weapon against the forces of Indian liberalism and the Indian National Congress.

Natesan describes the popularity of his second election victory:

"Sir Mancherjee was the recipient of a signal compliment and distinction when, in July, 1901, about three hundred ladies and gentlemen including Lord George Hamilton, the

Secretary of State for India, numerous Members of Parliament of both sides and prominent Anglo-Indian officials, together with the leading members of the Parsee community and representative Hindus and Mahomedans resident in England, assembled in his honour at the Hotel Cecil to commemorate his second victory at the polls."

Bhownaggree had promised to keep abreast of his constituents' feelings and to take up individual concerns, without advocating 'any claim for India', although his subsequent record shows that Indian issues moved to the forefront of his Parliamentary agenda. Some three-quarters of Bhownaggree's interventions in the Commons, and nearly all his Parliamentary time, concerned Indian affairs, suggesting he was making an earnest attempt to win the support and sympathy of his compatriots. In an echo of Naoroji, he referred to the drain on India of British policies, warning that political firebrands might start stirring up discontent. He particularly objected to India being required to contribute to the cost of a garrison in South Africa, calling the charges 'a flagrant act of injustice', and later opposed the demand for Indian taxes to fund a campaign in Tibet. He also argued energetically for British investment in Indian education, particularly in scientific, technical and vocational subjects, saying that every school in India should be provided with workshops and scientific laboratories. He pressed the Viceroy to implement an educational plan involving forestry schools, polytechnic and industrial schools and an industrial exhibition. He protested when a British engineering college was closed down for lack of students, pointing out that this was no excuse as the obvious solution would be to fill the vacancies by admitting Indians.

He also fought for the building of railways, arguing that rather than being a financial burden they would improve trade, allow easier transport of supplies and help to unite the country. In the Commons in a debate in 1898, he stated: "Railways are not merely means of necessary transport in times of famine, but they actually carry with them a moral and material development of the country which cannot be too highly valued. They bring under cultivation, in the first place, large areas which for want of railways would remain in future uncultivated as they have remained for generations. They bring in their train education of a sort that India needs most, by creating a tendency among her different communities which are separated by restrictions of caste and custom which we do not understand here, to bring them together in their ways of life, in their modes of thought, and in other multifarious respects, which alone can lead to a development of the resources of the country, and to their eventual progress and prosperity".

There are some signs that by the turn of the century Bhownaggree had won rather more support among his fellow Indians and managed to allay the scepticism of some of his enemies. In 1901 the *Indian Spectator* reported: "Sir Mancherjee is undoubtedly popular with all sorts and conditions of men. Those who do not see eye to eye with him in public life can yet appreciate him as a friend."

Bhownaggree's role in fighting for justice for the weak has not received due recognition, according to Ralph and Hinnells. In 1900 he complained that qualified Indian medical staff were being restricted to inferior posts and denied promotion. He complained: "Capable men of long experience have to relinquish their posts, or retire, after a service of more than thirty years without having had any appreciable advance in pay and position from where they began early in life", and reminded his audience, as Naoroji had done, of Queen Victoria's 1858 proclamation of equality.

In 1904 he stated, with regard to the salt tax: "I would point out that the very poorest classes, who feel the weight of this tax to be intolerable, are in a condition of existence which can be likened to those who seek Poor Law Relief in this country. By their toil and thrifty ways of living they contribute to the wealth of agricultural and trading interests, so… they should not be subjected to any further exaction of the state." The Government reduced the tax the following year, but refused to abolish it.

Bhownaggree campaigned particular forcefully for Indians in South Africa who had been expelled from the Transvaal during the Boer War and were now, he pointed out, living in unacceptable conditions. He raised this matter 44 times in Parliament, mainly during his second term in the House, arguing that South African Indians "were treated in a manner that was a disgrace to the Empire, were robbed of the rights that belonged to them not only as citizens of the Empire, but as human beings, without a word of protest from statesmen who have the direction of foreign and colonial affairs." He was told in a reply from Lord Ampthill in the Prime Minister's office that "it would be idle for [Joseph Chamberlain, Secretary of State for the Colonies] to seek to disguise the fact that there exist in Natal strong feelings against the influx of immigrants from Asia in large numbers as to threaten to outnumber the European population" – in other words, equality for Indians was all very well, as long as there were not too many of them.

This campaign did not achieve much in the short term,

but it was appreciated in India, and won the support of Naoroji and of Gandhi, who had been Bhownaggree's main source of information. In 1898 Gandhi wrote to tell him: "The Committee of the British Indians resident in Natal, having heard of work done by and on behalf of the British Indians in South Africa, hereby places on record its thanks to Sir M. M. Bhownaggree KCIE, MP for the splendid support extended to the cause of the British Indians in South Africa."

From his early days in office, Bhownaggree shared Naoroji's concern that India imported goods worth many times more than her exports. In July 1900 he wrote: "90% of the population subsists on agricultural pursuits[33], and if we succeed in withdrawing, say, even 10% from this occupation, we at once reduce by so much the burden on the soil, and increase the productive power of that 10% by teaching them to turn raw materials into articles of domestic use, every one of which nearly they now import from foreign countries."

Two years later in the House of Commons (10.11.1902) he criticised the poor level of agricultural training, saying:

"The cultivator is left to his ancient methods of eking out a bare subsistence as best he can... One man in a thousand brought up to a scientific training in agriculture, who can analyse the clay, handle an improved harrow, know how to keep his cattle in good condition, and take account of the economic and natural conditions amid which he has to work, would prove a benefactor of the 999 who in normal times live from hand to mouth, and with the first touch of a drought lapse into abject helplessness. But where is this one man to acquire his training? I say, sir, without fear of contradiction, that there is no means at his disposal for the purpose. True,

33 In 2016 the figure was down to 23%, lower than the figures for manufacturing and petrochemicals

there are a few classes, sparsely spread in the neighbourhood of some towns, meant to give agricultural instruction. Even if they were efficient, they are not numerous enough... What we want in India today is a multiplication of such a farm as I had the good fortune to see in Allahabad last January... The organiser of this enterprise was a military officer who had some knowledge originally of agricultural pursuits, which enabled him to develop it, stage by stage, from a small experimental farm into what is today a model and highly reproductive institution, having well-equipped departments for all kinds of dairy produce, and breeding fine stock of cattle which would bear favourable comparison with anything of the kind in this country. This gentleman has not only conquered the difficulties of climate, and introduced such new industries as the manufacture of bacon, but drawn to his work many willing hands from the agriculturists of surrounding districts by his kindly treatment and such concession to their feelings as abstaining from killing cows reared on the farm... I do not see why what has been shown to be possible in Allahabad should not be multiplied in every province of India. The country should be dotted over with such model farms."

On several occasions Bhownaggree pointed out that the British Government was blocking the development of Indian industry through its controls; the sugar cane industry was not allowed to manufacture rum, and the tea industry was heavily taxed. He also campaigned, successfully, for the reduction of tax on salt, as a burden which disproportionately affected the poorest people, and complained about duty-free imports of tobacco to India, and about the high export duty on chutney (1901). He sought reductions in land revenues, especially in the most poverty-stricken areas, and proposed to increase the lower tax threshold. He argued that the children of labourers should receive educational and medical care and sought to protect the rights of Lascars (Indian sailors) working on P&O liners. In all these respects he was fighting for the poorer Indians, just as Naoroji had done.

One of his longest speeches to the House, on July 21 1904, concerned Indian labour in the Transvaal. He rejected a statement by Sir Joseph Chamberlain, who had said that 'a large influx of Indian labourers' could not be permitted because it would 'practically swamp the white people'. He complained that this was 'an abuse of the powers and authority that rested with the British Administration whether in Africa or any other portion of our dominions, to exclude Indians and prefer men of other nationalities for such fields of labour... Time after time, in spite of pledges which the right hon. Gentleman had willingly given, determined attempts had been made in South Africa, even with the countenance of the responsible administrators there, to oppress and tyrannise British Indian subjects and trample underfoot their few remaining rights... statesmen might well pause to consider what would be the ultimate effect of giving grave cause for discontent to millions of His Majesty's Indian subjects for the sake of pleasing a few thousand colonists in South Africa."

Bhownaggree's longest speech to the Commons, extending to some 30 minutes, was a wide-ranging one made during an Indian budget debate on August 12 1904, when he argued in support of his motion that the British Exchequer should pay a large part of the expenses of an armed mission to Tibet, to quell rebellion there. He disputed an assertion by the Secretary of State for India that the Tibetan question was 'essentially an Indian interest', saying that it was of great importance to Britain, and the fact that the road to Tibet just happened to run through India was no reason to lay the costs at her door. He also pointed out that a 'healthy surplus' in the accounts (of £1.2 million) was not so healthy from the perspective of the Indian people, and aired a range of related economic and cultural issues. He again queried the high tax on salt, which unfairly penalised the poorest people, and the unwillingness of the Government to invest appropriately in education.

Bhownaggree got to his feet in the House for the last time on August 8, 1905, to ask once again about the treatment of British Indians in African colonies.

Bhownaggree has received criticism from historians over the years, along with a few snubs from his fellow Parsis. In 1974 Eckehard Kulke published *The Parsees in India*, which has become an authoritative work on the subject. He described Bhownaggree as 'an unconditional advocate of Britain's imperialist politics', citing his support for the annexation of the state of Chitral and for the British military expedition to Lhasa in 1907, and his direct opposition to Naoroji with regard even to such issues as simultaneous Civil Service examinations in Britain and India. He stated that Naoroji would have preferred not to see Bhownaggree in Parliament (this may be true, though given Naoroji's reluctance to express overt criticism of anyone, we would be unlikely to find any evidence of it). He also gave an account of the opposition Bhownaggree faced on his tour of India in 1896. The account finished with a quotation from *The Gujarati*, which expressed satisfaction at Bhownaggree's loss of his parliamentary seat in 1906:

"The news of Sir Muncherjee Bhownagree's defeat will be received with unfeigned satisfaction by the entire Indian public, in as much as it roves from Parliament an enemy in the path of India's political progress. He has always danced to the tune of his Anglo-Saxon patrons and has lost no opportunity to strike a blow at India's political advancement... Sir Muncherjee's unpopularity in India can be gauged from the fact that the Bengalis recently burnt his effigy out of indignation at his attitude towards the Bengal partition."

Ralph and Hinnells do not agree with Kulke's assessment. They sum up Bhownaggree's true reputation as follows: "It is clear that the political estimate of Bhownaggree needs to be reassessed. He warned that the British were straining Indian loyalty; he complained at the unjust drain of taxation on India; he described the British actions as parsimonious; he spoke of flagrant acts of injustice; he called for more radical educational change than the INC thought was reasonable: he pressed for India to become more economically independent: for educational opportunities and equal career opportunities for the educated. He protested at the British government's failure to honour the pledge of the Empress, and accused it of showing prejudice on the grounds of colour, and of making hollow promises. The image of Bhownaggree purveyed by scholars as craven in his unquestioning loyalty to Britain owes more to the personal campaign of Wacha than to a careful study of historical records which suggests that, in his own way, Bhownaggree was a more radical reformer than has been appreciated."

In a letter to Naoroji of 1896, Bhownaggree writes that he had asked to meet Wacha, but the latter had refused, further evidence that his old foe was determined to avoid any *rapprochement* between them.

A gathering at the House of Commons in July 1905.
Sir Mancherjee Bhownaggree is on the far left.

By 1905, when the next general election was called, Bhownaggree's popularity had fallen, not helped by the many personal attacks. The *Morning Leader* criticised him for supporting Lord Curzon's partition of Bengal, which was bitterly opposed in India, and suggested that his personal financial interests were behind his support. When the paper accused him of buying votes through his support of local charities, implying that his money came as a large pension from India at the expense of his poverty-stricken compatriots, he sued them and won, but more damage had been done.

In the election, which took place in January and February 1906, Bhownaggree lost his seat to Sir Edwin Cornwall, the Liberal candidate, by 1997 votes. Cornwall would go on to hold the seat until 1922. Bhownaggree remains the only Conservative ever to win a Parliamentary election in Bethnal Green.

He might well have lost his seat in 1906 in any event, because in the election the Conservatives were struck by a Liberal landslide, thanks mainly to a split over free trade. Sir Henry Campbell-Bannerman's party gained 214 seats for a total of 397, leaving Arthur Balfour's Conservative and Liberal Unionist coalition with only 156.

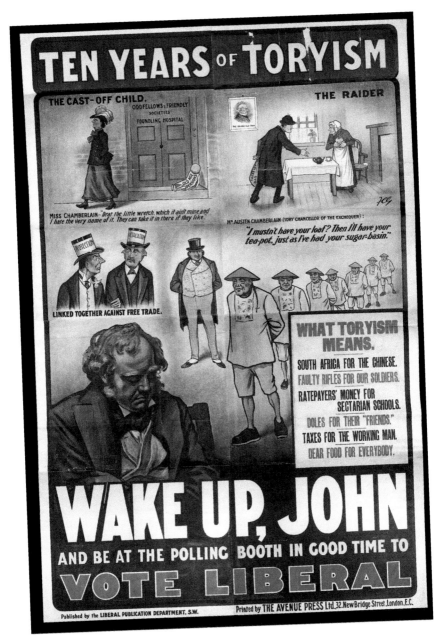

A Liberal election poster from the campaign which helped to topple the Conservatives, including Bhownaggree, in 1906

CHAPTER 8

A life after politics

After his Parliamentary defeat, Bhownaggree did not attempt re-election. Instead he spent most of his public time on local affairs and in continuing his legal work as a barrister. He continued to live in London, in the affluent Cromwell Road, meeting with Gandhi in 1906. Gandhi's support for Bhownaggree is clear from several communications. In 1903 he wrote to express the hope that Bhownaggree was not planning to retire from Parliament, stating, "We in South Africa had begun to rely upon the fruits of your continuous labours in the House on our behalf". When Bhownaggree lost his seat, a disappointed Gandhi said he had been "our greatest champion in the House of Commons".

In his later years, Bhownaggree worked hard on behalf of the Zoroastrians. After succeeding Naoroji as President of the Religious Society of Zarathushtrians in Europe,

Bhownaggree's home at 177 Cromwell Road as it is today.

he took legal steps to transmute the organisation into a properly-constituted body called the Incorporated Parsee Association of Europe. Its aims were similar, and included providing charitable help for funerals, supporting indigent Parsis and funding academic research into Zoroastrianism. Bhownaggree served as President of the Religious Society of Zarathushtrians from 1908 and then became the first president of the IPAE on its formation in 1909, remaining in post until his death. Under his leadership there was more emphasis on caring. He was a trustee of Broacha House in Edinburgh, the first Zoroastrian property to be established in Britain, in 1909, to be run as a hostel and club for

Parsis[34]. He was also closely involved in the provision of a 'chapel' or *sagdi* for the Parsi burial ground at Brookwood Cemetery, near Woking, which opened in 1901, and from 1908 he began to introduce a social calendar, with river trips on the Thames and banquets to which notable non-Parsis were also invited, including Field Marshall the Earl and Countess Haig and Lord Ampthill from the Prime Minister's office. His aim was to position Parsis in the higher echelons of society, distinguishing them from rank and file Indians whose presence in Britain was growing. He also established a Parsi centre, Zoroastrian House, first at 168 Cromwell Road, South Kensington (opposite his home at no. 177, and now part of the site of a large Bupa hospital), later moved to no. 11 Russell Road. It was run on social club lines, with a billiards room, a prayer room and visitor accommodation, very close to the modern concept of a community centre.

Among Bhownaggree's other acts in these later years was petitioning the Shah of Iran, in collaboration with Dadabhai Naoroji, on behalf of the Zoroastrians in that country, seeking fairer treatment for them. He arranged, or helped to arrange, the presentation of an address calling on the Shah to 'grant to our co-religionists... the same rights, privileges, and protection which His Majesty has evinced his desire to extend to the Persian nation under the constitution which has been recently inaugurated in his Empire'. By this stage of their lives, there is no doubt that he and Naoroji were co-operating as allies. It was Bhownaggree who conveyed the news to Naoroji that the Shah wished to decorate him, a proposal which, like all other such honours, the Grand Old Man turned down.

---

34 The project was abandoned and the property sold off some years later, mainly because the lease was passed to a woman who proved to be prejudiced against non-whites.

The outbreak of the First World War in 1914 led to a coalition government, and Bhownaggree is said to have hoped he would be given a Cabinet post within it. At the end of the war he called a meeting of 'all Indians resident in Great Britain' to mark the victory and thank the King for the creating the first Indian peer, Baron Sinha of Raipur (see final section). According to the Indian National Herald, quoted by Marc Wadsworth, Shapurji Saklatvala and his supporters hijacked the meeting, removed him from the chair and passed a vote condemning him for convening the meeting.

Just as Naoroji and Bhownaggree had crossed paths in their public lives, there was an overlap between the career of Bhownaggree and that of Shapurji Saklatvala, who in 1922 became the third Parsi Member of Parliament. As political opposites, Bhownaggree and Saklatvala were fierce enemies – at least, at first. According to Ralph and Hinnells: "There are many memories of Bhownaggree 'cutting' Saklatvala at Zoroastrian House, and of other Parsis walking out of meetings in protest at Bhownaggree's rudeness to his successor in Parliament". However, when Saklatvala wanted to put his children through the *navjote* Parsi initiation ceremony, which required special approval because he had married an Englishwoman and had been baptised a Catholic in his youth, the Zoroastrian House Managing Committee, under Bhownaggree's presidency, was happy to give the green light. A letter[35] from the Secretary, Spitam Cama, stated that he 'greatly appreciated' Saklatvala's sentiments about Bhownaggree, which must have been very positive. Bhownaggree also approved Saklatvala's wish nine years later to have a full Parsi funeral and to have his ashes

35   Ralph & Hinnells

interred in the Zoroastrian burial ground at Brookwood.

In a letter to Saklatvala in 1930 (quoted in the section on Saklatvala), Bhownaggree wrote: "The couple of generations that have elapsed since my notions of men and matters political were taking shape have not shaken the foundations of my beliefs; and as I have never cared to shift them in accordance with popular, that is to say mob, moods, I have been content to look while groups of favoured leaders have enjoyed their transient day of fame and passed into oblivion, or been surpassed by others of their kind, feeling firm in the belief that I, or rather my beliefs, shall be in some remote future justified." These comments portray a man who consistently did what he believed in, rather than pandering to public taste.

In 1916 Bhownaggree agreed to write a booklet for the War Publications Department aimed at Indians and designed to counteract German propaganda about the role of Britain in their country. The aim was 'to project Indian confidence in British rule and emphasise its advantages for India'[36]. *The Verdict of India* was designed to refute rumours put about by the Germans concerning British rule in India; the Kaiser was said to be counting on an Indian revolt to help Germany in its ambitions. The booklet asserted that Indians were proud of being British citizens and that it was 'by right and title of that citizenship' that they could 'revive the ancient glory of their motherland, taking their proper place in the community of nations'. Reporting a meeting of prominent Indians in London immediately after the 1914 declaration of war, Bhownaggree stated that the German regime "...were evidently obsessed with the idea that in spite of all the professions and practical proofs of India's

36   Rozina Visram

adhesion to the British throne, she could be counted on to add to its difficulties in a time of grave peril, that she was one of those weak links in the chain of the Empire on the snapping of which they reckoned for the ultimate fulfilment of their ambition to effect its humiliation and possibly dismemberment".

Bhownaggree reported the meeting's declaration of Indian loyalty to the Crown in typically high-flown language:

"From the lips of all there assembled, there sprung one accordant expression, viz. that India's princes and peoples would, on learning of the titanic struggle in which the Kaiser of Germany had sought to engage their Sovereign, place all their resources, their armies, and even their own lives, in support of British arms. So confirmed were they in this conviction, that without waiting even for the few hours in which the telegraph would bring them the news of the actual feeling aroused in India, they, one and all, resolved to incur the heavy responsibility of becoming the spokesmen in public of the thoughts and sentiments of upwards of three hundred millions of their countrymen, and entrusted me with the drafting of an address to His Majesty giving expression to that conviction."

Much of the rest of the booklet is taken up in championing British rule in India and demolishing complaints against it, in a style reminiscent of a (very lengthy) courtroom summing-up. Perhaps unsurprisingly, he dismisses the question of unfair British taxation in a few lines: "This is not the place to enter into considerations of the incidence of taxation, or of the allocation of revenue raised for the provision of administrative and national expenditure". He reports that a 'regular flood of literature' had been disseminated in India by official German sources, designed to inflame Indians against their British overlords. These were "full of the most hideous descriptions of the sufferings of the people by famines... insinuating and even asserting that they portrayed the results of British rule". A typical title was *Indien unter der britischen Faust* (India under the British fist). He commented: "An excited party in a conflict is always apt to overstate his case and never recognises that by that very exaggeration he puts himself out of court. The German at present is overwrought and highly inflamed, and no wonder he fails to see that his fierce diatribes against his foe have no bearing on the direct issue between them but betray his own weakness and malice."

Finally there is an attack on the German people which appears just as explicitly racist as the comments of less enlightened people about Indians: "The people of India, from whose proudest races these troops are furnished, were civilized and cultured long anterior to the period when, according to Julius Caesar, Tacitus, and other Roman writers, the Teutonic savages roamed the German forests. Caesar describes them as *feri ac barbari*. Tacitus says they had not even an alphabet. Gibbon calls them a herd of savages."

The Indian Government declined to translate *The Verdict of India* or distribute it widely, believing it would serve little purpose.

Having been a staunch supporter of the Empire in his early years, towards the end of his life Bhownaggree began to see Indian independence as inevitable; it finally came, of course, but not until 15 years after his death.

In the 1920s the Incorporated Parsee Association of Europe made several attempts to make a presentation to Bhownaggree, their President, but he consistently blocked their efforts. Perhaps, wounded by the many attacks on him, he was trying to avoid anything which would make him appear self-satisfied. On July 27 1927, at a function in his honour, they finally achieved their aim by presenting him with an address on vellum, placed in a silver box, without giving him a chance to stop them. In his response he pointed out that his lifelong goal had been the same as that of Naoroji, stating: "In respect of my career in another place, it was a privilege, which I have always cherished, to follow, doubtless at long distance and by methods which, in spite of some of them seeming different, were yet designed to arrive at the same goal, the course pursued by that venerable patriot of India Dadabhai Naoroji, whose friendship I had the honour to enjoy from early years".

In 1931 Sir Pheroze Sethna, a leading figure in the National Liberal Association of India, spoke of Bhownaggree's achievements during a visit to Zoroastrian House: "Sir Mancherjee was regarded as the one to whom not only their community but their countrymen looked for advice, guidance and help in difficult situations. The constitutional security of the Association and its funds were his conception, and it was the confidence which he had inspired in the community, and especially among its leaders, which had induced large-hearted benefactors... to endow the Centre in which they met".[37]

The last tribute paid to Sir Mancherjee Bhownaggree was the presentation of a portrait in oils by Mr E A Bhiwandiwalla, to mark his 25 years as President of the Association. The painting was handed over on October 8 1933; he was now 82 years old.

---

37   Hinnells, p 126

PRESENTED BY HIS PARSEE FRIENDS
TO
SIR MANCHERJEE MERWANJI BHOWNAGGREE, K.C. IE.
IN APPRECIATION OF HIS SERVICES
AS PRESIDENT PARSEE ASSOCIATION OF EUROPE, LONDON.
27TH JULY, 1927.

The painting of Sir Mancherjee Bhownaggree by E A Bhiwandiwalla

Bhownaggree died six weeks later, after a short illness, on November 14 1933, and on December 5 his ashes were interred in the Zoroastrian burial ground at Brookwood.

His obituary in *The Times* read: "Bhownaggree was of a different mould [from Naoroji and Saklatvala] and possessed a versatility that they lacked. He had a practical outlook and with great tenacity of purpose there was nothing quixotic or crusading in his temperament. To the mortification of the National Congress politicians of his day, he sat for North East Bethnal Green as a Unionist and helped Lord George Hamilton, then Secretary of State for India, to repel the attacks of Sir William Wedderburn and other members of a

Bhownaggree's tomb in the Parsi cemetery at Brookwood Crematorium, Surrey

small group of radicals known as the 'Indian Opposition'...
during his ten-year membership he impressed the House
by the vigour and eloquence of his speeches on Indian
subjects. It will always be to his credit that he originated
and unflaggingly maintained, in and out of the House, the
struggle against the disabilities of Indians in South Africa
and other overseas possessions of the Crown... Bhownaggree
was also one of the first Indians to press forward the need of
technical and vocational education".

A simpler obituary in the *Bethnal Green News*, November
18 1933, read: "Kind-hearted and benevolent, he was popular
wherever he went, and his short, stout figure and smiling
countenance were prominent in any gathering".

How does history look back on Mancherjee Bhownaggree?
He appears to be a man who got off on the wrong foot among
his fellow Indians with his often pretentious manner and his
display of pro-British, right-wing, conservative and racist
attitudes, although it was this platform which put him in the
House of Commons. From early adulthood, he saw himself
as an honorary Westerner and a cut above his compatriots,
which certainly did not endear him to many other Indians
of the time, yet there is evidence that behind a life which he
split between two great countries he bore a deep love for both;
he wrote in a letter in 1892, "still my heart leaps back to dear
old England". A tendency to self-importance, pomp, bombast
and high-flown rhetoric, a great contrast to the modest
gentility of Dadabhai Naoroji, clearly alienated many people
and gave the impression that he was far more self-seeking
than was in fact the case. He seems to have accepted much
of the racism of the period and did very little to fight the
cause of ordinary Indians in Britain, despite championing

them abroad. Nevertheless, he was a determined and a very gifted and clever man, and he spent most of his energies, once he was in a position of power, fighting for the underdog, for the Parsis and to a lesser but worthwhile extent, for his fellow Indians in general. Undoubtedly he was one of those who helped to persuade the racist white West that Indians were every bit as good as Europeans.

Rusi K Dalal, in his preface to the booklet about Bhownaggree by Hinnells and Ralph, stated: "Sir Mancherjee Bhownaggree's life can be picked out as a worthy example of the way that one individual's effort can speak for his community's values and endeavours." Dalal goes on to say: "His detractors in the INC and its British supporters alleged that becoming an MP was all that mattered to Bhownaggree and that principles and the welfare of India were of little concern to him, a perception that has remained to this day".

According to Mike Harris in *Little Atoms*: "His rise to the House of Commons, knighthood and prominence in English high society came from his lifelong passion for the empire. Yet his support for imperialism has made him one of history's overlooked figures, both in British and Indian history."

The Bhownaggree Corridor which housed his gallery at the Imperial Institute disappeared when the Institute was demolished in the 1960s to make way for the new Imperial College of Science and Technology of the University of London. The exhibits remained on view for a time in the Bhownaggree Gallery at the Commonwealth Institute in Holland Park, but in 1999 that institute too was closed, leaving the Bhownaggree Silver Medal at the Alexandra Institution and the stained-glass window in St Luke's as the only surviving physical reminders of Ave, or of her brother's devotion to her.

PART III

Shapurji Saklatvala
1874-1936
The middle-class communist

Just as Mancherjee Bhownaggree was born a generation after Dadabhai Naoroji, Shapurji Saklatvala was born a generation after Bhownaggree, on March 28 1874. Saklatvala was also born in Bombay, and he too was a Parsi, but his political leanings could not have been more different; a man of deep convictions, he was an ardent socialist from the beginning, despite being born into a well-to-do family, and he became one of only four communists to win seats in the British Parliament to the present day. His dedication to the cause, his incisive intelligence and his skill in debate would make him a leading figure in the party's history.

CHAPTER 9

The man who turned his back on a business empire

Shapurji Saklatvala was the second of five children born to Dorabji Saklatvala and his wife Jerbai, the younger sister of Jamsetji Nusserwanji (J N) Tata (b. 1839), the founder of Tata and revered as the 'Father of Indian Industry'. Dorabji Saklatvala was a 'famous merchant' as Saklatvala's first biographer, Panchanan Saha, put it, whose father, also called Shapurji, was Tata's close ally and business partner. The name 'Saklatvala' is apparently derived from 'Saklat-wallah', denoting the family's connection to the serge cloth industry.

The second child and the eldest of four sons, young Shapurji appears to have been his father's favourite.[38] They lived modestly but comfortably in the Fort area of Bombay.

When Shapurji was 14 in about 1888, they moved to the Tata family home, Esplanade House, to live alongside J N Tata and his wife and two sons, Dorab and Ratanji. Jamsetji, a great traveller and an avid reader, had a well-stocked library, and he had made a home there for all his nephews. Esplanade House was built in classical style around a courtyard and furnished in European fashion.

Esplanade House, Bombay (courtesy of Tata Central Archives)

Sir Jamsetji Nusserwanji Tata (1839-1904), the father of the
Tata Group and Saklatvala's uncle

This sounds like an auspicious beginning for young Shapurji, and not one which seemed likely to lead him along the path towards rebellion, but the reality was different; he soon became estranged not only from the wealthy middle classes to which he owed his origins but from the Tata dynasty. In about 1926 he wrote a letter which revealed a long-festering bitterness towards the family. It seems from this letter, quoted in his daughter Sehri's biography of her father, *The Fifth Commandment*, that Shapurji's grandfather had trusted J N Tata to look after his heir Dorabji, Shapurji junior's father, who was then still a teenager, after his death. Shapurji junior wrote:

"When [grandfather Shapurji] died, he left entirely to the honour and discretion of [J N Tata] the fixing and distribution of the fortune to surviving heirs, of whom my father Dorabji was the sole male heir and a special favourite... An ordinary trustee would have safeguarded the business rights of such an heir and also created a careful trust for the future safety of such an heir, who was then a helpless minor of fourteen. This was not done, but the unusual course was adopted of handing over all jewellery, house property and rupees 90,000 to the widow, without trust conditions and with further assurance that the son Dorabji, being about to become the Trustee's own son-in-law, would have nothing to want. Well, he had to lead all his life in want and from this age he was dispossessed of all wealth as well as business rights in the firm. Further, all throughout we, his children, were brought up positively to disrespect and even to despise him with the open doctrine that every Saklatvala influence must be wrong and every Tata quality the crystal-clear virtue. The open misappropriation of the rights of our father was explained to us as a thing to be made up to us and in us. Nothing of the sort has been done... The economic wrong stood for all these years under the excuse that Dorabji as a ward was disobedient, vicious and uncontrollable."

So, for reasons we may never understand in detail, Shapurji believed his father had been dispossessed by his father-in-law's family before he could take his first step into adult life, although there is no evidence of a family rift at the time. He was rarely seen at head office during his years working for the firm, as he was sent to work in branches far from Bombay.

This story must have had a formative influence on his son Shapurji, born more than a decade later but clearly well aware of this alleged wrong. The Tata Iron and Steel Company (TISCO) grew into an industrial giant and remains so; Shapurji Saklatvala senior, though he had not realised it, had died without passing on any benefit from his role as founding partner to his descendants. Perhaps seeing his father treated as an underdog after his grandfather's death awoke in the young Shapurji the socialist instincts which would later become the *raison d'être* of his life. Several witnesses from the time noticed his concern about the all-too-obvious gulf between the rich and poor of Bombay. He greatly appreciated the kindness of the Jesuit Fathers in providing free education for his brother Beram, Dorabji's fifth and last child, for whom there was no family money left. That lack of material support for a scion of such a wealthy family must have been a bitter blow.

When young Shapurji was old enough to join the firm in the 1890s, he apparently clicked immediately with J N Tata and to some extent came to regard him as a father figure. Jamsetji saw his potential, and favoured him to the extent of arousing great jealousy in his own son, another

Dorabji, who was 15 years older than Shapurji. It is not clear when Saklatvala first heard the allegations of unfair treatment of his father, but it did not stop him enjoying a good relationship with J N Tata and his other son, Ratan or Ratanji, throughout their lives.

As with most Parsi families at the time, the Zoroastrian faith was the cornerstone of daily life, and at the age of seven Shapurji undertook his *navjote* ceremony (comparable to a Jewish *Bar Mitzvah,* though taking place as early as seven years of age) to formally initiate him into the faith. When all four brothers were in their teens, like Dadabhai Naoroji they passed through the first two stages in the road to becoming a priest, essentially a job which was handed down from father to son. This occupied a year of their lives. Afterwards Shapurji was transferred to St Xavier's Jesuit school. He had developed an interest by now in spiritual matters, and tended to adopt a serious attitude to life. His brother Beram wrote later: "As he grew up, his tendency was to take things much more seriously than other boys of his own age. Personally I believe he was very greatly influenced by the austere and simple life of the Jesuit Fathers... he seldom took part in any games and did not seem to enjoy the company of rowdy boys. He had a circle of friends of his own. Though in fairly good health he was physically never very strong... he was willing to be helpful to others and was fond of joining debating societies and similar organisations... Philosophy and religion attracted him to such a degree that he even neglected his other studies."[39]

It is clear that Shapurji took a great interest as a young man in the Catholic faith, and studied it closely. This led to some disapproval among his family, although it seems

39   Sehri Saklatvala

clear that he was never intending, as some of them feared, to convert to Catholicism. Later he sent his children to a convent school, believing that nuns with no family ties of their own were best positioned to care for the children of others, although he forbade them from receiving Catholic religious instruction or attending services.

Beram's letter goes on to say that Shapurji failed to take an arts degree because of prolonged illness, and this 'filled him with bitterness', and changed his outlook on life. He was 'greatly perplexed by life's vagaries' and was struggling to decide what profession to take up.

At this time Shapurji's closest friend was Kaikoo Mehta, son of Sir Pherozeshah Mehta, the prominent Bombay lawyer who gave such vital support to Dadabhai Naoroji. Kaikoo was later described by Shapurji's daughter Sehri as 'like a second father' to her. He stated that even in the early days, Shapurji always had a feeling for 'the poor and the underdog'. "He used to go about and see these people in their cottages, discuss matters and sympathise with them and discuss the forces which kept them poor," said Mehta.

Shapurji was 'altogether a brilliant student', according to another friend, Spitam Cama, and excelled in mathematics and English literature. He made his first attempt at public speaking at St Xavier's College, to members of the 'Gwalia Circle', a literary group of which he was a member, and quickly became a leading figure in the society.

Shapurji's parents separated relatively early in their marriage, and he missed his father's presence during his boyhood, though there seems to have been plenty of contact between them.

In 1896, when Shapurji was 22, bubonic plague struck Bombay. The fight against it owed a great deal to Professor

Waldemar, or Vladimir, Haffkine, a Russian Jewish bacteriologist who had been imprisoned three times for his opposition to the Tsarist regime. Haffkine worked alongside the great Louis Pasteur and developed the first vaccine for cholera. Despite this, the Russian government refused to

Vladimir Haffkine

allow him back into his homeland to tackle cholera there, so in 1893 he moved to Calcutta to look into ways of tackling the disease at its source. When bubonic plague reached Bombay, Haffkine was sent there. With hundreds of people dying every day, the plague had reached devastating proportions. Within three or four months he had developed an effective vaccine, which he first tried upon himself before making available to the public. He was supported from the outset by the Tata family, who were among the first to benefit from the inoculations, and the students at St Xavier's were recruited to help him.

Shapurji Saklatvala was one of those who worked most closely with the professor, and he soon became a trusted ally. While the vaccine was overwhelmingly their priority, it is clear that they also discussed politics and the state of India. The professor was highly critical of the imperialist British government, having seen the appalling conditions in which poor Indians lived, and it seems likely that he found a sympathetic disciple in Shapurji.

Despite the success of Haffkine's work it took six years for the plague to be brought under control[40], not least because of the scepticism of many ordinary Indians, who, terrified of the disease and unable to understand how vaccination could prevent it, refused either to be inoculated or to be given hospital treatment. By then Shapurji had seen at close quarters how the poor of India lived, crowded together in desperately insanitary conditions and living on a semi-starvation diet. It is not hard to image how he must have become disaffected with his own middle-class background and the capitalist ethos of the Tata clan.

During his work with Professor Haffkine, Saklatvala

---

40 Bubonic plague was almost wiped out during the 20th century, but small-scale outbreaks have continued to occur right up to the present day.

found himself suffering the racial discrimination prevalent at the time. Some 25 years later, he recalled the experience in a speech to the House of Commons:

"The Governor of Bombay... sent a telegram to Professor Haffkine to go to him with certain facts and figures because the matter was becoming of vital importance. Professor Haffkine asked me to go and assist him. I gave up my work in the office and went to the place where he was staying, and that was his European club. People talk about untouchability! Although I had facts and figures at my disposal, I was actually prevented from entering the white man's club. Ultimately, the messenger of the club, after telephoning to various government officials, took me to the back yard of the club, led me through the kitchen and an underground passage to a basement room, where the professor was asked to see me, because I was not a white man."[41]

It is not entirely clear why Shapurji never sat his finals for his BA Arts degree; in addition to his illness, it may have been because he was too busy with his work for Professor Haffkine, researching the progress of the plague and the effectiveness of the vaccine.

In about 1901, Shapurji suffered a serious, though apparently undiagnosed, illness and was sent to a sanatorium in the hills of Panchgani, in Maharashtra, not far from Bombay. During his convalescence he is said to have become very depressed and spent long hours walking in the hills. In 1902, following tensions at the Tata family home, he went to live with his mother and sister in Hornby Road nearby.[42]

Shapurji's next practical concern was in connection with his work for the Tata company. He was charged with

41   Mike Squires
42   Marc Wadsworth

the job of researching sources of iron ore, as the basis of a steel production business. India had discovered iron several thousand years earlier, but as yet there was no organised industry based upon it. Jamsetji Tata had obtained the British Government's permission to prospect for iron in two areas of the Chanda District (now Chandrapur) in Maharashtra, and rather surprisingly he delegated to the somewhat frail Shapurji the exploration side of the business, which involved finding coal and limestone as well as iron ore. Perhaps he felt the job would be good for him.

Shapurji had experienced urban hardship at close quarters, and now he found himself encountering the rural kind, in the heat of a Maharashtra summer. The rice, linseed, gram and wheat harvests had been failing in the Chanda district, and most of the scattered population were living in abject poverty. Shapurji's team slept in the bullock carts in which they were travelling, but at times they accepted the hospitality of the country people. In this way he once again saw at close quarters how poverty made people suffer.

On a visit to the United States, Jamsetji met an American consulting engineer, C M Weld, who was recruited to join Shapurji's party; the two got on well together and were happy to rough it on their prospecting expeditions. Dorabji Tata, however, appears to have been jealous of Shapurji because Jamsetji so often entrusted him with jobs in preference to giving them to him, according to Sehri Saklatvala; he dismissed their prospecting mission as a 'wild goose chase'. He may have had a point. We do know that not long after C M Weld's arrival, the party gave up prospecting in Chanda and moved to try another area, Dondi Lohara, far to the east in the province of Chattisgarh.

Jamsetji Tata wrote of this episode:[43] "In April 1903 Mr Weld and Mr Dorabji Tata joined Mr Saklatvala and entered upon a period of adventurous wanderings which was often marked by much privation. The heat in the Central Provinces in April, May and June is intense. The prospectors were generally moving far from the railway line, and sometimes had difficulty in obtaining food. Water was frequently scarce and bad, and they were often compelled to make their tea with the soda water they carried on their carts. There were times when they could not make any progress at all. The district includes large forest areas, which are the joy of the hunters because tigers are numerous, but prospectors for iron and coal regard a multiplicity of tigers with more apprehension than delight. Roads were few and indifferent. Sometimes the party found shelter in a village house, but there were nights when they had to sleep in their carts. At first they lived very roughly indeed." (Quoted by Frank Harris, in his biography of J N Tata.)

Shapurji was saddened and depressed to hear of the death of J N Tata, in 1904 at the age of 65, not living to see the fulfilment of his dream through the creation of the Tata Iron and Steel Company. He may also have felt more vulnerable in the company without his protection, a fear which proved to be well justified.

The search for iron ore was becoming more competitive, but the family had something of a breakthrough soon after the death of J N Tata when the Maharaja of Mayurbhani invited them to go prospecting on his patch. Mayurbhani State proved to extend to 4000 square miles of densely-forested hills and was tough going for the explorers, but this time they struck gold, or rather iron. Shapurji was

43   Marc Wadsworth

able to head off a rival Bengal-based iron company and sign an agreement with the Maharaja on behalf of Tata, an agreement which he described as 'the birth of the Tata iron company'.

Unfortunately Shapurji paid a price for his success on the Mayurbhanj expedition. He succumbed to malaria, and was then given too large a dose of medicine, which led to the permanent paralysis of his toes, a handicap he would carry with him throughout his life. Ever after he had to wear soft boots especially made for him.

Lacking his late uncle's protection, Shapurji was now at the mercy of Dorabji Tata and Dorabji's cousin R D Tata, who seems to have been equally antagonistic to him. It was soon after this that Shapurji complained that he was being eased out of the business following a difference of opinion, apparently over the direction the company should be taking; Shapurji was focused on the mining side, which Dorabji regarded as less important. It appears that although he was almost universally liked among those who knew him, Shapurji had, in common with Mancherjee Bhownaggree before him, one seemingly implacable lifelong enemy. In Bhownaggree's case it was Sir Dinshaw Wacha, while in Saklatvala's it was Dorabji Tata. In the same letter quoted at the beginning, Shapurji wrote: "Then comes the unjust financial treatment of myself in business matters. Regardless of our ability… JNT with his patriarchal guardianship destined us to work in and live for the firm of the family… Our compensation for work and loyalty was fixity of tenure. Sir Dorabji's disregard of these unwritten moral contracts is really an abuse of his legal might. The iron scheme was impossible without the part I played."

Dorabji's way of ridding himself of this pestilent rebel was to send Shapurji away from Bombay and then out of India, using his poor health as a pretext. The exile that followed may also have owed something to his conflict with the Indian authorities; on his mining travels he had flouted convention by paying his labourers far more than the going rate and – quite unheard of – allowing them to rest in the afternoon heat. His biographer Saha, who knew Saklatvala and interviewed him several times, relates that on one occasion he arrived at a village to find it deserted. He guessed that the police had warned the villagers that a British expedition was coming and would give them a hard time, thus deliberately making them flee for cover. The police scheme was then to round up them up again for the prospectors and accept an appropriate reward for doing so. They had reckoned without Saklatvala, who saw through the trickery, grabbed the key of the station and locked the officers inside until they agreed to bring the villagers back without reward.

Saklatvala's exile began when in November 1905 he was escorted to England by Dorabji and his wife Mehrbai, ostensibly to give him a chance to recover his health. It is unlikely that he was happy about this arrangement. He was ill and still walking on crutches, and in retrospect it is clear that his career with the Tata organisation was coming to an end, although he was not yet ready to accept that; a year later he was still writing that ultimately he intended to return to the Tata office and focus, as he had always wanted to, on the mining side of the business.[44]

The Tatas took him on the long journey to London, and after a few days there they went on to Matlock, in the hills of the Peak District, whose health-giving mineral springs were sought by many invalids as an aid to their recovery. There

44 Mike Squires

they very soon left him, alone and very far from anyone he knew. Fortunately, life was about to smile on Shapurji Saklatvala once again.

CHAPTER 10

Love at first sight

Matlock was, and is, a delightful spot, the perfect setting for health spas and hydros designed to help the affluent convalescent. The leading hydro at the time was Smedley's[45], which could accommodate 250 guests, and it was here the Bombay party checked in. Dorabji and Mehrbai Tata stayed only a few days before returning, leaving Shapurji on his own.

He was sitting at dinner on his 32nd birthday, March 28 1906, when Sally Marsh first walked into his vision. He was immediately captivated. Sally (christened Sarah), was only 17 years old, the fourth of a brood of 12 working-class country children from the neighbouring village of Tansley. Like her brothers and sisters, she had had to get used to going out to

---

45 Smedley's went on to cater for many famous names, including Robert Louis Stevenson, Sir Thomas Beecham and Ivor Novello. Today the building is the headquarters of Derbyshire County Council.

work when still a child, but fortune smiled on her when she found a job as a pantrymaid at Smedley's Hydro. There she enjoyed far better food than she was used to and according to Sehri Saklatvala she 'blossomed in the unfamiliarly lavish surroundings', and soon graduated to the dining room, where she worked as a waitress. It was this that brought her to the attention of Shapurji Saklatvala. In a letter much later, Sally gave her account of their meeting and what followed it:

"He asked Maria Marsh who I was. She told me I was her cousin, so he asked her to call me over to his table and introduce me to him, which she did. With his beard, I took him for an old man. He gave me flowers almost every day and asked me to go for walks. I was too frightened to do so, but I kept saying I would just to satisfy him for the time being. Whenever I went out he would walk behind me. One afternoon I went to Matlock Bath by bus; when I offered my fare, the conductor said a gentleman behind had paid. I gave a blind man a penny in the afternoon without knowing he [Shapurji] was following; afterwards he told me that he had given the blind man two shillings and told him what a lucky man he was, as he had been given a penny by the sweetest girl in the world.

"One day I got a note from a shoe shop... would I go in and try on some shoes. There was a note inside a special pair of shoes which I was to try on from him, saying that he hoped to be able to buy all my shoes from now on.

"The day he left the Hydro, he asked me to see him off on the 2:19 train. I said yes but had no intention of going... I had a phone message to say that he was on Matlock Bath station and he intended to remain there however long it was until I went to see him. I went at nine o'clock at night and said goodbye to him."

A youthful portrait of Sarah Marsh

Smedley's Hydro, where Saklatvala met Sarah Marsh (Ann Andrews Collection)

Shapurji was clearly besotted. He wrote to Sally twice a day, and soon took the opportunity to visit again, just for the day. That September he went to Tansley for Sally's 18th birthday, when he saw Mr and Mrs Marsh and 'got them on his side', according to Sally. Finally on November 6, she accepted an engagement ring from Shapurji.

Early in the courtship Shapurji changed Sally's name to Sehri, a name of his own invention designed to combine 'Sally' with 'Sarah'; this was apparently because 'Sally' sounds like a swear word in Gujarati. Shapurji's mother Jerbai clicked with Sehri, and the couple were married on August 14 1907 in the Parish Church of St Thomas, Oldham, the town to which the Marsh family had now moved in the hope of finding more work.

Saklatvala with his new bride

With Sehri in Indian dress

Not that love, and the recovery of his health, were all that were on Shapurji's mind during his sojourn in Matlock. He had wasted no time in involving himself in political and trade union affairs and would attend meetings of the National Union of General and Municipal Workers.

Early in his stay he had got into the habit of visiting a

Mrs Richards, who kept a glass and china shop opposite Smedley's, and he would talk to her of the injustices suffered by the working classes. She later wrote, "His whole thought and actions were how to get people interested in helping to bring about a better life and improved conditions for the workers... he was very frail, but so great mentally."

Shapurji became good friends with Mrs Richards, and he asked if her husband would be his best man (In the event Mr Richards was away in Scotland and this was not possible).

After the marriage the couple moved to London, where they occupied a modest bed-sitter at 730 Holloway Road. Shapurji had by now largely relinquished his remaining involvement with the Tatas and had taken a job with British Westinghouse, the UK arm of the American company which made generators, switchgear and other equipment for the distribution of electricity. He had also tried joining Lincoln's Inn with the aim of becoming a barrister, but soon abandoned that idea, either because of the predominantly right-wing politics found among lawyers or because he wanted to focus on a political career – or both.

At this stage Shapurji was politically a Liberal, the Labour movement still being very new, and was giving the National Liberal Club as his address when in London. This lasted only a matter of months. He soon became disillusioned with the party, feeling it was not doing enough for the working classes. Rajani Palme Dutt, a contemporary communist who was half Indian and half Swedish, wrote: "He speedily saw through the very limited outlook and snobbish hypocrisy, crossed swords with Lord Morley, then Secretary of State for India, and turned from the liberal politicians to the working class. Travelling all over England, he saw the slums and unemployment, the ruthless exploitation of the industrial and agricultural workers... he came to realise that poverty was not just an Indian problem, but an international problem of the workers all over the world, and that its solution required the international fight of the working class against class society and for socialism."

Saklatvala addressing crowds in Trafalgar Square

Reg Bishop, who became Saklatvala's secretary when he was an MP and built a strong friendship with him, wrote of this time that his family had made him a life member of the National Liberal Club "so that he would meet all the really respectable friends of Indian freedom. He did, and he didn't think much of them. Among those he met was Lord Morley.

The outcome of a furious argument with 'Honest Jack', as Morley liked to be known, was Sak's resignation from the Liberal mausoleum and his entry into working class politics via the Independent Labour Party."[46]

By 1907 he was actively involved with the Socialist Party in East Finchley, and joined the Social Democratic Federation (later renamed the British Socialist Party), a Marxist group founded by H M Hyndman, which had a branch in Battersea that became important to Saklatvala later. The SDF was one of the organisations which later merged to create the Communist Party of Great Britain, although his main focus was the Independent Labour Party. At a meeting of the SDF in East Finchley, he heard George Bernard Shaw speak. He gave active support to the suffragette movement, joining in demonstrations, and came to know Sylvia Pankhurst well. In 1908 he joined one of the suffragettes' protest events, probably the first time he joined a political demonstration.

His old friend Kaikoo Mehta came to live in London at this time; he was a frequent visitor to the Saklatvala household and later a great favourite among the children. Sehri Saklatvala described him as much more light-hearted than her father, who was 'always somewhat stern and aloof'.

Shapurji's mother Jerbai Saklatvala died in November 1907 in New York, apparently as a result of the anaesthetic administered during an operation, and was brought to England to be buried in the Parsi burial ground at Brookwood, alongside her brother Jamsetji; we do not know if this was her stated wish or Shapurji's decision, although the latter seems likely, as he said later that he wanted his home to be near her. She did not live to know her first grandchild, Dorab, who was born soon afterwards.

46   Mike Squires

In 1908 the family moved to a cottage on Hampstead Heath, where Sehri, who was understandably missing her family up north, was very pleased to discover that their neighbours were an elderly couple from the same part of the world; they became close friends and no doubt helped to fill the gap left by Sehri's beloved parents.

Shapurji left his post at Westinghouse in 1909. It seems the firm had appointed him partly because of his involvement with the Tata family, potentially a very

Mr and Mrs Saklatvala with three of their children in 1908

Saklatvala family group at York House in 1912, young Sehri on her mother's knee

valuable business contact, before his estrangement from them became clear. Instead he joined a firm of consulting engineers in Manchester, and he, Sehri and Dorab moved to the nearby town of Ashton on Mersey. Sehri gave birth to a daughter there on her 21st birthday, and she was named Candida, after the play by George Bernard Shaw, whom the family had met in London; she became better known, rather incongruously, as Candy. Next came the third child, Beram, named after his uncle, an outgoing and highly entertaining child who from an early age would often entertain the family with self-composed verse. Sehri describes Beram as the brains of his generation; he became a successful writer and had his paintings hung in the Institute of British Artists, as well making a successful career with Tata.

In Manchester Shapurji joined the socialist Clarion Club, where he found an ally in Bipin Chandra Dal, a great orator and campaigner for Indian freedom, whom he already knew from Bombay. He attended meetings of the County Forum and spoke up eloquently for his beliefs. It was in Manchester that he first met Ramsay MacDonald, who in 1911 became leader of the Labour Party, and later the first Labour Prime Minister. He did not support MacDonald for the leadership, believing he was not the right man for the job; instead he backed John Clynes, who would become leader of the party in 1921. Clynes later wrote, "We had very pleasant conversations, and as I learned later he gave me some credit for turning his views in the socialist direction".

Saklatvala clearly changed his mind about MacDonald, because by the time of the 1918 election he was giving him his unstinted support and travelling to MacDonald's seat in Leicester to campaign for him.[47] This appears to have been partly because of their shared disagreement with the British decision to go to war in 1914, and partly because of MacDonald's support for Indian freedom. He would change his mind about MacDonald again after joining him in Parliament, and indeed MacDonald would change his mind about Saklatvala when he realised the extent of his devotion to communism and his inclination towards revolution.

Ramsay MacDonald

47   Squires

In 1911 there came an unexpected development: Saklatvala was invited to return to India to do some work for Tata. His father wrote to warn him that he risked being arrested there, presumably because of his opposition to the authorities at various points, so he delayed the visit until the following year. In the meantime he worked as personal assistant in London for his cousin Ratanji Tata, and for a short time managed his cotton mills department. When he did return to Bombay he took his family with him, intending to settle there once again. Instead of playing a role with Tata's main businesses, however, he was sent off by Dorabji to investigate some irregularities in the running of a company-owned hotel; clearly yet another attempt to sideline him. Neither at this nor at any other time did Shapurji criticise the Tatas publicly, however. It was not until much later that the extent of his bitterness towards them emerged.

In May or June of 1913, Shapurji and his family found themselves packing their bags once again for England. This was a company decision, taken without his agreement; he had fully expected to become settled back in his homeland. He wrote later: "Within 12 months, to my bitter astonishment, I received a sudden notice to return to England with my family and restart a home... I have never been allowed to know why this was done but my kindly-disposed cousin, who told me about it, allowed me to understand that he was not doing it of his choice."

When his father Dorabji, who was based in Manchester, remonstrated with the head of the family about this, the reply was, according to Saklatvala: "As my politics were displeasing to the Government of India, any improvement in my condition would bring trouble upon their heads in their business and other activities in India, for which they had largely to depend upon and co-operate with the Government".

The cousin was the wealthy but kindly Ratanji Tata, who had bought a palatial property in Twickenham called York House, and the Saklatvalas were invited to live there until they could find a home, which they did the following year, at 51 Lebanon Park. Ratanji took little interest in the

Ratanji Tata

family company and preferred to live the life of an English aristocrat. Beram, Saklatvala's son, said of him: "Work was not his line. He was the artistic dilettante, chestnut-headed, frock-coated, picture-collecting, armour-loving member of the family".

Shapurji was invited to work as Ratanji's personal assistant, an arrangement which continued until 1918. In fact he continued to take an annual salary from Tata even after he later became elected as an MP, which was a 'considerable embarrassment to the Communist Party' according to Marc Wadsworth, author of the 1998 political biography *Comrade Sak*. In 1922 it appears to have stood at £750, the equivalent of around £34,000 today. He finally relinquished it in 1925.

Despite that income, Saklatvala recalled this as a difficult period. He wrote: "After returning to England I had to pass through a period of extreme hardship, having to live through the entire war period with a family of young children on £22 a month with periodical warnings and notices from my English superior in the London office." He had of course received no financial support of any kind during his years of campaigning, and even as an MP he received only the fixed parliamentary allowance of £400 (first introduced in 1911), now worth about £18,000 but still far less than MPs are paid today.[48] Perhaps his privileged background gave him a different perspective of what a reasonable income amounted to. He was able to send his children to a fee-paying preparatory school in Twickenham, although later they attended a state school.

It was during this time that Sehri gave birth to their fourth child, Kaikoo, named after his great friend, and finally, in 1919, came his daughter Sehri, the author of his

48   Wadsworth

1991 biography. When Sehri senior's father died in 1916, her grandchildren were devastated, although they did receive the news that he was dying in time to travel north to his bedside before he departed.

Adding the conscientious objectors to his list of political

With Walton Newbold, who became the first communist Member of Parliament

causes, Shapurji now involved himself deeply in campaigning politics. In 1916 he joined the City of London branch of the Independent Labour Party, and began to acquire a national reputation for his campaigning and the power of his speeches. The branch contained a large number of revolutionary socialists, including Walton Newbold, of whom more later. In 1917 he was made a delegate to the ILP's divisional and national conferences, which gave him an opportunity to raise the issue of Indian independence. That he did not rise to greater prominence in the ILP at this time was down to one main factor; his wholehearted support of the 1917 Bolshevik revolution.

Herbert Bryan from the *Daily Herald* commented on Saklatvala's 'striking and original way of speaking' and said that at this time his reputation was spreading fast and he was constantly being asked to speak at meetings of various bodies. Bryan later wrote, "The points that stand out most in my memory about him are 1) his grasp of British political affairs and his great command of English on the platform... and 2) the fact that he was absolutely tireless and never considered sparing his physical powers in the least if he thought there was something to be done to advance the cause he had at heart."

He "became totally absorbed in the various political movements to which he subscribed and spent hardly any weekends at home," wrote his daughter Sehri. She stated that although he was called up to fight in the 'Great War', his call-up papers were withdrawn, presumably because of his politics.

A physical portrait of Saklatvala at this time comes from his daughter's biography: "He was of only average height, with a neat, trim figure, vigorous in his speech and general deportment. He had dark, wavy hair, shining hazel eyes that were most expressive of his earnestness, his anger or his twinkling and mischievous humour. Everyone who knew him was impressed by his kindliness, his warmth, his sincerity." And now that he had fully recovered from his earlier illness, he had 'limitless energy'. He had "an impish, ebullient yet quiet sense of fun and humour, and often used jocularity to prick the bubbles of pride or false dignity in others... Wide reading and powers of observation together with a prodigious memory and a facility with figures bestowed upon him an encyclopaedic knowledge which enabled him to make long political speeches laden with accurate statistics, extempore and without reference to written notes". Indeed Saklatvala was unusually fluent as a speaker and rarely if ever troubled to write out his speeches. In an edition of *Who's Who* he gave as his hobbies 'playing chess and silence'. He was 'generally somewhat stern and aloof towards his children'.

Saklatvala did have a less attractive side. Sehri wrote that "some minor domestic incident could trigger off a spate of shouting that frightened us all". He expected his own way at all times and demanded absolute obedience and total rectitude from his children. When Dorab was five, he defied his father by saying 'thank you' to his grandfather in English, and a furious Saklatvala struck him with a cane. A year or so later, Dorab came home one day with a cork in his pocket, saying he had brought it from the chemistry lab at school. His father insisted on marching him to the Headmaster's home to return it and confess.

In 1915 Arthur Field took Shapurji along to the City Branch of the Independent Labour Party, where he spoke from the floor. His performance led to invitations to speak at ILP meetings around London, and before long, around the UK. His performances drew large audiences, and he became increasingly well known. One of his key messages to his working-class audiences was the damage being done to their livelihoods by the cheap labour in the Empire under British imperialism – 'sweated labour in the Empire means unemployment at home'. He would explain that supporting the fight for better treatment abroad, apart from being fair and just, would benefit them economically by pushing up wages globally.

In 1917 Arthur Field and C F Ryder founded the Workers' Welfare League of India, and Saklatvala was an early supporter. He took an enthusiastic interest in the 1917 Russian Revolution, which helped to convince him that communism was the way forward. The *Daily Herald* reported that in its aftermath he was a co-founder of a short-lived group called the People's Russian Information Bureau.[49] He went on to visit the USSR, as Russia now was, in 1923, 1927 and 1934, lecturing and giving talks. In appreciating the relatively positive attitude towards communism which the establishment was taking at the time – the attitude which helped to make it possible for Saklatvala to stand for Parliament as a Labour candidate – it is useful to remember that in the wake of the Bolshevik Revolution, the Russian working classes were being widely hailed as heroes, and communism had not attracted the scepticism and fear in the West which crept in later in the 20th century. Lloyd George sent the Duma his 'heartiest congratulations' for their victory against the 'autocratic militarism which threatens the liberty of Europe'. *The Observer* called it 'one of the great and best things of our time'. The potentially negative aspects of communism were not yet appreciated; that would change.

49   Mike Squires

A principal objection many people expressed to communism at this time was simply the 'not invented here' argument – supporting communism, a relatively new political idea imported from elsewhere, was seen as unpatriotic, rather than evil or threatening.

Perhaps because England had moved on a little in its attitude to people of other colours (with the exception, perhaps, of Jews), Saklatvala did not endure the casual racism with which certain members of the establishment had attacked Dadabhai Naoroji. He dealt with hecklers with humour and logic and knew exactly how to control his audiences. But his principles overruled his manners at state occasions; his daughter wrote that he sat down when 'God Save the King' was sung at banquets and would not toast the Royal Family.

When a General Election was held in 1918, Saklatvala travelled frequently to Leicester to give his support to Ramsay MacDonald's campaign there; MacDonald had been the sitting MP for Leicester, but it was now being split into three constituencies. MacDonald, whose reputation had taken a severe knock in the past few years with accusations of treason and cowardice, fought for the new seat of Leicester West, but lost to Joseph Green, standing for the National Democratic and Labour Party, which had the support of the Liberal-Conservative coalition government. Herbert Bryan of the *Daily Herald* reported that 'Sak' travelled from London to Leicester evening after evening in the weeks before the election, returning the same night.

That same year the People's Russian Information Bureau was formed, and Saklatvala joined. "Like many other socialists," wrote his daughter, "he thought the Russian pattern was a prelude to a radical change in the politics of the whole of Europe, and this was a period of much hope and optimism."

It seems that by the time Saklatvala had become an MP his left-wing political views had made him a suspicious character in the eyes of the establishment, and Ramsay MacDonald is known to have requested and studied regular Special Branch reports on his activities.[50] By now MacDonald, alarmed by the wave of radicalism that swept through the Labour movement after the Russian Revolution, had become a firm enemy of communism, and therefore of Shapurji Saklatvala. According to Mike Squires in *Saklatvala, a Political Biography*, sourcing MacDonald's private papers, "he was kept under close scrutiny during his period as a Labour MP, and Ramsay MacDonald was particularly interested in his activities". MacDonald received weekly reports from New Scotland Yard and "read meticulously" the reports on Saklatvala. His house was raided on a number of occasions and his private correspondence was opened. MacDonald was clearly alarmed at Saklatvala's propensity for rebellion and stated in the House of Commons that Saklatvala's party had been officially instructed from Moscow to remain inside the Independent Labour Party in order to disrupt it.

Saklatvala's daughter wrote that her father was under personal surveillance for much of his life in England, something he became accustomed to; one rainy day he invited the detective who was following him to come into the restaurant where he was having lunch, to save him from getting wet. When he was on his way to speak at a meeting in London and forgot where it was being held, he simply asked at the local police station, confident that they would have all the details, as indeed they did.

50 Squires

The authorities' chief concern was his activism on behalf of India. Most British people still laboured under the illusion, thanks to centuries of Government propaganda, that British rule was essentially benign and the Indian National Congress was not much more than a collection of troublemakers. The Indian struggle for independence was little appreciated, and certainly little credence was given to it. Saklatvala certainly supported the INC, but he wanted them to rise to the challenge by rising up in a concerted campaign rather than working towards *swaraj* (self-rule) on several diplomatic fronts.

Also in 1918, Ratan died at the age of only 47, which came as a 'bitter blow' to Shapurji, as the two had become close and Ratan was his only friendly link with the Tata family. In 1920 Shapurji's father Dorabji died in Manchester, a further great blow to Shapurji and an event which left him without any members of his Indian family left in England.

In 1921 or 1922, Saklatvala bought a home of his own, a four-storey house at no. 2 St Alban's Villas, Highgate Road, NW5. He was still 'working in a modest capacity' for Tata, perhaps encouraged by having the chance to work alongside Kaikoo Mehta. He had plans to improve the house but lacked the funds to do so quickly, although he did not delay in completing the most important room, the bedroom he shared with Sehri senior, at great expense, having it kitted out in some style with fine French furniture, marble and brass. Bit by bit walls were knocked down, other walls erected, the garden was dug to lower level to match the house, the kitchen became the dining room and a new kitchen was built at the back. Large quantities of marble bought by Saklatvala at auction were used to line many of the floors. Electricity came early – the house was one of the first in London to use it – but Sehri recalled that the stairs remained bare of carpet for five years.

He was keen on classical Western paintings, and was derided by his enemies in the House for allegedly concealing wealth while posing as a friend of the working classes. They accused him of having spent £250 on having a marble fountain installed in his garden; the truth was that there was no fountain, but he did have a substantial fish pond.[51]

Much information about Saklatvala comes from letters of condolence and reminiscence written to his son Beram in the months after his father's death. Around the time of the outbreak of World War I, his friend Spitam Cama was one of a group of London Indians who would meet in a restaurant; they included Mancherjee Bhownaggree. Spitam wrote that Saklatvala had said their aim should be 'to kill as many Englishmen as possible' and suggested that British troops in India could be killed by infecting the Bombay water supply with cholera. Bhownaggree left the group after this outburst. Sehri Saklatvala believes that these words were simply an expression of anger against India's English rulers and did not constitute actual intention (it would hardly have been possible to target the infected water only at British troops), but they reveal how angry and rebellious he felt at the time. "Words and humour were his most potent weapons and refuge" wrote Sehri.

After the First World War, many in the Independent Labour Party wanted it to become affiliated to the Third International, an international Communist organisation, successor to the Second International, which was campaigning for world communism. Saklatvala and a group of allies campaigned for affiliation under the umbrella of the

51   Marc Wadsworth

Left Wing Group of the ILP. This proposal was rejected at the 1921 ILP annual conference in Stockport, and it was at this point that Saklatvala decided to leave the ILP and join the Communist Party. In his resignation letter, he accused the ILP of 'seeking municipal and parliamentary advantages at the sacrifice of the spirit of true socialism'. Nevertheless, he and the ILP parted on good terms.

CHAPTER 11

'Bolshie Battersea'

The seat Saklatvala chose for his entry to front-line British politics was Battersea North, a new seat created by the Representation of the People Act 1918. His entry as a Labour candidate might seem surprising, given that he had recently left the Independent Labour Party to join the Communist Party, but the Labour Party at that time was an umbrella party gathering in various supportive factions in order to unite them against the common enemy of the Right. Even so, his application was not rubber-stamped; while 13 of 14 prospective parliamentary candidates were approved without further ado by the Executive Committee of the party on October 18 1921, Saklatvala's was deferred. Only after national party officials had met him with Battersea Labour Party and secured his acceptance of the party constitution did the Labour Party give the go-ahead.

Presumably his formidable reputation as a campaigner and debater secured his acceptance. No communist had ever been elected to Parliament at that time. Indeed another communist, a Mr Foulis, was rejected as a Labour candidate at that time by the Leith constituency specifically because (unlike Saklatvala) he would not accept the conditions for candidacy laid down by the Labour Party.[52]

In the 1920s Battersea was an urban industrial area comprising four wards, Church, Latchmere, Nine Elms and Park, with a large number of working-class residents.[53] It took in the whole of Battersea Park, with Clapham Junction on the south-western border. In 1924, the Church of England newspaper *British Weekly* portrayed it thus: "Smoke and dust thicken the flat, marshy air. Trams zoom along and buses rattle past, packed with men in caps and dungarees... acres and acres of grey streets, monotonous with dingy, low-browed little houses, the criminal legacy of jerry-builders – cramped, rickety and crowded. Recently the demolition of slums in Chelsea flung a fresh torrent of poor into Battersea, which now shelters nearly 168,000 souls. The Medical Officer of Health would condemn scores of these homes but for the intolerable hardship to their packed inhabitants, who could find no other accommodation in the borough."

"People lucky enough to be in work still had to suffer low wages and bad housing" wrote Marc Wadsworth in *Comrade Sak*. "It was not unusual for families to be cramped into one or two rooms in rented accommodation. Because they did not have basic amenities in their homes, the working-class population had to use public bath houses and laundries."

The area had already been known for some decades as a

---

52 In the event the Leith seat was won by William Wedgwood Benn, the father of Tony Benn; he was standing in that election as a Liberal, but in 1928 he switched to Labour.

53 Marc Wadsworth

Battersea in the early 20th century

stronghold of radical politics; *The Times* described it as 'one of the chief centres of the Socialist and Communist movements'. The *British Weekly* stated that "North Battersea was a constituency predisposed to support anyone who prefixes his creed with 'anti'." It was "one of the first parts of London where organised labour began to exert a political influence in local affairs" according to Mike Squires' 1990 book *Saklatvala – a Political Biography*. The Battersea Trades and Labour Council was formed in 1994, an amalgamation of various unions and labour groups including such organisations as the Battersea Street Traders' Association and the Battersea Liberal and Radical Association. An alliance of Liberals and Labour supporters retained council control until 1909, when a split between them briefly allowed the Conservatives to capture the council, but it was firmly in Labour hands again by the time Saklatvala first set foot in the constituency.

Battersea was also a centre of opposition to imperialism, as became clear during the Boer War (1899-1902), when locals formed a Stop the War Committee, and George Lansbury, later to become the Labour MP for Bow and Bromley, addressed a meeting of 5000 people.[54]

The Battersea constituency had been held by John Burns for the Liberal Party from 1892 until 1918, after his resignation from the Government in protest at the declaration of war on Germany; he had been undefeated in six elections. Burns, like Saklatvala, was a radical who upset the establishment with his left-wing views and incitements to break the law. He was arrested twice on charges of conspiracy and sedition, and in 1887 he was imprisoned for six weeks.

As mentioned in Part 2 of this book, at the end of the war Mancherjee Bhownaggree called a meeting of 'all Indians resident in Great Britain' to mark the victory over Germany; it was hijacked by Saklatvala and his supporters, who removed Bhownaggree from the chair and passed a vote condemning him for convening the meeting. After that they became sworn enemies, at least for a time. At public functions Bhownaggree made sure that Saklatvala and his wife were

54   Mike Squires

seated well away from the top table, and avoided naming him in his speeches. At one dinner in 1923, S R Bomanji, a prominent member of the community, walked out in protest at this deliberate snubbing of Saklatvala.[55]

In 1919 Labour left-wingers won control of Battersea council, and two communists, Alfred Watts and Joseph Butler, were elected to represent the borough's North Division, joining three other communists who were already on the council. By the 1920s, Battersea housed some 5-6000 trade unionists and at least 48 union branches and had gained the nickname 'Bolshie Battersea'. The *Daily Telegraph* wrote: "The communists found, in the casual labourers who drifted into the district in large bodies and were subject to periods of fluctuating unemployment, the natural seedbed for extreme and alien doctrines, and this was developed until representation on municipal bodies was attained by all sorts of extremists." Street corner protests were taking place before Saklatvala came on the scene, and the police were watching the situation closely. In 1921 the unemployed of Battersea made national news when they took over the local workhouse and hoisted the red flag.

In 1913 Battersea had been the first place in Britain to elect a black mayor, John Richard Archer, a 50-year-old professional photographer from Liverpool, whose father was a ship's steward from Barbados and whose mother was Irish. Archer was a member of the Progressive Alliance, which collapsed a few years later, and thereafter he represented Labour. In 1921, as chair of a session of the second Pan African Congress in London, he introduced Saklatvala to the delegates. Soon after this Archer gave up his council seat to focus on working to support Saklatvala's election campaign,

55   Wadsworth

and was described by a fellow councillor as 'Saklatvala's most loyal and doughty champion' (although he became his opponent later, after the split in the Battersea Labour movement). It was probably Archer who played the central role in inviting Saklatvala to contest the seat, but Saklatvala had other political friends in the borough thanks to his years of activity in the ILP and other bodies, such as Arthur Field, the former secretary of his old ILP branch, and Duncan

Charlotte Despard

Carmichael, treasurer of the Battersea Labour and Trades Council.[56]

Another ally was Charlotte Despard, a fervent feminist, suffragist, pacifist, novelist and communist, who co-founded the Women's Freedom League and even built (with her friend Kate Harvey) a hospital for women and children. Despard had stood for the Labour Party in Battersea North at the 1918 General Election, losing to the Liberals but winning 33% of the vote.

So with all these allies, Saklatvala was certainly not tackling Battersea cold. His selection for the seat was probably helped by a much-praised speech he had given in Battersea Town Hall in April 1921, two months before his selection, in support of the striking miners of South Wales. When the local Labour Party met to discuss the selection, he was chosen by an 'overwhelming majority' according to R C Kiloh, the Council's secretary. There were no rules to stand in his way, nothing to prevent a communist standing as a Labour Party candidate, although the Labour leadership had considerable reservations over his selection, given that he had opposed the party in several respects, not least attempting to form a secessionist ILP group favourable to the Third International. His candidature was sanctioned only on the understanding that he would take the Labour whip and support the party constitution, which he did.

Under the banner 'Labour's united front' he fought a vigorous and effective campaign and was strongly supported by his many admirers, not least his wife Sehri, who attended many of his meetings. His daughter Sehri sometimes went along too, although she was only three at the time, and she recalled 'packed halls, where smoke from the dark streets

56   Squires

outside made it hard for me to breathe'; she was relieved by the gift of some Fishermen's Friend throat pastilles.

Saklatvala put forward a manifesto which reflected the official Labour one, including commitments to nationalisation, state housing, welfare benefits, full adult suffrage (votes for everyone over 21), and women's rights.

The seat had been won at the last election in 1918, after Burns' resignation from the Government, by Richard Morris for the Liberals. In 1922 Saklatvala's main rival was Henry Hogbin, the National Liberal candidate, a privately-educated businessman. His attitude to Hogbin and his party is clear from a statement distributed on the eve of polling under the heading 'Mr Saklatvala's Last Word To the Electors of Battersea':

"The Liberal Candidate for North Battersea claims that the Industries of Britain have been built up by Capitalists, and he says 'Heaven help us if the wash-outs get hold of them!' Workers of Britain, with your superior workmanship YOU have built up British Industries, and when you take control of them periodical stoppages will cease, unemployment disappear, and British Industries generally become stronger... The Liberals and the Conservatives do not like to see a community of property. They flourish on a community living in slums, on high rents, and low wages, for the benefit of landlords, profiteers, and royalty owners. Mr Hogbin comes to you on behalf of the National Liberal Association with an avowal to support Mr Lloyd George. It is rather a rash guess on behalf of my friend to suppose that North Battersea wants to support Lloyd George, whose dishonourable methods have ruined this country and have shocked the whole world... Self-help alone will save the People!"

Henry Hogbin, Liberal candidate for
Battersea North in 1922

A 1922 election poster

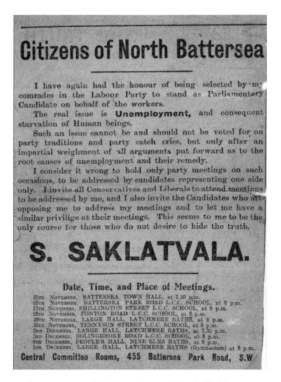

A press appeal to the voters of North Battersea

Here is part of the text of a long letter to voters distributed by Saklatvala immediately before the election:

GENERAL ELECTION, 1922.
North Battersea Division.
VOTE FOR SAKLATVALA
THE LABOUR CANDIDATE.
Polling Day Wednesday, November 15th.
8 a.m. to 9. p.m.
ELECTORS OF NORTH BATTERSEA.

I DO know where I am, though Mr Bonar Law does not. After our folly in the 1918 Election you ALL do know where you are today and where you want to be!

Our gullibility in December, 1918, has shut down workshops to a million and a half honest British Workers, with degrading cuts in wages to four million others. Our Tory-Liberal Rulers have devastated three fourths of Europe, and have antagonised practically the whole of Asia, and wonder why we are workless.

If elected, I pledge myself to the fullest extent to support the well-known programme of the Labour Party. To meet the changing positions which will arise, I promise to present myself to my Labour electors, about once a month, to ascertain their wishes on all fresh issues. The spirit of the Labour Programme may be summarised as under:

1)   A Levy on massed fortunes exceeding £5,000, for the specific purpose of unloading the weight of National Debt. Mr Bonar Law said, to a deputation in the House, on November 14th, 1917, "My own feeling is that it would be better, both for the wealthy classes and the country, to have this Levy on Capital, and reduce the burden of the National Debt; that is my own feeling. TAXATION, FOOD PRICES, and HOUSE RENTS, can NEVER be LOWERED OTHERWISE. "

2) A more just distribution of the INCOME TAX, relieving the Middle-Class Wage-earner, and abolition of TAXES ON FOOD and the necessaries of life.

3) Prompt NATIONALISATION of such Industries, to begin with, where grievous harm by private ownership has already been proved. This would lead to re-organisation of all Industries and International Commerce, and ABOLISH UNEMPLOYMENT and periodical Reduction of Wages.

4) An immediate transformation of the Imperial relations of England with Ireland, Egypt, and India, and an equitable and honest inter-relationship with all the peoples of the world through a UNIVERSAL INTERNATIONAL MACHINERY, in place of the present conglomeration of armed nations.

5) Immediately to provide for the long-neglected social and intellectual needs of the people, in the shape of better STATE HOUSING, the highest possible type of STATE EDUCATION, and ample financial provision for Aged People, Mothers, Widows, Orphans, Ex-Service victims, and Locked-out Workers.

6) To strengthen the House of Commons, elected on an ADULT SUFFRAGE for Women and Men, and to strengthen the Working-Class Organisations, as effective weapons of defence of mass rights. At present the two Houses of Parliament are used as convenient tools against the people by Political and Financial cliques, and the Organisations of the Working Classes, really representing the majority of the population, are continually defrauded and defied. THE TRADE UNION CONGRESS OF 1869 STARTED WITH A DEMAND FOR DIRECT INDUSTRIAL REPRESENTATION, WHICH IS YET TO COME.

The letter goes on to state 'THE LABOUR PARTY IS TODAY THE ONLY PARTY IN GREAT BRITAIN THAT STANDS SOLIDLY TOGETHER' and warns that the 'scare cry of "Communist" which is sure to be raised by eleventh-hour leaflets' must be ignored. It ends "I have always remembered one thing, that I have to fight for and to work for the Working Classes, as through them alone I see a chance for a truly humane world".

While he was talking to people who still remembered the election, Marc Wadsworth was given the words of a popular electioneering song:

Vote, vote, vote for Saklatvala
Kick old Hogbin out the door
For Sakky is the man who will give us bread and jam
And we won't go hungry any more.[57]

Minnie Bowles, Harry Pollitt's secretary and a member of the Young Communist League, recalled: "He would come in at the end of the hall and walk right down the centre aisle, and the whole audience would rise and applaud. He had the most beautiful speaking voice which had the crowd quiet in seconds". A Hogbin supporter said in a newspaper interview: "He would turn up at a street corner on the coldest of nights and by sheer personality and his wonderful eloquence would rivet the attention of the audience so completely that they soon forgot their discomfort. One of the great secrets was the humility of mind he displayed... he knew how to time his arrival at a meeting to the minute and with a few witty sentences and excruciatingly humorous remarks, very quickly had his audience spellbound by his oratory... His

57   Wadsworth

rage on the platform could be frantic if he found himself discussing any piece of legislation hostile to his ideals. Every fibre of his frail body seemed to quiver with overwhelming indignation, which, irresistibly, seemed to transmit itself to his audience."

Immediately before the election, *Lloyd's Sunday News* advised its readers that 'local betting is now on [Mr Hogbin's] return by a substantial majority, but the *Daily Telegraph* was less confident, warning its largely Tory readers: "Viscount Curzon has a straight fight with Labour in Battersea South, but in the Northern Division the vote will be split by the Independent Liberals. Fortunately the Conservatives and National Liberals have joined forces against what in this constituency is a very real socialist menace".

When the result came, there was momentous news for Saklatvala and his supporters. Aided by that split, he had beaten Hogbin by 11,311 votes to 9,290, a majority of 2021, winning 50.5% of the vote. He had more than doubled the vote secured in 1918 by Charlotte Despard. Nationally the coalition government of David Lloyd George (Liberal) and Andrew Bonar Law (Conservative) benefited from a landslide, totalling 509 seats between them.

Five days later, on November 20, Saklatvala was sworn in and took his seat in the House of Commons. Looking back on his victory in an article in *The Communist* magazine, he wrote: "If ever an election fight was a series of pitched battle, it was at North Battersea. Yet they were all bloodless battles full of good cheer, and though a serious fight, it was at the same time a sing-song fight all the way. The great plank in the opponent's fight was the Labour candidate's membership of the Communist Party. But this plank never even once balanced itself on two firm ends... all of [his supporters'] laughed at the scare-cry of against their candidate being a Communist."

Having been elected as a Labour candidate, Saklatvala left the honour of becoming the first officially communist Member of Parliament to another man, John Turner Walton Newbold (known as Walton Newbold), who was sent to Parliament in the same election by the Motherwell constituency, as an official Communist Party candidate. A lecturer in history and politics, Newbold, 14 years younger than Saklatvala, had also been an ILP member, and like 'Sak' he had joined the Communist Party in 1921, having become a committed Communist the year before. Newbold had Labour Party support in standing for the seat, but he was not allowed to take the Labour whip or sit with the Labour group. He focused on producing communist propaganda, in which he was helped by Saklatvala, but he was not considered effective in Parliament and soon became disillusioned with communism, rejoining the Labour Party in 1924 and never sitting as an MP again.

The Communist Party chose to play down, even ignore, the fact that Saklatvala was actually a Labour MP. Immediately after the election, the party's official newspaper wrote: "In the name of the whole Party, the Executive Committee greets the new communist faction in Parliament, Comrades Newbold and Saklatvala."

It is worth remembering that the Communist Party had a different view of the role and value of an MP from the major parties, regarding the House of Commons as a platform from which the demands of the masses could be put across and not in itself an instrument of the change it sought; the Party did not imagine that Parliament was ever going to bring about socialism. The workers should never 'fool themselves with dreams of an easy victory over capitalism', as Saklatvala put it in 1928.[58] In fact many communists were sceptical about the value of participating in Parliament at all, although Lenin himself was firmly in favour.

Saklatvala did not wait long to deliver his maiden speech, which the House heard on November 23 1922. He began the 12-minute speech with all the traditional courtesy, apologising in advance for the direct approach he planned to take: "If we are found especially wanting in certain mannerisms or if our phraseology is not up to the standard, it is not for want of respect or want of love for any of you, but simply because we of the people shall now require that the people's matters shall be talked in the people's voice." Flouting the tradition of keeping a maiden speech non-controversial, he then – still very courteously – went on the attack. He dived straight into unemployment, attacking the Conservative Prime Minister, Andrew Bonar Law, for his 'unfortunate attitude' to the issue and his reluctance to meet a deputation of the unemployed which had been waiting in London to put their case to him. Then followed an attack on the policies which had led to 74 jute mills being erected in Bengal by British capitalists and industrialists, some of them paying workers as little as 14 shillings a month and thereby 'depriving workers of another country of their legitimate livelihood', because mills in the UK had closed, unable to compete with Indian prices.

Saklatvala continued with another attack on the Prime Minister, for dubbing those protesting on behalf of the unemployed 'a set of criminals'. He then criticised the Irish Treaty, drawn up to end the Irish War of Independence, saying it would not, as promised, bring peace to Ireland because it had been forced upon the Irish people and would

58   Squires/The Encyclopaedia of the Labour Movement

not bring full self-determination. Finally he attacked the Foreign Secretary, Lord Curzon (George Curzon, 1ˢᵗ Marquess Curzon of Kedleston), for 'sitting in consultation' with Mussolini, the founding father of fascism in Italy, who had already taken power in his country by deposing King Victor Emmanuel III.[59]

So Saklatvala demonstrated his willingness to play the maverick from his earliest days in the House, in particular with his stance on Ireland. He tabled (unsuccessfully) an amendment to the Irish bill, although it had both Conservative and Opposition support, to give himself the chance to vote against it. The *Manchester Guardian* said the amendment was of an 'obviously irresponsible character'. His daughter wrote of this: "That needs a very special courage, in my view; unlike a heroic act of courage which evokes praise and adulation, this kind of courage evokes derision, rejection and the jeers of your peers; it isolates you from your colleagues. Father was to show this particular brand of courage in full measure throughout his political life".

Saklatvala himself wrote that when he took his stance on Ireland, "Ridicule, contempt, sneers, showered from all sides and a look of 'cut him out – he's no good to us in this assembly' seemed to be on the faces of all of my colleagues".

According to Marc Wadsworth, the Government was attempting to undermine Saklatvala from the moment he set foot in the House. He stated that a senior civil servant had written, "No opportunity has yet been afforded for a disclosure in the House of Commons of his real nature and personality because there has been only one Indian debate, in which it would not have been possible to deal with him personally; moreover, practically none of his violent speeches

59   The Fifth Commandment, p 160

outside have been reported in the press... If, however, he ever became really objectionable in the House itself, there is a certain amount of 'stuff' which could be used." Of course, Sak knew better than to become 'really objectionable', in the House of Commons or anywhere else – at least, most of the time.

He was the victim of many racist sneers, the perpetrators including Lord Winterton, the Under Secretary of State for India, who commented: "He has a flow of what is commonly known as Babu English which greatly amuses the House". Lord Gisborough (a Tory MP before he was made Steward of the Chiltern Hundreds and sent to the Lords in 1917) stated in a speech to the British Israel Congress that Britain had "given [Saklatvala] hospitality, allowed him to become a Member of Parliament, and that he should be allowed to run round and bite the hand that fed him was a scandal... Either he ought to be deported, or if that was illegal, shut up in some room where he would be safe... that would be a lethal chamber".

Conversely, the Labour Party held out hopes for a while that they could lure him to their own side. His private secretary, Reg Bishop, said later: "For the first year or so after his election there were many who tried to get him to break from the Communist Party. The Under-Secretaryship was held out if only he would be more 'orthodox' in politics."[60] Some hope of that.

When Parliament reconvened after Christmas 1922, Saklatvala had his first opportunity to address the House on the evils of imperialism in India, and he did so eloquently and at length. On February 27 the Indian States Protection against Disaffection Act 1922 was presented, a piece of

60   Wadsworth

legislation designed to stop Indians protesting against the tyranny and malpractice of some of their princes. Saklatvala spoke angrily against it, accusing Parliament of 'believing in a dictatorship over a foreign people through a man whom they have sent out, in whose selection 300 million people had no voice whatsoever" (he was referring to the Viceroy). He went on to call any form of political imperialism 'mere barbarity' and stated "the world has come to realise that no country and no nation can now live at peace and in prosperity by crushing other nations economically". He sarcastically attacked the civil service: "The Indian Civil Service is not Indian. It has no reputation for being civil, and it is a domination and a usurpation. Barring these three great defects, they are all right."

The following day he attacked the problem of sub-standard housing in his new constituency, highlighting the rogue landlords who were using a loophole in the law to avoid paying for compulsory repairs carried out by the council, with the result that the council could not afford these repairs.

On July 5 1923, in his last major speech before the summer recess, he excoriated the British capitalists for their excessive profiteering in the Bengal jute industry:

"In Bengal our British financial friends have raised 74 jute mills. The Bengalis have a right to see these jute mills erected in their midst, and the financier has a perfect right to go anywhere and direct any factory, if the people are simple enough to allow him to do so, but the real position is this... I have found that on a capital investment of £6,140,000 they earned, in the four years 1918, 1919, 1920 and 1921, £22,900,000 as dividends and that 41 jute mills had, besides their profits, set aside £19,000,000 as reserves.

The wages in these jute mills never reached 5 shillings a week in the spinning department and 10 shillings in the weaving department... I can quite realise that this great jute industry may have increased the wealth of a few Scottish families... but does it not appear to Members on the other side of the house that the position above means starvation for thousands of workers in Dundee and also for the workers of Bengal?"

He went on to point out that the Government of India was responsible for this situation because it had failed to introduce trade union legislation. The same applied to the iron and steel industry. Quoting some harrowing statistics for infant mortality in India, he suggested that it was not enough to blame 'Indian conditions', and stated, "The people must have either an Eastern or Western life, an agricultural peasant life or an industrial life." He called for a Committee of Investigation to be appointed to look into the disparity of wages and how conditions were leading to want of education, want of sanitation and human dignity, and starvation and unemployment.

At home, the lobbying and campaigning went on in a domestic setting. His daughter wrote: "He was seldom home and when he was, he was almost always entertaining political friends, Indian journalists, doctors, businessmen. Our house was always full of strangers... they were entertained to breakfast, lunch, tea, supper. We all took it for granted that we sat quietly by while political discussions went on around us."

In 1923 Saklatvala paid his first visit to Russia. He and Walton Newbold had been invited to Moscow for a private meeting with members of the Communist International – 'more an order than an invitation', as his daughter described it, although she believes that her father was there to advise and discuss, as well as to take party orders, and stated later that year that he had 'never received a single letter or telegraphic instruction from Moscow'. He took his wife with him. It is likely that the Communist Party wanted the British MP's help to try to gain a closer affiliation with the Labour Party. En route to Moscow he attended an international conference of MPs in Copenhagen, and a Special Branch report stated that he had received the sum of £500 from Communist International while in the city.[61]

This was Saklatvala's first taste of communism in Soviet Russia, and his daughter wrote that he was more impressed than her mother, who hated being parted from her children (they were accommodated by their Aunt Annie during their absence) and was horrified at the idea of children being put in a creche while their mothers worked. However her husband gave her firm instructions not to express her views while they were the guests of Russia.

Since Saklatvala's election Bonar Law had stood down as Prime Minister through ill health, and the Chancellor of the Exchequer, Stanley Baldwin, had taken his place. The Parliamentary recess ended on November 13, when Baldwin called a new general election to increase his mandate after dispute on the issue of trade tariffs. So ended Shapurji Saklatvala's first term in Parliament.

CHAPTER 12

In and out of office

The next General Election was held on December 6 1923, and Saklatvala campaigned as vigorously as ever for the working classes he continued so determinedly to champion. In his election address he stated: "When militarist jingoes of all nations work together it is called 'Council of War'; when intriguing politicians of all nations conspire together it is called 'Council of Ambassadors'; when armed financiers meet together to rob unarmed nations they are called the 'League of Nations'; when workers of all nations meet and work together, they are called 'Alien Bolsheviks'. We MUST HAVE UNIFORM STANDARDS FOR ALL THE WORKERS ALL OVER EUROPE AND ASIA."

Frequent references in the press to Saklatvala's membership of a wealthy industrial family drove him to repeatedly deny any capitalist sympathies, and in his election address he stated: "I would here warn you against the attempt to misrepresent my position in the Labour world by identifying me with others of a like name connected with finance in India and in America".

Racism seems to have barely tainted the campaign; in fact it seems clear that Saklatvala's race helped rather than hindered him, underlining his anti-imperialist stance. When Henry Hogbin's agent, Captain Godfrey, made the mistake of stating that he had 'an instinctive preference for an Englishman', he brought a torrent of abuse upon his head. Certainly Saklatvala was better known, and much more widely attacked, for being a communist than for being an Indian. There was a fair amount of scaremongering designed to awaken people's fears of communism, and Hogbin actually claimed that his meetings were being broken up by Saklatvala's thugs. Among many similar reports, the *London Evening Standard* alleged that the communists had a gang of armed gunmen in Battersea and were out to eliminate the Liberal candidate. It is likely that few people believed such wild claims, given the lack of any trace of real violence. By polling day, reported the *Daily Telegraph*, the only violent incident was one in which someone had thrown a lump of coal at a Liberal official.

In the event, although Stanley Baldwin's Conservatives won the most seats (258), they did not take enough for an overall majority, and the result was a hung Parliament. Labour, led by Ramsay MacDonald, took 191 seats, while Herbert Asquith's reunited Liberal Party won 158, the last time the Liberals managed to win more than a hundred seats in a General Election.

Unfortunately Saklatvala was one of the victims of the Liberal resurgence. He had been unanimously reselected by the Labour Party for the seat he had held for barely a year, but this time Henry Hogbin was not hampered by a split vote, as he stood alone against Saklatvala. He turned the tables to reverse his defeat of the previous year, pipping Saklatvala to the post by 186 votes.

In retrospect, Saklatvala's victory in 1922 coincided with the high point of the Communist Party's fortunes in the UK. The growing rift with the Labour Party left it increasingly isolated and relegated to a minor party. Only in 1924, 1935 and 1945 would the communists again win any seats at all in Parliament, and only at the end of World War II in 1945, in a last hurrah, did they manage to capture two (Mile End, to Phil Piratin, and West Fife, to Willie Gallacher).

In the wake of his 1923 defeat Saklatvala came under some pressure, his daughter wrote, to leave the Communist Party and commit himself fully to the Labour Party. He was not tempted, knowing full well that his beliefs and ambitions matched only one party, the Communists. The gap between the parties was in fact widening, largely because of the deep division between their approaches to achieving their aims. Many communists became disillusioned and drifted to the right, contributing to the long-term erosion of the party's support, but Saklatvala would remain, throughout his life, unwaveringly devoted to the Communist Party and its cause.

In July 1924 Saklatvala submitted an 11-point blueprint outlining his ideas for Labour's policy on Indian independence, under the title 'The British Labour Government and India'. It proposed a substantial pay rise for government employees, the abolition of forced labour, trade union rights, and judicial reform, including trials by jury. The Secretary of State for India, Lord Olivier (uncle of the famous actor), failed to respond to it, increasing Saklatvala's disaffection with the party. Olivier's appointment had dismayed those who had expected the India post to go to Josiah Wedgwood, a supporter of the Indian independence movement; Olivier simply maintained Conservative policy on India and ignored his own party's agenda. As it happened, he was in office for less than a year before Ramsay MacDonald's government was replaced by the Conservatives under Stanley Baldwin.

At the 24th annual Labour Party Conference in October 1924, Saklatvala stated that his party refused to accept a 'sham democracy' in the form of Parliament as it was then constituted. He spoke against three resolutions – to exclude communists from the party, to prevent them standing as Labour candidates and to deny the affiliation of the Communist Party to the Labour Party. All three were carried. Despite this, he remained a member of the Labour Party for a further four years – although the resolutions ensured that he would not be standing for Labour in another election.

It was a vote of no confidence that led to another election being called in 1924, the third in less than two years. The vote followed a charge of sedition against the editor of the Communist *Workers' Weekly*, who had published an article calling on the armed forces not to obstruct striking workers. The Attorney General withdrew the charge, giving the Conservatives and Liberals the chance to move a vote of censure. Ramsay MacDonald's minority government was defeated, and an election was called for October 29.

The result was a Conservative landslide, Stanley Baldwin's government returning to power with 412 seats. The Liberals were annihilated, losing 118 of their 158 MPs. The Labour Party also took a beating, losing 40 seats; the damage to the Left was partly attributed to the notorious affair of the Zinoviev Letter, a letter purporting to be from the head of the Communist International to the Communist Party of Great Britain and ordering it to engage in widespread sedition. The letter later turned out to be a fake, and most commentators believe it did not have a major impact on the vote, but it certainly did not help the Labour Party or the Communists. It does not, however, seem to have affected Shapurji Saklatvala and his campaign. He managed to reverse his 1923 defeat, beating Henry Hogbin by 15,096 votes to 14,554.

Saklatvala had presented himself this time as a Communist Party candidate, supported by the Labour Party and the Trades Union Council. He took his seat in Parliament on December 2, the sole Communist member (Walton Newbold did not stand; the other six Communist candidates were all defeated). He had to walk with the help of crutches following a fall at home which had broken his ankle. Soon after he was told that he was not to be given the Labour Whip, to which he replied that he had not asked for it. Being free of the Whip liberated him from having to adhere to Labour policies. He was soon in full flight, propounding communist ideology to the House. As his daughter put it, "He acted as the irritant within the oyster-shell of the House of Commons and frequently produced pearls which were quoted by the press of the day". He cut a lonely figure in the middle of the Labour benches, dismissively referring to his neighbours as 'my comrades who aspire to be socialists' (*Manchester Guardian*).

Issues Saklatvala addressed over the following months included the defence budget; a recurrent theme in his speeches was Britain's long record as a warmongering nation. Frequently he returned to the issue of working wages, pointing out in one debate that people who worked with their hands should not be considered inferior to those who worked with their brains: "No spinner, no weaver, no smelter, no miner, no carpenter, no bricklayer, no stonemason, can do his work correctly if does not use his brain just as much as the Lord Chancellor and the judges and lawyers and architects". When Winston Churchill, Baldwin's new Chancellor of the Exchequer, accused working people of cheating over unemployment benefits, Labour members were outraged. Saklatvala told the House, "The Chancellor of the Exchequer has brought about this disorder, and it falls upon a revolutionary communist to restore order."

In 1924 he produced a pamphlet called *The Class Struggle in Parliament*, which consisted entirely of extracts from his speeches. The first 10,000 copies quickly sold out, and it had to be reprinted. Two more similar publications followed, selling for a penny a copy.

Saklatvala's regular attendance in the House did not prevent him from travelling up and down the country to address crowds of workers. He kept in regular contact with home at these times, frequently telephoning his wife. In 1925 he helped to found a new workers' periodical, the *Sunday Worker*.

Also in 1925, Saklatvala made arrangements to attend a conference of the Inter-Parliamentary Union in Washington. His brothers Pherozeshah and Beram were both settled in the USA, which was part of his motivation for going, as he had not seen either for some time. Beram, described as the brains of the family, enjoyed a successful career there as a metallurgist, while Pherozeshah ran a steelworks.

Then on September 16, just before his departure, Saklatvala was told his visa for the USA had been revoked. According to Panchanan Saha's biography, this was on the instructions of Frank Kellogg, the US Secretary of

State, on the grounds that 'the United States did not admit revolutionaries', though there was speculation that the British Government had put him up to it. This prompted an outcry among Sak's supporters and much concern in the press. A protest meeting in Battersea drew large crowds, more than 2000 people squeezing into the Town Hall. Saklatvala told the gathering: "I stand by every word of the columns I have spoken. I have not spoken these words with any feeling of hatred for the people of Britain, or through any nationalist emotion at being an Indian. Great Britain has no right to rule India, any more than Germany had a right to rule Great Britain."

The prominent Labour MP George Lansbury, the Member for Bow and Bromley, who later joined the Cabinet as part of Ramsay MacDonald's 1929 Government, wrote: "The American Government, by its action, has made Comrade Saklatvala a political figure of international importance". So it had. When the British delegates arrived, the Civil Liberties Union held a huge protest meeting at the absence of Saklatvala.

It was in 1925 that he finally made the decision to cut his ties with the Tata company; he had continued to serve as manager of the Cotton Mills Department. His brother Sorab had visited him to express the family's concerns at his political stance. In a gracious letter of resignation, Saklatvala agreed that his political activities could be damaging the firm's standing and assured his colleagues at Tata of his continuing goodwill. He did continue to receive a pension of £500 a year, but he complained that at the instigation of the authorities a 'promised settlement' of £5000 for his children's upkeep was withheld.[62]

62   Marc Wadsworth

Two years later he was in direct conflict with Tata over a railway strike. He wrote to the company saying that he was astonished that the firm, which was being supported from public funds, was participating in strike-breaking activity against 'half-starved' railway workers.

A debate on the expenditure of the India Office in July 1925 gave Saklatvala an opportunity to return to the subject of the misgovernment of India by Great Britain. He started by attacking the attitude of his colleagues in the House: "I pay homage to the British spirit of hypocritical statesmanship. We are talking of the Indian Empire just in the same strain of common agreement, with that very placid attitude of mind and phraseology of speech as if we were discussing some matters relating to the renewal of furniture in the library or cooking utensils in the kitchen of the House of Commons... We are debating here as if the Bengal ordinances were never promulgated, as if the shooting of Bombay operatives during the cotton strike had never taken place, as if a great strike of thousands of railway workers is not even now going on in the Punjab."

Referring to the accepted statistic that only 10% of India's 300 million population were educated, he went on: "You take jolly good care to see that the other 280 million remain ignorant, illiterate, uneducated, with no freedom to call their souls their own... There would not be a man or woman [in Europe] who tomorrow would not rise and fight to the bitter end to claim their rights if the monarchy claimed one tenth of the privileges which in the name of the Crown are exercised over the people of India."

Saklatvala played an important role in the establishment of the Communist Party of India in 1925; it was recognised by the Communist International the following year, and promoted by Saklatvala in his tour of the country in early 1927. His lobbying for the communists was not announced as a part of his tour agenda, but according to the testimony of a communist who had turned police informer, Jamark Prased Barjerhatta, he arrived in India with a plan to organise communist groups in each city he visited.[63]

Saklatvala's focus on India during his time in the House did draw some criticism from those who had expected him to be fighting constituency issues first and foremost. He had rather indiscreetly told the local paper, the *South Western Star*, that he was 'not concerned with local interests', that 'local affairs were for local bodies' and 'Parliament's concern is that of nation and empire'.[64] However he was so active in Parliament, with more than 500 interventions during his career, that even if most of these concerned India, there were a very healthy number of speeches and comments on matters nearer to home.

In the months before the General Strike in 1926, Saklatvala pressed the Government repeatedly to explain the Army Supplementary Reserve it had set up, which was widely suspected of having been created to replace striking workers, if that proved necessary. He managed to ascertain that the men recruited to date were from the four British railway companies and 'certain engineering and transport companies', and that negotiations were with the National Union of Railwaymen and the Transport and General Workers' Union. This was a strong clue that the recruits were being taken on to ensure that coal and other vital goods could still be moved around the country in the event of a strike. He was highly suspicious of the statement that no

63 Squires
64 Wadsworth

figures were available for the numbers of engine drivers, signalmen and other key transport tradesmen recruited.

On June 30 1925, the coal mine owners announced the termination of all existing wage agreements, an end to a minimum wage rate and an immediate reduction in miners' pay, to put the industry back on its feet; its output and profitability had fallen dramatically since World War II. The TUC response was an embargo on all movement of coal. To try to pacify the miners, Baldwin offered to maintain wages at their current level for another year, and in the meantime a Royal Commission started looking into the problem. When it concluded that although it was not the miners' fault, they would have to accept reduced wages, both owners and miners rejected its findings. In the following weeks 12 leading communists were arrested and tried and five of them jailed, while 50 miners also received jail sentences for 'riotous assembly'. Saklatvala was one of 70 MPs who wrote to the press demanding the immediate release of the prisoners.

All this reunited the working classes as never before. Saklatvala told a Labour Party meeting in West Fulham that the situation would make communists of all of them within 12 months. On February 24 1926, he physically carried a 300,000-name petition demanding the release of the imprisoned men into the House.

The temporary Government subsidy came to an end on May 1 1926, and vast crowds of workers assembled for a march to Hyde Park. The *Manchester Guardian* described Saklatvala as 'the hero of the day': "He was followed to his platform by a swirling wake of enthusiasts, and his meeting was much the biggest. He is, one imagines, the most powerful mob operator of his day. This sallow Indian, with a face worn by fanatical passion, dominated the whole scene, as with outstretched, claw-like hands he harangued for a good half hour. With a sort of sombre joy, he acclaimed the General Strike against their oppressors."

The meeting was entirely peaceful and there was no call for violent uprising, but two days later the law called at the Saklatvala home, in the shape of two detectives in raincoats and trilby hats. He was charged with sedition, the offending words apparently having been the following: "Whether Joynson-Hicks [the Home Secretary] likes it or not, whether he calls it sedition or not to suit the financiers and his rich friends, we have a duty towards the men to say to them that they must lay down their arms." A few days later he was arrested and appeared before the magistrates, where he was bound over to keep the peace for 12 months. There the matter would have ended, but he refused to be bound over, prompting a call of "Hear hear!" from his wife, and instead received a two-month prison sentence.

So the General Strike took place without Shapurji Saklatvala. At its peak, a total of 1.7 million workers took part, but it ended in ignominious defeat. After nine days, the TUC called it all off with very little achieved, and the miners all eventually drifted reluctantly back to work. Before long they had accepted the necessity of working longer hours for lower wages.

Prison was not too great an ordeal for Saklatvala. His daughter wrote that when he was asked at Wormwood Scrubs to give his religion and stated 'none', he was advised to say he was Church of England, as this would permit him to attend church services on Sunday mornings as a break from the normal prison routine. This he did, and it apparently gave him some comfort. At home, his family received visits from a stream of supporters, many of them ex-prisoners. He was allowed to have copies of Hansard and to receive visits from his solicitor, to discuss litigation which was proceeding against Tata and his cousin Dorabji.

His wife's attitude to his imprisonment is revealed by a letter to a well-wisher in which she stated: "I have considered the many messages of sympathy rather out of place, because I was really very proud to see my husband make the firm stand he made, and go to prison rather than go back on his word and pretend to be sorry for what he said". She took the opportunity of her husband's absence to buy a puppy for young Sehri (Saklatvala had feared it would add to his wife's workload, but he raised no objection when he returned home to find it already installed).

Saklatvala was released at 10.30 in the morning into the arms of a delighted Sehri senior, and by 12 noon he was speaking in the House of Commons. Commenting that he had been much better cared for during his absence from society than the 'poor miners', he attacked those who objected to sympathisers in other countries sending money to help the miners.

Not surprisingly, he attacked the Emergency Powers Act in the House on several occasions, complaining that it was being used primarily as a weapon against the workers. He even accused the Government and Ministers of the Crown of being the 'hired agents of the coal owners'. "They have ceased to be Ministers of the Crown, and it is a falsehood to describe them as Ministers of the Crown" he told Parliament. "From today… they are going to use the police, the Army and other forces of the Crown, and even the Civil Servants, in a class war to fight their friends' battles… Every policeman, every soldier and every civil servant who is a man of honour and conscience should either chuck his job or act against the

Government rather than lend himself to be a tool in their fight against the nation."

It seemed that by imprisoning Saklatvala, the authorities had only managed to increase his public standing. He was even more celebrated on his release than he had been before, addressing rapturous crowds wherever he went. The Home Secretary, Sir William Joynson-Hicks, did his best to prevent these gatherings by using the Emergency Powers Act, which resulted in many meetings due to be addressed by Saklatvala being cancelled, sometimes when they were already under way. The police told him that they were aiming to prohibit or suppress any meeting he was going to address in his own constituency, which threatened to make life somewhat awkward all round, given that the people had democratically elected him to represent them.

'This sallow Indian, with a face worn by fanatical passion' (The Guardian, 1926)

Sir William Joynson-Hicks, who as Home Secretary did his best to suppress Saklatvala

Saklatvala told an anecdote which demonstrated the ludicrous consequences of the Emergency Powers Act. He had been banned from holding a meeting 'at or in the vicinity of Hoelycue' (Heol y Cyw) in South Wales, and in trying to establish what exactly 'in the vicinity' meant had come up against the predictable official waffle and vagueness. In the end he solved the problem by holding the meeting some 12 miles from Heol y Cyw, without obstruction.

That October in the House, he went on the attack over the cheap coal produced outside the UK. "There are 50 million tons of coal now raised in the Empire under conditions which are a disgrace to anyone who calls himself a decent human being," he said. "Not only do the present Government permit this, but Members of the Government take a share in the profits, and as long as this game is allowed to go on the state of affairs cannot be regarded as a mere accident of the trade, but as a weapon of the class war."

In December 1926, Saklatvala set sail for his homeland (he had now been granted a new passport, after appealing to Stanley Baldwin, the Prime Minister, telling him that he should 'stop interfering with legitimate functions and duties of an MP'), arriving there in mid-January 1927, his first sight of India in 13 years. During the voyage the *Sunday Worker* praised his punishing schedule and wrote: "Bad health, including a very 'dicky' heart, does not deter Sak for a moment. On one page of his diary you may see entries showing that on two successive days he spoke at four meetings in Northumberland and Durham and two in his own constituency... during the intervening night he travelled south by train, sleeping as he always does, wrapped in his overcoat, even on the floor of the corridor in a crowded train – certainly never in a 1st class sleeper – but he did say to the pressmen of Marseilles [en route to India], 'I am tired and need a rest..."'

In Bombay he received a hero's welcome, with flowers and garlands. A fulsome tribute printed on cloth and presented to him read in part: "You have been from your very youth a true Friend of the Poor, the Suffering and the Sorrowing. Whether in India, or in Europe, you have felt and fought for the Suppressed and the Oppressed... you are a Citizen of the World. Castes and Creeds, Colours and Sex, Continent and Countries, do not affect you at all. To you, Humanity is One Great Family of the Divine Father; and you strive and struggle to bring mankind together, in loving links of Unity, Amity and Harmony."

As always, he hit the ground running. In Navsari, his birthplace, he received the Freedom of the Municipality and addressed a gathering of thousands. Having laid his welcome garlands at the feet of Bombay's statue of Dadabhai Naoroji, he addressed two meetings on the day of his arrival and continued on his tour to speak for the unity of all the Indian peoples, speaking equally freely in English, Hindi and Gujarati as the local population required. The *Bombay Chronicle* wrote: "Whether he is at a tea party or a reception, a Labour meeting or a public reception of thousands, he avails himself of every opportunity to drill his fresh and dynamic views into the hearts of his audience with his magnificent oratory, of which indeed there is no parallel in India today. Wherever he goes he enlivens the atmosphere and electrifies his hearers".

But the accolades and the celebrations did not go down well with his enemies. The British Government, according to Marc Wadsworth, was now 'obsessed' with what they perceived as the communist threat. "Reports on communist activity were a common feature at Cabinet meetings," he wrote. "The Foreign Office wanted the Government to find a way of banning all communists from entering India." The activists who had travelled there included Philip Spratt and Ben Bradley, who played key roles in setting up the Communist Party of India. Soon after Saklatvala's arrival, Lord Birkenhead, the Secretary of State for India, sent a message to the Viceroy saying, "I do not quarrel with the decision to grant him a visa for India, but I do hope you will not scruple to act at once if his activities become really mischievous". A month later he followed this with a telegram urging him to act if he had the opportunity.

Saklatvala focused his message on the need for trades unions and a peasant organisation. He also used every opportunity to promote communism. This caused particular alarm with the authorities, because India was beginning to be seen as a key country for the spread of revolution by the Soviets. In fact he did not by any means receive a universal welcome. Even in Bombay, the city powers denied him an official reception.[65]

He attacked the Indian National Congress, using a mass rally in the Gujarat state capital of Ahmedabad to criticise the party's programme – "Awake your peasantry from slumber!" he exhorted them. He complained that the party had made the error of not setting a clear goal, and as a result the various factions within it were defining *swaraj* (self-rule) in different ways. On the eve of his departure he made a speech calling for peasants and workers to rally round Congress and work within it, rather than attacking it from the outside: "Nothing can be national in India if the peasants and workers are not in it, for they form the largest majority".

65   Wadsworth

This did not please other activists, those who believed that the future they were fighting for could never be achieved by the INC.

The visit provided him with an opportunity to meet Gandhi for the first time, and letters between them were published later that year. The two saw India's struggle, and the possible route to victory, very differently. In particular, Saklatvala detested the cult of worship which Gandhi had engendered in his followers. He opened the exchange by challenging Gandhi on his 'charka' movement. 'Charka' means spinning wheel, and Gandhi was aiming to bring this humble device back as a token of simplicity, peace and economic freedom, and a symbolic antidote to the ills of the modern technology which was making so many Westerners rich at the expense of the Indians. Saklatvala was strongly against this philosophy, believing that working people should be organised and given the tools to escape from poverty; to him, the spinning wheel was a symbol of that poverty. Attacking Gandhi's apparent lack of recognition of the 'class war' which he felt was raging in India, he wrote: "To defend such a position is criminal, but to go even further and throw dust in the eyes of the world that class war is not operating acutely in India is inhuman and monstrous, and I have always felt that through your misguided sentimentality you have preferred to be one of them. Class war will continue to be there until any successful scheme of Communism abolishes it. In the meantime, not to struggle against its evil effects from day to day is a doctrine which cannot appeal to any genuine humanitarian."

Saklatvala also told Gandhi that he should stop allowing people to address him with the honorific 'Mahatma', because it was a term of veneration which was inappropriate for someone who was supposed to be representing the ordinary people. Likewise he should 'rigorously stop crowds and processions' passing him with 'folded hands and downcast eyes', and he should not allow them to touch him as a gesture of worship. "You are ruining the mentality and the psychology of these villagers for another generation or two. Politically this career of yours is ruinous… come forward and live with us as a brother with brothers, and work with us in a manner and form in which we all consider your service to be most valuable… be a good old Gandhi, put on an ordinary pair of *khaddar* trousers and coat and come out and work with us in the ordinary way." His scornful treatment of Gandhi may have been motivated to some extent by jealousy; his daughter wrote that he would have very much liked a following as large as Gandhi's.

Gandhi's reply was published in an open letter in the *Bombay Daily Mail* on March 17 1927. He wrote that 'Comrade' Saklatvala's sincerity was transparent and his passion for the poor was unquestioned, but he had to say no to this appeal. The two continued to disagree politely but profoundly throughout Saklatvala's remaining years.

Gandhi was a lifelong leader of the Indian National Congress and became its president and then its lifelong spiritual leader and icon. This was another point of difference between them, because Saklatvala, while fully supporting the party's aims, disagreed with its roundabout and unfocused approach, as he saw it, to achieving *swaraj*.

When in 1930 Gandhi led his people on a 240-mile march to challenge the tax on salt, Saklatvala was not impressed. He wrote: "He does not call upon millions of Indian villagers to expel the Salt Police from their villages and he does not call upon his own friends, the big Indian salt manufacturers, to refuse to pay the taxes and go to prison. He does not call upon his propertied and mill-owning friends to refuse to pay income tax and have their property confiscated... There is a great warfare, more cruel than that waged with firearms and bullets, between rich and poor all over the world. Almost all of our Indian politicians, including Mr Gandhi, do not care for Indian labourers."

Saklatvala was something of a lone voice in his criticism of Gandhi. He does not seem to have persuaded many people, either in Britain or India, of the error of the Mahatma's ways. His attacks on Gandhi did not go down too well even with some of his own supporters, and he was criticised in some quarters for it on his return to England.

His determination to wage war on the establishment in India, along with the great popular success of his three-month tour of his homeland, finally led, in September 1927, to a letter from the Foreign Office advising him that the endorsement for India on his passport had been cancelled. The Minister for India, Lord Birkenhead, wrote to the Viceroy: "There was some difficult in persuading the Foreign Office to issue the letter, their hesitation being based upon the apprehension that the action proposed conflicted with the principle, which is generally accepted, that no country can refuse to accept back one of its own inhabitants if his nationality is not in doubt". The limp excuse the FO fielded was that Saklatvala had had 'no connection' with India for nearly 20 years.

This time the decision was never rescinded. When the Labour Party returned to power in 1929, there were hopes that the ban would be lifted, but the Secretary of State for India, William Wedgwood Benn, and the Foreign Secretary, Arthur Henderson, kept it in place. When Saklatvala was invited to represent the London branch of the INC at their 1929 Congress, he assumed the cancellation would be rescinded for that, but it was not. C V Vakil, representing the London branch, wrote furiously back to the FO: "Your letter gives us a clear proof that the present Labour Government's policy of repression and suppression is a faithful continuity of the old imperialist policy of your predecessors, regardless of any consideration of human rights or fair play". Saklatvala, in his own letter of protest, called the decision a 'monstrous inhumanity'.

The cancellation of his passport meant that Shapurji Saklatvala was never able to see his homeland again. His daughter wrote: "To hold him as an enforced and permanent exile from his country and from his family who lived there was a cruel transgression against human rights and liberty and one that cannot be justified or forgiven. It was without doubt the greatest hurt that was ever inflicted on him."

After Saklatvala's exile, his influence in the communist movement in India inevitably suffered. M R Masani, biographer of Dadabhai Naoroji, wrote: "his special position vis à vis India was undermined and Rajani Palme Dutt emerged as the rising star in the firmament".

During Saklatvala's visit to India, the Government had begun sending Indian troops to fight for Britain in China. He joined the widespread protests against this, saying that it was 'a great abuse of power' and showed that Britain was 'a danger to the world'. Even here he managed to entertain his audience, and his speech was reported as 'full of wit which threw his audience into roars of laughter, while his cogent arguments transposed them into serious and thoughtful mood'.

His daughter believed that this was 'probably the most

emotionally demanding and rewarding period of his whole political life', and perhaps it would have been even more so if he had known that he would never see his homeland again.

CHAPTER 13

A rebel in exile

While Saklatvala was in India, his sister took the opportunity to reproach him for having failed to bring up any of his five children in the Parsi faith. She protested that he had no right to withhold the family's religious heritage from his children, and Saklatvala clearly took the point, as one of the first things he did on his return to London was to arrange for all five of them to undergo the Parsi initiation ceremony of *navjote*, only the third time it had ever been performed in Britain, according to Sehri. The navjote is the ritual whereby a young Parsi (any age from seven upwards) is initiated into the Zoroastrian faith and introduced to wearing the *sudreh* and the *kushti,* the traditional garment and the belt used to secure it. Preparations normally begins years before hand, but in this case this was hardly practical. The child has to bathe in sacred water before the ceremony to 'purify'

him or her and a tray bearing a mixture of fresh coconut, pomegranate, raisins and almonds is on hand, ready to be sprinkled on the child. A sacred fire is lit, while the initiate recites a declaration of faith. Further prayers follow, and finally a garland is placed on the initiate and blessings and good wishes pronounced.

Kew Gardens supplied the necessary fresh pomegranate leaves. Saklatvala wrote out all the prayers in Roman text and gave his brood, then aged between eight and 19, daily lessons before school. "We were not released to go to school until we had learned the day's quota by heart, and there were therefore some very fraught and tearful mornings, for to be late for school was unthinkable," wrote Sehri. "For my part, the fear of unpunctuality put me in such a panic that the unfamiliar words became a nightmare, but Father was relentless, stern and unyielding."

The *navjote* ceremony was carried out at Caxton Hall, Westminster, in July 1927 in the full glare of press publicity, and among those present, despite their previous hostility to Saklatvala, were Sir Mancherjee Bhownaggree and Viscount Curzon (no relation to the previous Viceroy), the Conservative MP for Battersea South. The event got Saklatvala into trouble with the Communist Party, which announced its 'public disapproval' of the ceremony and wanted to know why they had not been asked permission, to which he replied that he knew they would not have given it. The party's resolution was reproduced in *Worker's Life*, and in part it stated: "The Communist Party of Great Britain recognises that in capitalist society many revolutionary workers who are sincere enemies of capitalism have not yet succeeded in fully shaking off the religious prejudices and traditions in which they were brought up... the Communist

Party insists that they shall not actively participate in religious propaganda. Comrade Saklatvala... knows the particularly disastrous effect of religious prejudices and quarrels among the masses of India, and the unscrupulous and successful use made of religion by British imperialism to perpetrate the enslavement and exploitation of the Indian people." Saklatvala published a conciliatory response in the newspaper, pleading that the arrangements had been 'outside his control'.

Saklatvala's health had deteriorated again, confirmed by his appearance at the ceremony looking pale and drawn with a bandaged neck following a severe throat infection, and from this time on he suffered from almost continuously poor health. Nevertheless he continued to campaign as vigorously as he could, addressing a meeting with Harry Pollitt in Hyde Park on May Day 1927 and attending other meetings with that leading Communist, who had recently served a jail sentence for incitement to mutiny.

Also in 1927, the Government introduced the Trade Disputes and Trade Unions Bill, designed to restrict and in some cases outlaw strike action. Saklatvala joined the left-wing campaign against it and pledged to do all in his power to fight the 'iniquitous' Bill, recommending an 'energetic campaign' which should culminate in a 'real General Strike'. In the House on May 5, he called the Bill an 'act of treason' against parliamentary government. Despite all protests, the Bill became law before the summer recess.

In October 1927 the Soviet Union celebrated the tenth anniversary of the October Revolution, and Saklatvala was among those invited to join in, his second visit to the USSR. He made the visit as a member of the British Workers' delegation, and addressed an international gathering of supporters of the revolution. He also had an opportunity to meet Nehru, and was able to discuss the political situation in India with him.

In his speech, he attacked the British attitude to democracy. "I sit in Westminster making laws for India, and as an Indian I am the despised slave of that Parliament and under the orders of an autocratic and idiotic Minister like Chamberlain, I am now told not to go back to my own country. That is parliamentary democracy."

He made a stirring speech appealing to those present to "carry with you that great image of the real and truly free men, the real and truly emancipated women and the truly cared for children here... I beg you to go back to your countries and wish, morning, noon and night for greater success for Sovietism in the Soviet republic."

The question of sending a Statutory Commission to India to look at its future administration was much debated in Parliament during 1927. Saklatvala and his supporters went on the attack, sure that the Commission's aim could only be to continue the subjugation and exploitation of the country they wished to see emancipated, and feeling it 'absurd' that one country should write a constitution for another. Opponents were outraged that the Commission, chaired by Sir John Simon, was not to include a single Indian member, particularly as two Parliamentarians were available – Saklatvala and Baron Sinha. Saklatvala attacked the proposal in a series of speeches in the House during 1927, setting out again all the reasons why British rule without the participation of Indians was continuing to damage India and its people. He stated, "I say that a nation which, after 150 years of hypercritical pretence, has kept the literacy of the people down to six per cent, ought to be pilloried in public in the eyes of the nations of the world... There is tremendous progress in the murder [through high infant mortality] of children all over India... famine is the constant lot of the people... the murder of four millions of the Indians who are dying because of British rule over and above the normal death rate which should exist in a tropical country like India is alone sufficient reason to tell the British people to get out bag and baggage." In November he proposed that Motilal Nehru of the Legislative Assembly of India (a senior figure on the Indian National Congress and the father of Jawaharlal Nehru, who later became the first Prime Minister of India) should be invited to the House 'to explain Indian sentiments and to guide the House' before agreeing who should serve on the commission. But the Government of India Statutory Commission Bill had Labour Party backing, and there was no chance of its being defeated.

In December the Indian National Congress resolved to boycott the Commission. The League Against Imperialism convened an international conference in Brussels at which Saklatvala was elected to the Executive Council. Antagonism outside Parliament, its success was all but guaranteed, and the seven members of the Simon Commission, dubbed by Saklatvala the 'latest weapon of British imperialism', arrived in India on February 3 1928. It would be an understatement to say that it was not welcome. There were violent demonstrations, and an effigy of Ramsay MacDonald was burned in the streets. By this stage it was clear that Saklatvala was no longer a fan of MacDonald.

Saklatvala led a hostile reception committee to meet the two Labour members, Clement Attlee and Mr Hartshorn, on their return, at Victoria Station. In fact they decided that discretion was the better part of valour and escaped via a side exit. The police picked out Indians from the crowds, attacking them and their banners and placards and causing several injuries.

Now exiled from his homeland, Saklatvala continued to support the growing unrest there through the press, the League Against Imperialism (he served as secretary to the leader of the LAI, Reginald Bridgeman), the Workers' Welfare League of India and the Communist Party, as well as through the House of Commons. Through the Workers' Welfare League he extended support to the poor Indian workers in the docks, putting on a Christmas party for them and their families each year; the children were given toys and the wives packets of tea and other household items.

Saklatvala's house in Highgate became the 'unofficial London home' of the Indian independence movement, according to Marc Wadsworth. Among the visitors were Bal Gangadhar Tilak, dubbed 'the father of Indian unrest', who appealed to the British on their home ground, and Mohammed Ali, a Muslim member of the Communist Party.

In March 1929, two British men and 29 Indians were arrested and imprisoned in India as a result of their opposition to imperialism, charged with 'conspiring to deprive the King-Emperor of the Sovereignty of India'. The British men were the two activists mentioned earlier, Philip Spratt, a Cambridge graduate who was studying working conditions in India, and Benjamin Bradley, the Vice President of the All India Trade Union Congress (they were later joined by another Englishman, Lester Hutchinson). The Indians included union leaders, journalists, teachers and lawyers. Their trial in Meerut, near Delhi, did not begin until January 1930 and the men had to endure barbaric conditions in jail. It was not until 1933 that the hearing was concluded; most of the men were sentenced to transportation for life or three to four years' imprisonment. The Meerut Trial affair was another stain on British imperialism, and this time also on the Labour Party, which had come to power under Ramsay MacDonald by the time the trial took place; the new Government did nothing to come to the aid of the imprisoned men. As a result, the Communist movement in India was greatly strengthened.

In May 1928 Saklatvala launched an attack in the House on the Kellogg-Briand Pact, under which some 65 countries including Britain, led by the USA and France, agreed to renounce war as a means of settling disputes. Pointing out that many members of the House were officers in the armed forces, he accused signatory countries of making hollow promises, given that some of them were at war even as they signed the pact.

He spoke on a number of other matters during the year that followed, but as it turned out, that was to be his last major speech to the House of Commons.

Shapurji Saklatvala fought the 1929 General Election as vigorously as he had the previous two, addressing five or six meetings a day. This time, however, he stood without Labour Party support; in fact all the previous cooperation between the Labour Party and the Communist Party had melted away. By now the split between the two was deep and permanent. In 1929 the communists adopted a 'New Line' policy which positioned the Labour Party as the bastion of the ruling classes, and in effect the communists' chief enemy, to be opposed on all fronts. Communists stood against Labour candidates and under no circumstances were allowed to support them.

So this time Labour put up their own candidate, Captain William Sanders, while the Conservatives fielded a Unionist candidate, Sir Arthur Marsden, also a Captain, who had retired from the Royal Navy some years previously. Saklatvala was therefore up against tough opposition on two fronts. He was supported by his usual allies; Charlotte Despard, now 83, came over from Ireland to help, and Pandit Nehru sent £100 for his election fund.

Undoubtedly he had to endure more of the dirty tricks which had characterised the last two elections. Among other slurs, the Labour Party told the electorate that he was planning to promote Indian trade at the expense of the British and had been planning to desert North Battersea for North St Pancras, and even that his party intended to pull down Catholic churches. He fought with his usual fire and determination.[66] On May Day he appealed in Hyde Park to the British working classes, saying: "Let May Day be a pledge of our determination to rid the world of imperialism, breeder of war, poverty and pestilence. Let us fight on May Day against the British White Terror raging in India... Down with imperialism! Long live the world republic of the workers and the peasants!"

Saklatvala was optimistic about the outcome, and at a meeting during the campaign he stated that it was his firm belief that if the Communist Party could field 200 candidates they would win more seats than the Labour Party. But this time he had misjudged the popular mood. In the aftermath of the General Strike and the resultant beating the working

66   Wadsworth

classes had taken, with no sign that the Communist Party would ever be able to deliver on its promises of a better life for them, fear of unemployment haunted the streets, and the Left were on the run. On May 24 came Empire Day, fervently supported with demonstrations and festivities. When election day came on May 30, not one of the 25 Communist Party candidates was successful. In Battersea North, the victor was Captain Sanders with 13,265 votes, with Marsden in second place with 10,833. Saklatvala was pushed into third place with only 6,554 votes, his share of the vote having plummeted from 50.9% to 18.6%. On his way home he suffered another heart attack.

The election had clearly demonstrated that the Communist Party could not win seats on its own. As the *South Western Star* had put it three years earlier: "The votes of Communists alone would never have brought Mr Saklatvala within sight of the House of Commons. Cut off from the Labour Party, the Communists would be as impotent as the little band of red flaggers who used to plot at Sydney Hall."

Another factor in the outcome was the greatly increased number of women voting, thanks to those between 21 and 30 having been enfranchised by the Representation of the People Act 1928 (those over 30 had had the vote since 1918). In fact, for the first time, there were more women entitled to vote than men, and in fact 65 women stood for Parliament (including two for the Communist Party). Nationally, Ramsay MacDonald's Labour Party carried the day with 287 votes, but with Stanley Baldwin's Conservatives securing 260, the result was a hung parliament.

After the vote Saklatvala told the *South Western Star* that losing his seat to Labour had come as a shock. Even the Labour candidate, Captain Sanders, had expected the

Conservatives to win. Britain would have to wait nearly 60 years to see another MP of Asian origin in the house: Keith Vaz, whose family originate from the Indian state of Goa, was elected for Labour at the 1987 General Election. In the same election, the first black MPs for Britain were elected: Paul Boateng, Bernie Grant, and Diane Abbott.

In the aftermath of the election, the Saklatvalas went to stay in the family home in Surrey of Mrs Phair, mother of Erich Backhaus, who had become betrothed to Saklatvala's daughter Candida. "Father was more relaxed than we had ever known him" wrote his daughter Sehri.

Saklatvala had not quite finished with politics, although remarkably he kept his last two attempts at re-election to himself and did not tell his own family, according to his daughter; they did not find out until some time after his death. Very likely this was because he feared his nearest and dearest would try to stop him, fearful for his failing health. In 1930 he alarmed his loyal Battersea supporters by deciding to stand in a by-election in Glasgow Shettleston, 500 miles from home and the constituency and people he knew. Success never seemed likely, but he was surprised and disappointed to come fourth and last behind John McGovern (Labour), William Templeton (Conservative) and John McNicol (Scottish Nationalist), with just 1459 votes, 5.8 per cent of the poll. During the campaign he exchanged cordial letters with his former foe and polar opposite, Sir Mancherjee Bhownaggree, in the spirit of uniting against a common enemy, the Labour Party. In one, Saklatvala wrote: "There are several factors which often make me think of you. When you first started breaking the Indian superstition that all Liberals are really liberals and all Conservatives were cruel you were considered to be the only 'fool among all wise men'! Now in Labour we have worse impostors even than in Liberals, and in the so-called Left Wing Independent Labour Party we reached the maximum of political hypocrisy of the present day. My last few years are spent in fighting this error, if injustice and oppression are to be fought."

The following year he attempted to regain his seat in North Battersea, but by now the Communist Party had few allies, and he came a distant third behind his old adversaries Captains Marsden and Sanders. It was Marsden who won this time, with 55% of the vote. Sanders would turn the tables again at the 1935 election. His daughter believed that "he took part in these elections with no hope of success, but merely to carry the Communist banner into the fray". Also in 1931, he unsuccessfully contested a seat on London County Council; the campaign was not helped the a bout of the 'flu.

Something of a scandal erupted in the family in 1931. Saklatvala's second son Beram was enjoying a romantic dalliance with an older student called Mair with whom he was studying at Westfield College, London University. One day a letter arrived from a landlady in Wales, asking for settlement of a laundry bill. It transpired that she had accommodated Beram and Mair in the belief that they were husband and wife. This was scandalous news in those times, and the upshot, after a conference involving the families of both transgressors as well as the college Principal, was that they were forbidden ever to see each other again. The Principal, in an unpleasantly sexist decision, also announced that while Beram could continue his studies, Mair must leave the college without taking her degree finals. Saklatvala was appalled by this, and managed to persuade him to let Mair take her degree, although she had to study in isolation.

The couple continued to see each other clandestinely, and as soon as Beram reached the age of consent at 21 he announced that they were to marry. His parents were shocked, but Saklatvala was prepared to bow to the inevitable. When his wife announced that she would not attend the wedding, there followed one of the very few serious rows between them ever recorded. "Father became quite hysterically angry," wrote Sehri. "'If you refuse to go, I'll lay a curse on you!' he ranted. 'Your favourite child will be carried out of this house dead!'" But Sehri senior still did not attend the wedding.

An Oxford ex-student called Himmat Sinha told Panchanan Saha that Shapurji had once said to him that it was 'quite easy to learn any European language and deliver a fluent speech in it, provided one knew any of the Indian languages'. On one occasion he astounded a German audience by delivering a speech fluently in their own language. According to Sinha, he had written the speech in English, had it translated, then got someone to read it out to him while he copied the sounds down in Gujarati.

Saklatvala at the centre of a social gathering in the late 1920s or early 1930s

Shapurji and Sehri on their silver wedding anniversary, 1932

He had always said that he wanted his children to marry into different nationalities; according to Sehri, he envisaged 'a tribe that would be truly international'. Pherozeshah, who became a rich man, with his own steelworks in America, married an American woman called Mae. Dorab, who had become a doctor, and Candida both also married within the next few years, Candida in 1934 to Erich Backhaus, and in 1935 Saklatvala was able to see Dorab and his wife Janet's first child, Wendy, the only grandchild born in his lifetime. A 1954 photo of a production of Shakespeare's *Pericles* at Birmingham Repertory Theatre features an actress called Wendy Saklatvala, who is presumably the same young woman.

In 1934 Saklatvala made two final attempts to secure political office. In March he again tried to win a seat on London County Council, for North Battersea. He and his communist running mate, Bill Johnson, campaigned on slum clearance and better housing rather than more ideological issues such as the war on capitalism. They were unsuccessful. That November he tried to win a seat on St Pancras Borough Council, but suffered the ignominy of being beaten by a fellow communist, Maud Carter, and coming a disastrous 14th in the poll. He was also beaten by a young Indian, Krishna Menon, who was embarking on his career as a Labour politician.[67]

According to Marc Wadsworth, "Saklatvala did not contest North Battersea at the 1935 General Election because he wanted to ensure a socialist candidate won, and he accepted that the man who had ended his parliamentary career, William Sanders, the Labour candidate, had the best chance." Again he was putting the cause before his own interests.

More successful was his third and last visit to the Soviet Union, in late 1934. This time it was a lengthy lecture tour, starting in the north and taking him south-east across many of the wilder parts of the country. He was impressed by what

67   Wadsworth

he found and wrote in the *Daily Worker*: "I have finished a long and most interesting tour… I have learned things of which I could never have got a real grasp by 'collecting' information at home. New Russia is a wonderful place, but new Soviet Asia even more so. One can never fully realise the tremendous extent of human development made possible by the Revolution… No worker who sees for himself can leave anything but a friend of the Soviet Union. At large meetings in Tashkent, Fergana, Stalinabad, Ashkhabad, Baku, Batoum, Erivan and Tiflis I have been asked to convey resolutions of solidarity with British workers, Indian toilers and the Communist Party of Great Britain."

This experience gave Saklatvala a 'new and greater energy and impulse in all his later work', according to Panchanan Saha. Clearly his burning vision of a world made whole by communist revolution never faded. Yet as time went on, it was vision he shared with fewer and fewer people in the West. Marc Wadsworth quotes the Indian academic Bhagwan Singh Josh as pointing out a key difference between states where revolution had succeeded, like the USSR, and those where it could not be expected to. Authoritarianism and absolutism, Josh believed, invited revolution and made the state vulnerable to it. On the other hand, countries which were run on democratic principles, ie with the consent of the people, could not be smashed by revolution because state control was too great. This applied to India just as it did to the democratic nations of Europe. This was why Gandhi advocated a 'non-constitutionalist and non-insurrectionist' (and non-violent) strategy and why, Josh believed, European Marxist theory, based on the need to mobilise industrial workers against capitalism, was not applicable to a country where the workforce was overwhelmingly made up of rural peasants, like India. Saklatvala does not appear to have made this distinction in his lifelong fight for communism. "It was the Mahatma, not the Comrade, who had the more sophisticated view of the Indian state," comments Wadsworth. "Saklatvala's revolutionary vanguard strategy could only have worked if the British colonial administration had been universally detested, and it was not."

On his return from the Soviet Union, Saklatvala threw the household in turmoil by announcing that he had invited all the 40 crew of the ship, the SS *Co-operatzia*, to their home the following day. The captain returned the favour by inviting the family to dinner on board his ship before it sailed, and presented a small statue of Lenin to Saklatvala; it was later given to the Marx Memorial Library in London.

It was not until years later that young Sehri discovered by chance from a stranger that her father had suffered a severe heart attack on the return voyage from the USSR. In fact it was his second during the trip; he had passed out as a result of an earlier heart attack during a major meeting in Moscow. He consistently played down his ill-health and either kept his problems to himself or made light of them. Accordingly no one realised how near the end actually was.

On January 15 1936, Saklatvala gave a lecture to students at the Marx Memorial Library on 'the basis of socialism'. The next day, Sehri returned home to find him having an animated argument with a League Against Imperialism man called Yajnik. At one point he commented to Mr Yajnik, "Well, when I die I hope the dustbin men will simply take me away along with all the other rubbish!"

Saklatvala arranged to collect his daughter from a class that evening, but when the class finished she was given a message from home telling her to make her own way back.

When she got there, she was met by a tearful Dr Gotla, the family doctor, and knew immediately that her father was dead. He had been struck by another heart attack as he sat down to write a letter to his youngest son, Kaikoo, and had died before the doctor had got to the house. He was 62.

Saklatvala was laid on his bed, and some Parsi women lit a fire of sandalwood on a table at the foot. There came a stream of mourners, and the practical and efficient Candida, aged 27, took charge of the household and of her siblings. Tributes came from around the world, from Jawaharlal Nehru, Clement Attlee and his lifelong friend and ally George Lansbury, among many others.

The funeral took place on a day of drizzle at Golders Green Crematorium (coincidentally the funeral of Rudyard Kipling, who had died on January 18, took place on the same day in the same crematorium). The Zoroastrian ceremony was conducted by the priests who had held the *navjote* for the five children nine years before. Sehri and her children each placed a symbolic chip of sandalwood on the flames, and the Communist Internationale was sung. Letters from Saklatvala to his wife were burned with him (to their daughter's later regret), along with her wedding shoes. The *Daily Worker* ran a full report: "The crematorium was filled to overflowing by several hundred people who had waited for nearly an hour in the slight rain which was falling in order that they could pay their last tribute to one whom they had known as a great fighter for working-class emancipation and national freedom… For several hours friends and comrades brought wreaths and cut flowers."

After the ceremony his ashes were buried in the Parsi burial ground at Brookwood Cemetery. Beram Saklatvala composed his epitaph: "Shapurji Saklatvala, eldest son of

Dorabji and Jerbai Saklatvala, mourned by his sorrowing wife Sehri and their five children… nothing but death could end his courage and determination in the cause of humanity. Nothing but such determination could conquer death. His work lives on".

Saklatvala's grave in the Parsi burial ground at Brookwood.

The Tata mausoleum at Brookwood – Saklatvala's grave lies directly in front of it.

The next issue of the *Daily Worker* printed tributes from several prominent figures, notably Harry Pollitt, who wrote: "By the death of Saklatvala, the Indian people have lost their greatest and most sincere champion, the Communist Party one of its most devoted and self-sacrificing leaders... he will be mourned by millions of oppressed peoples, who appreciated his fight for liberation and independence from the yoke of imperialism. Never have the workers in Britain, and the workers and peasants of India especially, had a leader who did so much and sacrificed himself so much to their service... Another soldier of the revolution has passed on. We lower our red banners before your closed eyes, dear Comrade Saklatvala, we pay tribute to all that you have done and taught us... You have built better than you knew. Your work will go on. We swear before your open grave that the red banner you held so proudly aloft, the hope and inspiration you gave to millions living in the darkness of imperial slavery, shall be carried forward to other fights and victories... The workers of the world will unite. They will break their chains. They will build that new world of which you have been so mighty an architect."

Herbert Bryan of the *Daily Herald* wrote to Arthur Field: "I think there can be no doubt whatever that he wore himself out prematurely by reason of the strain of incessant propaganda work and the constant travelling involved, which brought about his premature death."

Clement Attlee wrote: "Mr Saklatvala was always a very pleasant man with whom to have dealings. He was ever courteous and was gifted with a very vivid sense of humour... I always got on well in my personal relationship with him."

Willie Gallacher, a founding member of the Communist Party of Great Britain, described him as 'the friend and champion of all who were oppressed... Physically frail, he had tremendous courage, both physical and moral."

Despite his deep and passionate convictions, Saklatvala was not always free of doubt about the course his life had taken. According to his daughter he once said to her mother, "Well, Sehri, have I been a fool? Should I have made money like the rest of them and given you and the children a comfortable life, instead of spending my energies on politics?" Yet she was convinced that he was in general optimistic about the future: "For the most part he fervently believed that communism, and with it human happiness, would be achieved, that the poor and oppressed would be rescued, that the mighty should be put down from their seats, those of low degree would be exalted; the hungry should be filled with good things and the rich would be sent empty away."

Saklatvala left a thriving brood of high achievers behind. His eldest son, Dorab, became a successful doctor; his father would have been less pleased to know that later he also became a staunch Conservative. Candida became a barrister and took a degree in psychology. Beram joined Tata and became managing director of the London branch, co-authoring an official biography of the firm's founder, J N Tata. He became a socialist, and died in 1976.

Kaikoo served with the British Air Transport Auxiliary in World War II as a pilot (Second Officer) and flew Spitfires, Mosquitos and Lancasters. He later became an engineer. Both Beram and Kaikoo died before their mother, who passed away in 1977 at the age of 88, having outlived her husband by 41 years. In place of a memorial stone, her daughter Sehri planted 120 trees on the hillside beside the cottage in Derbyshire where she was born. She said her mother had 'never stopped quoting [Saklatvala] and following his advice'.

Young Sehri had a career on the stage before working for India House and on the staff of Greater London Council. She lived until 2017, when she was 98.

PART IV

Baron Sinha of Raipur
1863-1928
A brilliant and dedicated statesman

Satyendra Prasanna Sinha was a gentle and diplomatic man who was also exceptionally intelligent, very highly motivated and an extraordinarily high achiever. These qualities brought him a string of firsts; he was the first and still the only Indian to be granted a hereditary peerage to the House of Lords, the first and only one to date to become a British Minister, the first to join the Viceroy's Executive Council and the first to be appointed governor of an Indian province. Yet in youth he rebelled against his family in order to follow his ambitions, an action which would colour the rest of his life, and despite his conservative and generally pro-British stance he fought for his countrymen by consistently arguing for reforms which would increase India's prosperity and independence.

CHAPTER 14

The zamindar's son

Satyendra Prasanna Sinha was born on March 24 1863 in the village of Raipur, Bengal, into a well-to-do family. According to an account of his life which appeared in a 1919 publication by the Natesan Press in Bombay, *Speeches and Writings of Lord Sinha*,[68] the Sinhas trace their descent from an ancient family of the Utter Rahri Kayastha caste (the Kayasthas being a group of Hindu castes) which had 'sent out many ramifications' throughout Bengal. The Sinhas were well-to-do people with position and prestige. They owned land and property and were trusted servants and adherents of Raja Chitra Sen of Semrupagarh towards the closing years of the eighteenth century.

Sinha's father, Sitikanta or Sitikantha Sinha, was a

[68] https://archive.org/details/speecheswritings00sinhuoft

munsiff (judge) under the East India Company. He died in 1865, when Satyendra was barely two years old. As a result, according to the Natesan biography, Satyendra "early in life lost the advantage of his plastic mind being moulded by the informed and instructed intelligence of his father, though his mother supplied the want to the extent that was possible for her".

Satyendra was the youngest of four brothers; the eldest became the Government Pleader of Birbhum, while the second looked after the family estate. The first two hardly feature in the rest of Satyendra's story, but he was close to the third, Narendra Prasanna Sinha, born in 1858.

Raipur, a village in the Birbhum district of West Bengal, was part of the Burdwan or Bardhama Raj, which covered 5000 square miles of Bengal. It lies in an open and largely flat agricultural area. For many years it had been a focal point for the weaving trade, and some time in the late 18th century, while the East India Company still ruled, a man called Shri Lalchand De set up home in Raipur on the river Ajay and brought in a thousand weavers to the area, settling them in Raipur, Mirjapur and other villages; ships' sails were among their output. Shri Lalchand De and the Sinhas shared membership of the Uttar Rarhi Kayastha caste, and it appears to have been this link to the weaving trade which made them rich, some generations before Satyendra was born. According to *The Structure of Hindu Society* by Nirmal Kumar Bose (1975), from which this information comes: "The trade was developing against a background of considerable military disorder, but the Sinhas were able to carry on their business with impunity because they were under the protection of a man called John Cheap, a factor with the East India Company, who employed Shri Lalchand

De's son". According to Bose: "In exchange for (their) wealth the ruling family of Rajnaga sold the *zamindari* [landowning] rights to the entire area from Seuri to Raipur to the Sinha family".

A date is not given, but the line of inheritance would place this four generations before the birth of Satyendra Sinha in 1863, or some time back in the last 18th century. Bose goes on: "Lalchand's son was Shyamkishore; Shyamkishore's sons were Jagmohan, Brajamohan, Bhubanmohan and Manamohan. The eldest of the four sons looked after the zamindari, Bhubanmohan supervised the office work, and Manamohan is believed to have spent his time in the cultivation of music and other arts. Manamohan had four sons and among these, Sitikanatha was the father of Shri Satyendra Prasanna Sinha." In other words, Lord Sinha, as he would one day become, was the great-great-grandson of Lalchand De.

Sinha's father was a zamindar controlling a large acreage of land in Raipur. The Kayastha, associated with north-central and eastern India, are part of the scribe caste and traditionally employed as administrators, writers and keepers of records. A zamindar had a great deal of power over the local people and extracted taxes from them. As the journalist Anusua Mukherjee put it, writing in the *Telegraph India* (2010): "Although the zamindars were not royalty as such, their affluence and power made it easy for them to command the obedience of the people, who addressed them as rajas". The British rewarded some zamindars who supported their regime by titling them princes.

Bengal in the 19th century was home to a very wide variety of people, from religious and social reformers to writers, journalists, orators and scientists, all playing their part in a renaissance. Bengal played a major role in the Indian independence movement, in which revolutionary groups such as Anushilan Samiti and Jugantar were dominant.

In about 1870, Satyendra followed his brother Narendra to Birbhum Zilla School in Siuri, about 20 miles north of Raipur. The Zilla schools were secondary schools established by the British Raj, generally based on existing schools and primarily aimed at educating talented local youngsters. The one in Birbhum was established in 1851 and in 1864 it was declared by Mr H L Harrison, Inspector of Schools for the South West Region, to be the best in his division.[69] After suffering for a couple of years from the competition from a new Baptist school established nearby, the school flourished once more in the 1870s under a new headmaster, Shib Habu.

Young Satyendra was 'a quiet, industrious and bright student who strenuously applied himself to his studies'. At the age of 14 in 1877, he passed the matriculation examination with credit and moved up to Presidency College in Calcutta, winning a scholarship. Students at Presidency College have included A K Fazlul Haq, Prime Minister of Bengal from 1939-43, Dr Rajendra Prasad, first President of India 1991-96, several presidents of the Indian National Congress and many government ministers and captains of industry,

The college was formally opened with 20 scholars on Monday 20 January 1817. The college's foundation committee, which oversaw its establishment, was headed by Raja Rammohan Roy, while the control of the institution was vested in a body of two Governors and four Directors. The new college mostly admitted Hindu students from affluent

---

69   https://www.slideshare.net/persona2020/history-of-birbhum-zilla-school

Presidency College, Calcutta

and progressive families, but it also admitted students who were Muslims, Jews, Christians and Buddhists.

At first the classes were held in a house rented by the college. In January 1818 the college moved to a house nearby in Chitpore. From there the college moved to Bowbazar and later to the building that now houses the Sanskrit College on College Street.

Sinha is recorded as passing his FA (final high school qualification) in 1879, although David Kopf in *The Brahmo Samaj and the Shaping of the Modern Indian Mind* (1979) states that he began his undergraduate career at 13. Kopf wrote: "The ferocious dedication to hard work and the unquenchable desire to achieve were conscious puritanical traits too often concealed by the later lordly manner of a Bengali *bhadralok* [English-style gentleman] emulating the English aristocrat."

In 1880, the 17-year-old Satyendra married Gobinda Mohini Mitter, the only daughter of another zamindar, Kristo Chunder Mitter; the couple would go on to have four sons and three daughters.

When Satyendra's elder brother Narendra attained his majority in 1878, he learned that his father had left on deposit the sum of 10,000 rupees as an inheritance for him – a little over £500 in English money, equivalent to roughly £60,000 today. This enabled him to make a dramatic change in his career plans. He had recently joined Calcutta Medical College, but he knew that this would involve many years of hard work for meagre returns at the end of it. As the Natesan biography put it: "The prospects of students who come out after a tedious and hard life in Indian colleges were, as now, very poor. The bright idea occurred to him that if only he had the money, he could go to England and qualify himself for the IMS (Indian Medical Service), and the timely in-coming of this money and the ardour of his younger brother, who himself desired to accompany him, fixed his resolution."

So armed with this wealth, the two Sinha brothers decided to head for England, Narendra to study medicine, Satyendra law. There was a formidable cultural obstacle in their way, however, an ancient Hindu prejudice which still prevailed at the time against crossing the *kalapani*, a Hindu word literally meaning 'black water', and referring to the ocean that had to be crossed to reach another land. Those who had crossed the *kalapani* were considered abased and unclean. This was partly because life on board ship made it impossible to adhere to the strict routine of daily life as a Hindu, and partly because sailing to a foreign country would inevitably bring the voyager into contact with the *mleccha,* or barbarians, of other lands. It would also cut the traveller off from the regenerating waters of the Ganges (although some captains tried to allay the travellers' fears about this by carrying cauldrons of Ganges water on board ship). If such a traveller returned (many did not), only an intensive ritual purification would make him acceptable to his people once again.

In the poverty of 19th century India, the kalapani taboo did not put off many people seeking a better life overseas. According to an account from the American Historical Association: "As British colonial rule expanded over India's many regions, diverse Indians, especially men born into high *varna* [class] groups, found overseas travel worth the risk. Simultaneously, the qualification and status that these England-returned claimed were challenged by those Indians who refused to undertake this polluting voyage."

Many impoverished sailors, servants and others crossed the kalapani to seek their fortunes in Britain in particular, often breaking promises to return, and sometimes being abused and abandoned en route, in a foreshadowing of the modern rush of illegal immigrants to Britain.

The kalapani issue must have posed a formidable obstacle to the Sinha brothers, who well knew that their family would try to stop them, and accordingly they made their plans in secret. So it was that early one morning in 1881 they tiptoed out of the family home in Raipur and set off to seek their fortunes. The alarm was raised almost immediately, and the brothers had only an hour's start over the rest of the family, several members of which pursued the errant sons all the way to Diamond Harbour, Calcutta.

The ship sailed just in time to allow the two young men to evade capture. Neither of them would see their homeland – or their wives – again for five years. It was not until 1887, seven years after Satyendra's marriage to Gobinda, that the first of their children, the boy who would become the second Baron Sinha, was born.

CHAPTER 15

A star at the bar

Once in England, the two Sinha brothers wasted no time in applying themselves to their chosen careers. While Narendra applied himself to the study of medicine, Satyendra joined Lincoln's Inn and devoted himself to a career in the legal profession. He was further helped by winning a scholarship worth £50 a year for four years, to study Roman Law (in which he excelled, helped by his earlier study of Latin), Jurisprudence, Constitutional Law and International Law. Later he followed this with a Lincoln's Inn scholarship, worth £100 a year for three years.[70]

Mancherjee Bhownaggree, 12 years Sinha's senior, started his law studies at Lincoln's Inn the following year, having made his own pioneering voyage from Bombay to England a year later, in 1882. Other prominent Indians called

70   http://www.open.ac.uk/researchprojects/makingbritain/content/s-p-sinha

to the bar at Lincoln's Inn have included Gnanendrahoman Tagore, the first Asian to be called to the bar in England, in 1862, and later Mithan Jamshed Lam, the first Indian woman barrister, in 1898.

It is clear that Sinha made a great impression on his tutors and colleagues. "No other lawyer, Brahmo or otherwise, was so courted by the British bureaucracy, and no other lawyer achieved so much in a single lifetime" wrote David Kopf in *The Brahmo Samaj and the Shaping of the Modern Indian Mind.* "Sinha was also given a professorship at City College in law, and might have been satisfied with the position had it not been for a driving ambition to achieve a much higher status... In terms of esteem by the British ruling class in England and India, Lord Sinha was undoubtedly the most famous Brahmo of the Calcutta Sadharan congregation. And he was a good lay Brahmo, who regularly supported his church both morally and philanthropically."

Called to the bar in 1886, Sinha rounded off his years of study by touring Europe and 'learning various European languages'. Presumably this was a tour of some months. While he made preparation to return home to India, his brother Narendra remained in England, attending University College and embarking on a medical career.[71] He joined the Indian Medical Service in 1886 and became a Major, and later a consultant physician in London. Narendra served in the Burmese Campaign and the Tirah and Chinese Expeditions, and also in Bengal as Medical Officer and Deputy Sanitary Commissioner. After he settled in London he made his home in Ealing, where he played tennis and golf. He was a member of the National Liberal Club.

71   Indian Biographical Dictionary

So when Satyendra Sinha returned to India in 1886, he did so alone. He received a hostile reception in his old family home, perhaps unsurprisingly after his unauthorised five-year absence abroad. According to Anusua Mukherjee's *Telegraph India* article,[72] he was forbidden to enter the household after the disgrace of his unauthorised departure. "Having crossed the *kalapani,* he had become a *mleccha* and was never allowed to see his parents again" wrote Ms Mukherjee. "He would sit on a *mancha* [a podium or platform] atop a cowshed to watch with binoculars his mother in the turret of their ancestral home." She went on to say that nothing remained of the zamindar *bari* (house) where the Sinhas held court except "skeletal walls overgrown with weeds... The turret still stands amid the desolation". It is still there today, derelict and overgrown.

"Bengali Brahmins who had crossed the seas to Britain became untouchables when they returned home," explains Ms Mukherjee. "They often had to go through a purification rite to wash off the stigma." She says that Badal Sinha, an elderly nephew of Lord Sinha, had told her how Debendranath Tagore used to come to Raipur to propagate the Brahmo religion and used a room there to meditate. Tagore (1817-1905) was a Hindu philosopher and religious reformer, active in the Brahmo Samaj, a religious movement founded in 1828 by Raja Rammohan Roy and devoted to a monotheistic approach, as an alternative to conventional Hinduism; the name means 'those who worship Brahman', Brahman being the 'highest reality' rather than a god in the conventional sense. Brahmo Samajists have no faith in any scripture as an authority, do not believe in avatars, denounce

72 https://www.telegraphindia.com/1100304/jsp/opinion/story_12141194.jsp

polytheism and idol worship, oppose caste restrictions, and do not insist on belief in the concepts of karma and rebirth. The movement had undergone a change in 1866, just after Sinha's birth, when Keshab Chandra Sen led the formation of a new Indian Brahmo Samaj focused on northern India. "In the 1870s this branch of Brahmo Samaj was very influential in the field of social and religious reform" wrote Frans Damen in his 1983 study *Crisis and Religious Revival in the Brahmo Samaj*. "It successfully brought Brahmoism to more than 100 provincial towns and villages all over the subcontinent". Bengal appears to have been a stronghold, with 26 local Samajes.

Among Sinha's friends by this time was Rabindranath Tagore, Debendranath's youngest son and a man of his own generation; he was a poet, writer, musician and painter and a leading figure in Bengali cultural life. In 1913 he became the first non-European to win the Nobel Prize in Literature. He denounced the British Raj and was a fierce supporter of Indian independence, although like Sinha, he was no peasant rebel but a land-owning zamindar.

Clearly his young wife Gobinda must have forgiven him for disappearing for five years almost immediately after marrying her; not that wives had much choice in these matters at the time, and they had both been mere teenagers, so perhaps she felt she could afford to wait, particularly given the wealth he was able to bring to the family on his return.

From 1886, the couple became members of the Brahmo Samaj community, a clear indication that they had parted company with their traditional Hindu faith, presumably in the aftermath of the *kalapani* affair, although later comments suggest that Sinha either soon left the Brahmo

Rabindranath Tagore, prominent Bengali and friend of the young Sinha

Samaj or never became fully involved with it, because much later in England he stated his 'avowed and active hostility to all pretensions of caste and class supremacy on the part of Brahmans or any others'.

According to Anusua Mukherjee, when Rabindranath Tagore set up an ashram in the little town of Santiniketan near Bolpur in Birbhum, Sinha helped him to get the necessary land. Here Tagore started Patha Bhavana, the 'school of ideals', whose central premise was that learning in a natural environment would be more enjoyable and fruitful. In 1921, after his Nobel Prize success, the school was expanded into a university. Three years later he founded an institution designed to educate and training people from the deprived parts of society. In 1951 the institution achieved university status.

Presumably Sinha, temporarily homeless but with plenty of money still at his disposal, had no trouble finding alternative lodgings in or near Calcutta while he applied himself to the practice of law. He was still only 23, and according to the Natesan profile, within eight years he had attained 'a fair measure of success' in his new career. "His sincerity, hard work and cool courage were noted and appreciated; his quickness of grasp, clear-headedness and penetrating intellect enabled him to master the intricacies of complicated cases with ease; and his wide knowledge of law and his power of rapid comprehension imparted strength and lucidity to his presentment. By 1894 he had become fairly well established in practice and within the next five years he came to occupy a pre-eminent position in the bar, partly owing to the passing away of the bright luminaries who had shed such lustre on the legal firmament and on the public life, and partly owing to the phenomenal prestige and reputation he had gained as an able, painstaking and brilliant advocate."

"By the beginning of the present century [Sinha] was one of the foremost figures at the Calcutta bar, where up to that time the European element had had an almost unchallenged supremacy" wrote Peter Unwin in *Newcomers' Lives, the Story of Immigrants* (2013).

Sinha's legal practice quickly became large and successful. He was based at Calcutta High Court, the first High Court to be established in India (in 1862). According to the Natesan profile: "Mr Sinha had not perhaps the dazzling wit or sparkling genius which astonish the world, nor the deep erudition or fine culture which bring on name and fame but fail to satisfy the inexorable mistress of law. Endowed with natural shrewdness and plenty of common sense, accustomed to hard and strenuous work, thoroughly versed in law and procedure and well-grounded in legal principles and maxims, Mr Sinha grappled with his cases with perfect ease and presented them in such a natural, pleasing, and persuasive fashion and in such simple, direct and unadorned language that he drew spontaneous admiration from his colleagues and respect from the bench. His keenness of perception and unerring judgment of men made him a fine cross-examiner, and his power of lucid exposition in which he made use of plain, simple but well-chosen words was striking to behold. When a lawyer once reaches the topmost ladder, it never rains but it pours, and Mr Sinha was engaged in almost every important case."

Published as it was well within Sinha's lifetime, this portrait could not have been expected to be too critical, but that reference to the lack of 'sparkling wit or dazzling genius' does appear to portray a man of sober dedication and methodical thought, rather than a charismatic crowd-pleaser.

Sinha would spend most of the next 30 years in India, taking on increasingly wide and varied responsibilities in law and administration. In 1896 he took part in the Calcutta Congress, where he moved a well-received resolution recording the opinion of the Congress that it was desirable that, in future, no Indian prince or chief should be deposed on the ground of maladministration or misconduct until this was proved at a public tribunal. He was cautious in speaking out on topical issues as the causes of popular unrest, the Bengal partition, industrial depression and poverty, particularly in the early years, although he did consider the demand of Indians to govern their own country as a matter of right and not as a concession or reward for loyalty.

Some light is thrown on Sinha's philosophy and approach to life at this time by this passage from *The Brahmo Samaj and the Shaping of the Modern Indian Mind*:

"It was the Puritan ethic that most typified his sensational climb up the ladder of social success in a foreign-imposed system. We learn from his diaries of 1902 and 1906 that Sinha scheduled his daily events with utmost care and that he put in an extraordinarily long working day. Like most Brahmo Puritans, he scorned idleness and believed in the utility of hard, productive work. Sinha kept meticulous accounts of income and expenditure, including his investments in numerous commercial enterprises. Later in life, Lord Sinha became more aristocratic, but in the early stages he was essentially the young Brahmo Puritan making government service his entrepreneurial activity."

In 1903 Sinha was appointed to the post of Standing Counsel to the Government of India, the first Indian (or possibly the second – sources vary) to hold this post.[73] This meant that he was the constitutional legal adviser to the Government of India as well as the Government of Bengal. The potential for disaster here was huge, as many of Sinha's own friends were campaigning for the partition of Bengal, which came under Sinha's legal jurisdiction, so he had to advise on it. But he was friendly and congenial and managed

73   Newcomers' Lives, the Story of Immigrants, Peter Unwin

to keep everyone happy – his friends, as well as senior figures in power.

Sinha considered Lord Curzon's partition of Bengal in 1905, designed to separate the largely Muslim eastern areas from the mainly Hindu western areas, a mistake, particularly for the brusque manner in which it was carried out.[74] "The great soreness produced in Bengal by that measure is not likely to subside in our time," he told the *Manchester Guardian* in 1911. "I think it would have caused much less heart-burning if all the Bengali-speaking people were left together." He considered that the great resentment it brought, particularly among the Hindus, would last for decades, in which he was proved right. Asked about the torture of some prisoners by the police in order to extort confessions, he replied: "There you touch the weakest spot in the administration of justice... measures are in contemplation to remedy this state of things. I think it has now been made sufficiently clear that the authorities both here and in India are practically agreed that legislative steps should be taken to prevent or at least to minimise the abuse in question."

From 1906-9 Sinha served as Advocate-General of Bengal (initially on an acting basis), a post he returned to in 1916; he was the twentieth holder of the post, and yet again the first Indian appointed to it. The Advocate-General's job was to act as legal adviser to the Government of the Bengal Presidency. By this time he had become 'the undisputed leader of the bar' and his 'sociability, amiable disposition and fine temper' enabled him to occupy a high position in the Indian and European society of Calcutta. According to *Newcomers' Lives, the Story of Immigrants*, "Such advancement might have been unwelcome to his English brethren at the Bar,

74   Natesan profile

if the selection had fallen on one less Europeanised in his habits and outlook on life".

In his early years in Calcutta, Sinha showed little or no inclination to become involved in politics. He was clearly a reserved, cautious man, always the moderate and the source of wise counsel, never one to act in haste or without thought as to the consequences of his actions. Natesan: "An Indian of his position, learning and tradition could not manage to be oblivious of his surroundings, and of the new impulses stirring the soul of India. But, with his habitual practice of careful sifting of evidence and impartial weighing of arguments, he always tested the aspirations of his countrymen with a view to see whether they were practical, reasonable and sound. He never allowed his impulses to get the better of his judgment, but at the same time, his robust patriotism never degenerated into mendicancy. His natural reserve and modesty combined with his solid worth were hardly calculated to push him into prominence and he always chose to remain a follower."

CHAPTER 16

On the Viceroy's Council

In 1909 Lord Morley, Secretary of State for India, appointed Sinha as the legal member of the Viceroy's Executive Council, once again the first Indian to achieve this and a somewhat revolutionary move, from the point of the view of the establishment. The Indian people had for some years been demanding the admission of Indians to the Viceroy's Executive Council, and Congress had been asking for this reform since 1904. In fact Morley had been preparing the Government to accept the idea for some time and had been courting the Viceroy, Lord Minto, on the point. In his memoir 'Recollections', Morley wrote: "A member of the Viceroy's Executive Council holds one of the most important offices in the whole system. Hitherto Europeans only had been raised to a post so responsible and powerful, though memorable assurances had been given in the great Charters of 1833 and 1858 that neither race nor creed should be a bar to employment in the public service."

As the Natesan profile put it: "Mr Morley, with that tact, judgment and persuasion which all the world has learnt to associate with his noble name, broke down barrier after barrier which lay in front of him, brought his colleagues to his way of thinking and by alternate threat and impassioned appeal to abiding principles of state action, rendered opposition ineffective and reached the final goal as few else endowed with less courage and less faith in democratic principles could have done." Lord Minto, who was a conservative Viceroy and a fierce champion of the Raj, havered on the question of an Indian on the Executive Council for some time, apparently meeting stiff opposition from some quarters, notably Lord Kitchener, then Commander in Chief of the Army in India, but he finally told Morley: "I have very nearly, on several occasions, suggested to you the possibility of a native gentleman on my Executive Council, but thought it would be premature to say anything about it." It appears to have been Minto who suggested, in 1907, that the first Indian to be admitted to the Council should be Satyendra Sinha.

Presenting his case for the appointment of Sinha, Lord Morley said: "Suppose there were in Calcutta an Indian lawyer of large practice and great experience in his profession, a man of unstained professional and personal repute, in close touch with European society, and much respected, and the actual holder of important legal office. Am I to say to this man, 'In spite of all these excellent circumstances to your credit, in spite of your undisputed fitness, in spite of the emphatic declaration of 1833 that fitness is to be the criterion of eligibility, in spite of the noble promise of

Lord Morley, co-architect of the   Lord Minto
Morley-Minto reforms

Queen Victoria's Proclamation of 1858, a promise of which every Englishman ought to be for ever proud if he tries to adhere to it, and ashamed if he tries to betray or to mock it in spite of all this, usage and prejudice are so strong that I dare not appoint you but must instead fish up a stranger to India from Lincoln's Inn or the Temple?' Is there one of your Lordships who would envy the Secretary of State who had to hold language of that kind to a meritorious candidate, one of the King's equal subjects?"

Despite this compelling argument, King Edward VII 'would not reconcile himself' to the idea of an Indian on the Council, but the Cabinet was convinced that he was the right man, and the King could hardly overrule the Government. Sinha duly took up the post. During his tenure the Morley-Minto reforms were introduced, in the shape of the Indian Councils Act 1909, which opened the door for more Indians to serve on legislative councils, thereby assuaging the Indian upper classes in the aftermath of the disastrous partitioning of Bengal and heading off fears that the Raj's credibility and authority would be undermined.

Sinha was closely involved in framing the rules and regulations. The Natesan profile reported: "During the one year he was on the Executive Council, he discharged his duties with great credit. His speeches in the Council were packed with information, he exhibited striking knowledge of questions which he dealt with and always showed great courtesy and good temper in dealing with those who differed in opinion from him. His marked independence gained for him the respect of his colleagues and the admiration of his countrymen, and it is believed that on one particular occasion it was his firm and unflinching attitude that saved the Government of Bengal from a critical situation."

However, barely a year after taking office Sinha resigned from the Viceroy's Executive Council, in somewhat opaque circumstances. According to *Speeches and Writings of Lord Sinha*, "His resignation after about a year and a half surprised, pained and astonished the public... His desire to lay down the office, which he did in the autumn of 1910, against the unanimous desire of his friends, official or non-official, European and Indian, was due to personal considerations".

According to Peter Unwin in *Newcomers' Lives*: "He had never coveted a post which involved for him heavy pecuniary loss and the necessity, painful to a man of his quiet domesticity, of spending large part of the year at Simla, away from his home and his and all his friends and connexions in Bengal." There was talk of a disagreement with Lord Minto over an unspecified issue, Minto having stated later

that Sinha had disagreed with 'a certain measure', although
the end of his tenure coincided with the end of Minto's term
as Viceroy, so it does not appear to have been a case of the
two being unable to work together. There was also talk of
Sinha's alleged exclusion from a 'supposed inner circle of the
Executive Council'. His greatly reduced income may well
have been a factor.

Lord Sinha in later life

On leaving public office and returning to the practice of law, Sinha quickly regained the dominant position at the bar which he had held before 1909, and his success was reportedly 'phenomenal'. He lived in a large house in Elysium Row, Calcutta, since renamed Lord Sinha Road. This was a genteel part of central Calcutta where names like Theatre Road and Park Street evoked the old association with England and the East India Company. Here is a description of it from *The Autobiography of an Unknown Indian*, by Nirad Chaudhuri (1951): "An area of large, still houses standing in their own grounds planted with canna and ixora and of wide, silent streets shaded by *gul mohurs* and cassias... The majority were impressive by their size and solidity, although not by their architecture, but a few had style. They were old buildings in the modified Georgian manner of the East India Company... the inhabitants of the area prized the silence greatly, and wrote angry letters to the newspapers against the tooting of horns by taxis prowling for fares at night." Lord Sinha shared the street with the headquarters of the Special Branch, the political police, where, according to Chaudhuri, "many [young men] had to go to be questioned, or to be tortured, or to be sent off to a detention camp".

In an interview in 1911, Sinha indicated his wary attitude to Indian independence. "I am decidedly in favour of my people being allowed an increasing share in the government of their own country, ie in co-operation and collaboration with the British Government," he said. "But I cannot conceive the idea of India governing herself, without the British being there as the paramount power, that is to say within any time that I can foresee."

Despite this cautious approach to independence, Sinha certainly agreed that reform was needed to give Indian

Lord Sinha Road, Calcutta, formerly Elysium Row (Google)

industries a fair chance of success in international markets. Asked by the *Manchester Guardian* in 1911 how the unrest among Indian workers could be allayed, he replied: "By doing all you can to help us to get rich, first by improving our agriculture and secondly, by helping our industries. The former must be for a long time yet our chief source of wealth." He said the opinion was widely held in India that without some sort of tariff its industries could not compete with foreign countries, that this protection was required against England herself and that the feeling of helplessness was one of the causes of unrest.

Later, in his presidential address, he stated: "Rich in all the resources of nature, India continues to be the poorest country in the civilised world... In India alone, with the exception of spasmodic efforts, the Government adheres to the exploded *laissez faire* doctrine that the development of commerce and industry is not within the province of the state."

In 1912 Sinha stated: "If India had been an industrially-advanced and self-contained country on a par with the other great wealth-producing countries of the world, then, by virtue of her position in the East and the volume, extent and variety of her resources, mineral and agricultural, she would have been the chief emporium of military stores, ammunition and ordinance, sufficient not only for her own requirements, but also for export both to the Near and Far East, and to the Dominions overseas. Why has her weight on the scale not been heavier and more decisive? Because her vast and limitless material resources are still undeveloped, because industrially she is still almost in the agricultural stage, and because the policy of trust and far-seeing statesmanship which might have given her a powerful national army has not yet been consistently pursued".

The following year he called for the industrial development of India, saying it had become 'the most essential need'. "Without an increase of prosperity it is useless to expect India to be contented and loyal to its connection with the Empire," he said. "Literally millions in India are on the border of starvation. Half the population never has a full meal in the day, and means must be found to remedy this. It is essentially necessary to take steps with regard to the Constitution as a means of bringing about contentment and prosperity. What is wanted is democratic government, and there is no reason why it should not work equally as well in India as in any other country."

In another speech at about the same time, Sinha protested at the aspersions cast on Indian loyalty and the 'vile abuse' of Indians indulged in by a certain class of English critics, notably in the British press: "I take this opportunity of entering a respectful but emphatic protest against the use of intemperate language and the substitution of invective and personal abuse for argument and reason on the part of responsible journalists in this country, in discussing the most grave political problem in the whole British Empire. I take it upon myself to utter a grave warning against descriptions of the masses of India as 'a vast block of uncivilised peoples' and 'a pack of animals outside in the dark waiting to be fed'." (These descriptions had appeared in *The Spectator*.) "Let not English people be lulled into a false sense of security by the comfortable belief that these masses will never know what is said in England. As sure as I am standing before you today, these words will be translated into every vernacular in India and spread throughout the length and breadth of India with both legitimate and illegitimate comments.

"Still more do I deprecate ill-natured attacks upon what is called the political section of the Brahmanical caste of India, whatever the limitation may denote. I hold no brief for the Brahmans, political or otherwise. I do not belong to that caste myself; [Sinha was a Kayastha] and everybody in India knows of my open, avowed and active hostility to all pretensions of caste and class supremacy on the part of Brahmans or any others. But I will take upon myself to repudiate the malicious insinuations against a class of my countrymen which includes such illustrious names as Ranade, Gokhale, W. C. Banerjea, Surendra Nath Banerjea and others. And I venture to point out that the ill-mannered and ill-informed attacks on a whole class held in respect and even reverence by large masses of the people of India will inevitably provoke reprisals which will seriously hamper all efforts for either political or social reform, and will in all probability create a ferment prejudicial to the best interests of the Empire in this crisis of its fortunes."

Sinha's exceptional achievements had not gone unnoticed in high places. In 1915 a knighthood was announced in the New Year Honours, and King George V, who had succeeded his father to the throne in 1910, performed the ceremony a short while later.

CHAPTER 17

President of Congress

Sinha had become a member of the Indian National Congress in 1896, and the esteem in which he was held by his countrymen was demonstrated by his election as President of the Indian National Congress of 1915 held in Bombay, at which he was given a 'royal welcome'. His friend Bhupendra Nath Bose (1859-1924), a fellow lawyer, who had presided in 1914, was instrumental in suggesting Sinha for this position and persuading him to accept it; Bose was keen to counter the efforts of the left wing on Congress.[75]

Sinha's address to Congress was described thus in the Natesan profile: "The address was a model of close reasoning, of arguments ably marshalled, of Indian demands concisely and precisely stated. There was admirable dignity, sincerity and force throughout the performance and if there were

75   *Newcomers' Lives, the Story of Immigrants,* Peter Unwin

no brilliant flashes of rhetoric or humour, there were solid thoughts and important pronouncements for which his countrymen are beholden to him." Sinha was clearly no entertainer, no master of repartee or humour; all his public pronouncements appear to have been equally measured and considered. In part, his address went as follows:

"Political wiseacres tell us that history does not record any precedent in which a foreign nation has with its own hands freed from bondage a people which it has itself conquered. I will not pause to point out what has been pointed out so often, that India was never conquered in the literal sense of the word and as very properly observed by the late Sir John Seely, India is not a possession of England in the sense of legally being a tributary to England any more than any of her Colonies. Has there been a situation before this in the history of mankind like that of India today? Has there been a nation whose ideas of political morality have ever reached those of the great English nation? Has there been another nation which has fought so continuously and strenuously for the freedom and liberty of other nations as the English? My faith is based not on emotion, unreasoning sentiment: it rests not on the record of what has already been achieved by the undying labours of far-sighted English statesmen and noble-hearted Indian patriots but those who are still working for the cause and those whose labours are done and whose spirits hover over us today and guide and inspire us. The East and the West have met not in vain. The invisible scribe who has been writing the most marvellous history that ever was written has not been idle. Those who have the discernment and inner vision to see will know that there is only one goal and there is only one path.

"Many of our difficulties in India arise from want of

understanding between ourselves and those to whom our destinies are committed. The English people profess the high ideals of Christianity, and though there might in many cases have been lapses from these high ideals, I believe the better mind of England is always ready to stand by those ideals. At the present moment there is, from all that I can gather, a great wave of feeling passing over England that many of their misfortunes are directly attributable to a neglect of those ideals. And it rests with those who call themselves the intellectual or educated classes of India to remind the English nation on every occasion that might arise of what those ideals are and what those ideals require in the dealings of England with an ancient people like ourselves whom Providence has placed in their charge."

Sinha had previously ridiculed those who had taken the term swaraj to imply independence to be attained by the murder of Europeans, rather than simply self-government. The picture of the future of India drawn by Lord Haldane and other English statesmen appealed to him, a future in which 'Englishmen and Indians will be fellow-citizens of a common empire and of a common and splendid heritage, all of us bringing our special talents to bear co-operatively for the common good of the whole'. Autonomy within the Empire was the accepted goal which should be reached in time, not by any sudden or revolutionary change, but by gradual evolution and cautious progress: "It is a commonplace of politics that nations, like individuals, must grow into freedom."

There were three obvious methods of reaching the goal, he told Congress. The first was by way of free gift, but this would not be worth having, for it militated against the grand principle of political growth that nations must grow into freedom, and it was not a question of practical politics, in view of the relations between England and India. The second method was by wresting it from England, which was unthinkable. "A few misguided youths with perverted imagination may think it feasible; but to the great bulk of Indians, the idea was abhorrent; it would retard and obstruct progress; it was unrighteous and criminal; it would alienate the sympathies of Englishmen; it would provoke the bitterest sentiments, and would proclaim our incapacity for self-government". He appealed in his address "to all sections of our people to express in unmistakable language their abhorrence of these dastardly crimes which besmirch the fair fame of our country and I pray to them so to co-operate with the authorities as to render their detection and punishment absolutely certain." The only alternative left was through 'patient and earnest endeavour and gradual, wary advance'.

He warmly defended the Morley-Minto reforms against 'unjust criticism'. These reforms, brought into law by the Indian Councils Act 1909, were designed to increase the involvement of Indians in the governance of their country. They were the Government's response to the Hindu backlash to the disastrously unpopular partitioning of Bengal, and although a step in the right direction, they were considered by many Indians to go nowhere near far enough. They certainly did not meet the demand of Congress for the same system of government which already applied in self-governing British colonies.

Urging the British to support the reforms, Sinha went on: "I appeal to the British nation to declare their ungrudging approval of the goal to which we aspire, to declare their inflexible resolution to equip India for her journey to that goal and to furnish her escort on the long and weary road. Such a declaration will be the most distinguished way of marking their appreciation of India's services and sacrifices for loyalty and her devotion to the Empire. Such a declaration will touch the heart and appeal to the imagination of the people far more than any mere specific political reforms. These latter may fall short of the high expectations raised by utterances of the responsible English statesman as to the future place of India in the Empire and they may cause general disappointment. But an authoritative declaration of policy on the lines I suggest will, without causing such disappointment, carry conviction to the minds of the people that the pace of the administrative reforms will be reasonably accelerated and that henceforth it will be only a question of patient preparation."

In another speech to Congress, Sinha criticised the failure of the British to allow Indians to join the British Army, or to allow the training and organisation they needed to defend their own country:

"Except certain warlike races like the Sikhs and Rajputs, the people generally are debarred from receiving any kind of military training. Not only are they not allowed enlistment in the ranks of His Majesty's Army, they are even precluded from joining any volunteer corps. Even with regard to the classes of men, Sikhs and Rajputs, Gurkhas and Pathans etc, who are taken into the regular army for the simple reason that the number of English troops is not in itself sufficient to maintain peace and order in this country, even with reference to these classes, it is an inflexible rule that though they may now obtain the highest badge of valour., viz., the Victoria Cross, not one of them can receive a Commission in His Majesty's Army, irrespective of birth or bravery, education or efficiency. While the humblest European and Eurasian and even the West Indian Negro has the right to carry arms, the law of the land denies even to the most law-abiding and respectable Indian the privilege of possessing or carrying arms of any description except as a matter of special concession and indulgence, often depending on the whim and caprice of unsympathetic officials."

Although social campaigning is not something Lord Sinha is remembered for, he certainly had a social conscience and shared the widespread concern about the poverty of many of his countrymen. In a speech at Calcutta University in 1917, he spoke to students of the importance of 'all classes' and 'particularly young men' doing what they could in the interests of social services: "When we remember that millions of our countrymen live and die on the borderland of destitution, that hundreds of thousands of them die through preventable diseases, that hundreds of thousands of children in Bengal alone well-nigh starve and perish of dirt and diseases and of ignorant handling, who is there amongst us but can help feeling that life is not worth living if we do not, each one of us, strive our utmost to prevent these things which ought not to be? Believe me, there is not the least amongst us who is not capable of doing a very great deal towards this munificent and benevolent work. If we cannot do anything else, each one of us can go and sweep the dirty floors, each one of us can go to the slums of Calcutta and wash the dirty clothes which are sources of disease and infection to millions of the people, both in Calcutta and outside Calcutta. Therefore I beg of you to remember that, however great the task may be, each one of you is able to help, and help considerably, not merely by money, because that to my mind is the least thing in the matter, but by your own personal work... I hope that my young friends here will profit by the example of an older man who regrets towards the end of his life that he did not learn when he was young that the object and aim of life is not to prosper for oneself, but to see that others are happy."

He went on to tell a press interviewer that the Morley-Minto reforms gave Indians in the Legislative Councils only influence, not power, going on to say "What we need is a steady increase of power to determine and control policy... we shall not be contented with a few crumbs. What we want is real power in the administration of our affairs."

In 1917 the Government decided to invite an Indian to assist the Secretary of State in his work at the Imperial War Conference, and Sinha was chosen to join the War Cabinet. The years in England that followed marked the summit of his fame and of his achievement. In a farewell speech at the Town Hall, Calcutta, on February 4 1917, he said: "Gentlemen, the present war [World War I] is a life-and-death struggle for the achievement of that freedom which is our ambition as much as it is the ambition of England herself. I believe, to repeat a phrase which I used on another occasion, I believe with the fervour of a religious faith that we shall find that freedom within the British Empire, and I mark my words within the British Empire alone. England as a nation is dedicated to freedom, is dedicated to government of the people by the people for the people, and the great issue involved in the present crisis is whether a nation so constituted shall endure and subsist."

Before he left for England, Sinha was interviewed by the *Christian Science Monitor*. His comments indicate that like most people in India, he was not quite as patient as he had been a few years earlier about the question of Indian independence:

"It is, from our point of view, less important now that we should have a perfect government than that we should govern ourselves. When we speak of self-government, not one of us ever contemplates any separation between Great Britain and India. We gladly recognise that the ties between the two countries are too strong to break, and, if they were not, we would not have them broken. Let the British Government retain the amplest powers of veto over all our affairs. But, subject to that veto, let us have now an instalment of self-government on colonial lines, and let the basis of these concessions be broadened as rapidly as we fit ourselves for their extension. Of course, we shall make mistakes; there will be many and big mistakes. Atrocities may occur. Never mind, even they will not prove that you have been wrong to trust us. Only be bold, and the outcome will be not merely a contented and prosperous India, but an India which will be ten times as strong a British asset as she is today... If we are to wait for true self-government until we are perfect, we shall wait for ever."

On arrival in London, Sinha suggested that an Indian prince should also join the team. This was agreed, and the Maharaja of Bikaner, a lifelong supporter and ally, was chosen. Sinha was said have worked without a break on behalf of India. He found time to interest prominent English politicians in Indian affairs and during his first visit he stayed for a short time with Sir William Wedderburn, the Bombay judge who became a great ally of the Indian progressive movement and co-founder and sometime president of the Indian National Congress, as well as a great foe of Sir Mancherjee Bhownaggree.

In 1918 came the Montagu-Chelmsford Reforms, drawn up by Edwin Montagu, Secretary of State for India, and Lord Chelmsford, the Viceroy from 1916 to 1921, and the subsequent Government of India Act 1919. The reforms split

The Maharaja of Bikaner, a staunch ally of Sinha's, whom he brought
to the Imperial War Conference

the Central Legislative Council into two houses, the Imperial
Legislative and the Council of States, and introduced
diarchy, or the Dual Government System. Predictably,

they were considered by traditionalists to be too radical and by reformers as not radical enough, and diarchy met with almost universal opposition in India. Sinha was a firm supporter of the reforms and the Act, although as usual he could see both sides. He commented at the time: "The only question is whether the steps recommended are sufficiently substantial or whether they go farther than ought to be the case at present". He stated that it would be difficult to present a more cautious and at the same time a more liberal scheme. He went on: "People holding one view or the other have every right to put their views before the public, for such criticism alone can provide material for constructive effort. I unhesitatingly believe that the report lays the foundation of an Indian constitution which will contribute to the solidarity and unity of the Empire in like degree as the genius of Sir H. Campbell-Bannerman achieved in the case of South Africa. What we in India have to remember is that we can contribute enormously to such periodic advancement by the co-operation we give in treading this path."

The Government of India Act 1919 represented a further step away from benevolent despotism and towards the delegation of responsible government to Indians, providing for the partial transfer of power to the electorate through the diarchy system. It marked the latest in a long line of cautious (some would say grudging) shifts of power from the Crown to the Indian nation, and explicitly stated that the aim was the gradual introduction of responsible government to India.

It is worth noting that after the First World War, the British appetite for life in India waned considerably. It was no longer seen as a desirable posting, where the natives could be relied upon to run around after their lords and masters

Edwin Montagu,
Secretary of State
for India 1917-1922

Lord Chelmsford,
Viceroy from 1916-1921

in loyal servitude. The great days of the Raj were long over, and the day was in the sight when Britain would have to relinquish its power over India entirely.

In an address to the Imperial War Conference in July 1918, Sinha sprang to the defence of Indian Army veterans who were aggrieved at their patronising and insulting treatment by some people in other parts of the British Empire. "It is difficult to convey to those who do not know India the intense and natural resentment felt by veterans who have seen active service under the British flag... when they find themselves described as 'coolies' and treated with contemptuous severity... a radically false conception of the real position of India is undoubtedly rife in many parts of the Empire".

In November 1918, Lord Sinha was chosen for the third time as Representative for India on both the Imperial Conference and the Peace Conference, the Maharaja of Bikaner being again selected to represent Indian chiefs and princes. He had hardly arrived back in Calcutta on his return when he was called back to Europe to represent India, in association with the Secretary of State and the Maharaja of Bikaner, at the 1919 Peace Conference in Paris following the end of the First World War, yet another first for an Indian.

CHAPTER 18

Raised to the Peerage

In 1919 the Coalition Party was returned to power under Lloyd George, and Montagu retained his position as Secretary of State for India, the only Cabinet Minister to hang on to his post. At the subsequent reshuffle at the end of the year, Sinha was made Under Secretary of State for India, and very soon afterwards he was elevated to the peerage, to the jubilation of the Indian people. He chose to celebrate the village of his birth in selecting the title Baron Sinha of Raipur. He was the first Indian elevated to the House of Lords, taking his seat in February 1919. He also became a Freeman of the City of London, and in the same year he took silk and became a King's Counsel, yet another first for an Indian, or for any lawyer practising in India. As *The Times* put it at the time: "The romance of his advancement from the obscurity of an

Indian village home is scarcely less remarkable that that of our own Prime Minister [Lloyd George]".

According to Unwin in *Newcomers' Lives,* it was said that Sinha was given only ten minutes to make up his mind to abandon his plan to return to his beloved Bengal in order to take up this post.

Sinha's maiden speech to the Lords on March 4 1919 was confined to procedural matters; the dates of publication of a Paper containing the opinions of the provincial governments of India on the Montagu-Chelmsford reforms, and another on Lord Southborough's committee, which had been meeting to discuss constitutional reform. On the same day however he responded to a more topical question from Lord Sydenham on the recent riots at Kartarpur, in which it was alleged that a mob of 3000 Hindus had murdered a number of Muhammadans (Muslims). He replied that the incident had been the result of a dispute over the sacrifice of cows by Muhamaddans, and a large crowd had attacked them and set their homes on fire. At least 17 people had been killed and 100 Hindus were on trial, he said. He explained that such outbursts of religious fanaticism were still common in India and had nothing to do with the campaign for home rule. He went on:

"In countries blessed with one of the noblest religions, one of the most civilising and humanising religions known to the world, we find people fighting with each other, and we find them doing so not for any supposed spiritual benefits but for mere material benefits; and, after all, when these Hindus and Muhammadans fight on the occasions of these religious festivals, they are fighting not for material benefits, but for what they believe to be the interests of their eternal souls. The only remedy is a closer cooperation of the officials with the more educated people for the purpose of spreading enlightenment and education amongst those poorer classes, and the more the people of the country co-operate with the Government and with the officials of the Government, the greater will be the checks and safeguards for the prevention of these deplorable occurrences."

A dinner at the Savoy in Sinha's honour on March 7 1919 was attended by a galaxy of famous figures, many of them titled. Sinha's ally the Maharaja of Bikaner commented that this showed that the Government was determined to carry through its reforms, that it underlined the fact that race and creed were no disqualification for admission to any office under the British Crown, and that it demonstrated a welcome improvement in understanding and respect between Englishmen and Indians. He also assured the gathering of the enormous support and approbation Sinha's appointment would receive from his countrymen, including the fellow princes whom he represented at the banquet.

In Sinha's homeland, *The Times of India* commented: "Sir S. Sinha is eminently qualified for the post by his devoted services to India, and his readiness to put his country's interests before his own entitles him to the high compliment and marked confidence which he has new received... he will find in the House of Lords unlimited opportunity of dealing with the arguments of Tory obstructionists, whose knowledge of India is, for the most part, hopelessly out of date."

After his ennoblement, Sinha navigated a bill through the House of Lords designed to regulate the government of India, and this became the Government of India Act of 1919. This Act transferred legislative power from the Governor-General to an Indian legislature as a step towards self-government. Lord Sinha successfully conducted the Bill through the House, even though some Conservative peers who had been associated with India opposed it vehemently. Sinha's negotiating and diplomatic skills were very much to the fore.

In 1920 Lord Sinha returned to India, and in December that year he was given the governorship of Bihar and Orissa, part of the Bengal Presidency, making him the first Indian to be appointed governor of an Indian province. In fact Bihar and Orissa had been under the control of a Lieutenant-Governor, and the role was upgraded to Governor on Sinha's accession. He was the only Indian ever to govern Bihar and Orissa; the four lieutenant governors who preceded him and the seven governors who succeeded him during the joint state's 36-year existence were all British. Sinha was assiduous in his duties and worked hard, never allowing himself to be distracted by the growing number of people who opposed British rule.

However it was by this time apparent that he was less robust than he had been, often suffering from severe tiredness. In November 1921, after serving as Governor for only 11 months, he retired on health grounds. After this, he wrote a series of articles advocating patience and restraint while moving towards democracy. In this he recalls Dadabhai Naoroji. He deplored the growing tensions between Hindu and Muslim in the subcontinent and was often castigated for his refusal to abandon his moderation. However, also like Naoroji, he was an Indian patriot at heart.

In 1926 he became a member of the judicial committee of the Privy Council, which meant going back to London (he was the second Indian to be accorded this honour, the first having been Ameer Ali (1849-1928), another prominent lawyer from Calcutta). Membership of the Privy Council qualified Sinha to become a member of the Athenaeum Club in Pall Mall, already over a hundred years old and dedicated to men with intellectual interests and achievements (no fewer than 52 members have been Nobel Prize winners). According to one of his friends, the two achievements of Sinha's life that pleased him most were his election to the Bench at Lincoln's Inn in London and joining the Athenaeum Club, where he said he felt more at home than in any other such place.

In 1927 he welcomed the Simon Commission, set up by Sir John Allsebrook Simon to look into India's constitutional progress and recommend appropriate reforms. Stanley Baldwin's Conservative Government feared defeat by Labour at the next election and set up the commission to safeguard India's administrative future. In fact the Commission, as mentioned in the section on Shapurji Saklatvala, enraged many campaigning for *swaraj* because no Indian member was included, despite the availability (initially at least) of two parliamentarians, Sinha himself and Shapurji Saklatvala. The members were Sir John Simon; Clement Attlee, MP for Limehouse; Harry Levy-Lawson, 1st Viscount Burnham; Edward Cadogan; Vernon Hartshorn; George Lane-Fox; and Donald Howard, 3rd Baron Strathcona and Mount Royal.

The Indian National Congress resolved to boycott the Commission and challenged Lord Birkenhead, Secretary of State for India, to draft a constitution that would be acceptable to the people of India. An All-India Committee for Cooperation with the Simon Commission was established by the Council of India. On their arrival in Bombay, the members of the Commission encountered violent protests.

According to Sukhchain Kaur, writing for the website

ijear.com:[76] "The excuse given for not appointing any Indian on the Commission was that the framers of the Act of 1919 intended to confine the Commission to only Members of Parliament. But it was a mere pretext. The Act, it is obvious, did nothing to specify any such restriction. But even if the British Government wanted to restrict the membership of the Statutory Commission to only the members of Parliament, the availability of two prominent Indians in the British Parliament was the relevant answer to this sudden and hasty decision of the Conservative Government. There were two well-known Indian members at the time to the British Parliament. One was Sir Satyendra Sinha, later Lord S.P. Sinha and the other was Shapurji Saklatvala. In fact, S.P. Sinha had been closely connected with the various stages of the constitutional reforms in India and his inclusion as a member of the Commission would have been of great consequence. These two Indian members were excluded from the Statutory Commission and ignored simply because of their race, and their exclusion thus saved the British Government from any future controversy and criticism which might have emanated from their prejudicial findings in the final recommendations of the Commission."

The Commission reported in 1930, recommending the establishment of representative government in the provinces. However, by that time it was too late for Baron Sinha to hear it. Lord Sinha's health had been deteriorating for some time, and in the autumn of 1927 he left England for the last time to travel to India. His condition became worse and he died in the city of Berhampore (Baharampur), 200 km north of Calcutta, on March 4th 1928, the tenth anniversary of his

76   IJEAR Vol 2 Issue 2 2012

maiden speech in the House of Lords and three weeks short of his 65th birthday.

On his death many tributes were paid. According to the Maharaja of Burdwan, Sinha was 'one of the finest statesmen India had produced' and had 'the welfare of his country and of the British Empire at heart'. The Secretary of State for India, Lord Birkenhead, praised Lord Sinha's 'singleness of purpose and high ideals' and called him 'one of the foremost rank of Indian statesmen'.

There now arose the question of succession. All of Sinha's seven children were at least partly educated in Britain. The sons were Arun (Aroon) Kumar (b. 1887), 2nd Baron Sinha, Shishir, the Hon. Sushil Kumar and Tarun Kumar. Lord Sinha was due to be succeeded in the title by his first son, Arun Kumar, but Arun had been born at a time when there was no system of registration of births and deaths in India, so initially he was unable to prove his claim to the title to the satisfaction of the House of Lords. When he presented a petition for a Writ of Summons to Parliament, objections were raised that Lord Sinha was a Hindu and so Arun was the offspring of a potentially polygamous marriage, which debarred Arun from inheriting the title. However, in 1938 the petition was referred to the Committee for Privileges, which decided that Arun had made good his claim.

In 1916 Arun married Pryatama Rani Chatterjee, the elder daughter of Rai Bahadur Lalit Mohan Chatterjee. Three years later, when Pryatama died at the age of 20, he married her sister, Nirupama Chatterjee. He died in 1967, aged 79, leaving two sons and three daughters.

The Hon. Sushil Kumar Sinha, Baron Sinha's second son and second in line of inheritance, was born in Calcutta in 1895. In 1907, at the age of 12, he moved to England and was educated at Colet Court, Kensington, for two years before attending St. Paul's School in West Kensington until 1913. He went up to Balliol College, Oxford, where he took a BA, and he went on to study at Cambridge from 1917-18. Later he became a magistrate. He married Romola Mullick, a Bengali who as Romola Sinha became closely involved with social campaigning and women's rights in India. In 1932 she co-founded the All Bengal Women's Union with a group of fellow activists.

The third Baron Sinha (1967-1989) was Sudhindra Prasanna Sinha (1920-1989), son of Arun Kumar Sinha and Nirupama Chatterjee. He was educated at Bryanston School in Dorset and became Chairman and Managing Director of Macneill & Barry, a shipping agency in Calcutta, and a director of *The Statesman*. He did not claim the title.

The fourth Baron was Sushanta Prasanna Sinha (1953-1992), a tea broker, who like his father did not claim the title, and died without issue, following a family tragedy. In November 1978 a fire broke out during the night in the Sinha mansion in Calcutta which resulted in the deaths of Sushanta's children Shane Patrick (4) and his three-year-old sister Sharon Patricia, the grandchildren of the third baron, Sudhindra Prasanna Sinha. Sushanta and his sister, Manjula Dorji, were subsequently charged with their murder, but the case never went to court. Shane Patrick would have been the heir to the title.

The fifth Baron, Sushanta's brother, was Aninda Kumar Sinha (1930-1999), who married Lolita Das and had four children. After his death the title passed to his son and successor Arup Kumar Sinha, a British citizen born in 1966. He has however not formally registered his title and so does not appear officially as the 6th Baron Sinha on the Roll of the Peerage.

A family portrait of Arun Kumar Sinha, 2nd Baron Sinha of Raipur,
with Lady Sinha and their son Anindo Kumar Sinha

Glossary

Avesta: the holy language and the holy book of Zoroastrianism

Baboo (Babu): man, chap, bloke (Hindi)

Bari: substantial house

Bhadralok: English-style gentleman

Charka: spinning wheel (symbolic)

Chokha: proper, genuine

Dewan: prime minister

Dordi: rope

Durbar: court

Durbari: courtier

Gathas: the hymns of the prophet Zoroaster

Gilli-danda: Indian cricket

Jonglo: Englishman

Kalapani: 'black water', a pejorative Hindu term referring to the act of crossing the ocean to another land

Kayastha: a Hindu caste

Kusti: sacred cord worn by Zoroastrians

Lakh: 100,000 rupees

Mancha: a podium or platform

Mleccha: barbarians or inferior races

Mobed/Mobad – Person qualified as a Zoroastrian priest

Munsiff: judge

Navar ceremony: a stage in preparation for the Zoroastrian priesthood

Navjote: Zoroastrian coming of age ceremony

Nazarana: gifts and favours bestowed on a person of rank

Pakardao: game of catch

Pateti: the Parsi New Year celebration

Purvoe: writer

Sagdi: chapel

Satyagraha: insistence on truth (Mahatma Gandhi)

Sudre: sacred shirt worn by initiated Zoroastrians

Swaraj: Indian independence

Varna: a Sanskrit word referring to social class

Zamindar: a landowner (Hindu)

Bibliography

DADABHAI NAOROJI

Dadabhai Naoroji, the Grand Old Man of India, R P Masani, 1939

Naoroji, the First Asian MP, Omar Ralph, Hansib Caribbean 1997

Dadabhai Naoroji, Speeches and Writings, D N Banerjea (paper)

Western India in 1838, Marianne Postans, Saunders and Otley 1839, text at https://archive.org/details/westernindiain00postgoog

The Twist in the Rope, Farrokh Vajifdar, World Zoroastrian Organisation 1992

WORKS BY NAOROJI

Poverty of India, Dadabhai Naoroji 1878, reprinted Forgotten Books 2015

The Parsee Religion, Dadabhai Naoroji 1861

Wants and Means of India, Dadabhai Naoroji 1878

Poverty and Un-British Rule in India,
Dadabhai Naoroji 1901

SIR MANCHERJEE BHOWNAGGREE
Zoroastrians in Britain, John R Hinnells,
Clarendon Press 1996

Bhownaggree, Member of Parliament 1895-1906, John R
Hinnells and Omar Ralph, Hansib Publishing 1995

*Zoroastrian and Parsee Studies, selected works of John R
Hinnells*, Ashgate 2000

Famous Parsis, Biographical and Critical Sketches,
Natesan, Bombay, 1930

'Mourning, Philanthropy, and M. M. Bhownaggree's Road
To Parliament', John McLeod, published in *Parsis in India
and the Diaspora* (see below)

WORKS BY BHOWNAGGREE

The Verdict of India (booklet), Sir Mancherjee
Bhownaggree, 1916, text at https://archive.org/stream/
verdictofindiaby00bhow/verdictofindiaby00bhow_djvu.txt
Other works include *The Constitution of the East India
Company*, Bombay, 1872; *Mahārāni Viktōriyā*, tr. and
annotated by M. M. Bhāvnagri; *Skātlandnā Pahādi
Mulakmām Karelā Pravāsōnum Varnan*, Bombāy, 1877;
"The Present Condition and Future Prospects of Female
Education in India," *Journal of the Society of Arts*, 1885;
"The Present Agitation in India and the Vernacular
Press," *The Fortnightly Review*, 1897; letter to Joseph

Chamberlain on the South African question, in *Transvaal: Correspondence relating to the position of British Indians in the Transvaal* (British Sessional Papers, House of Commons, Cd 2239), London, 1904; "The Industrial Development of India," in *Broad Views*, 1907. The author has consulted collections of his unpublished letters in the Sir George Birdwood Collection, Oriental and India Office Collections, The British Library, London, and the Dadabhai Naoroji Papers, National Archives of India, New Delhi.

SHAPURJI SAKLATVALA

The Fifth Commandment, Sehri Saklatvala, Miranda Press 1991

Comrade Sak, Marc Wadsworth, Peepal Tree Press 1998

Shapurji Saklatvala, a short biography, Panchanan Saha, People's Publishing House 1970

Saklatvala, a political biography, Mike Squires, Lawrence and Wishart 1990

History of the Communist Party of Great Britain Vol. 1, James Klugmann, Lawrence and Wishart 1968

WORKS BY SAKLATVALA

The Class Struggle in Parliament, Shapurji Saklatvala (1921)

Is India Different? The Class Struggle in India (1927)

BARON SINHA

Speeches and Writings of Lord Sinha, Natesan Press, Calcutta 1919, text at https://archive.org/details/speecheswritings00sinhuoft

The Brahmo Samaj and the Shaping of the Modern Indian Mind, David Kopf, Princeton University Press 1979

Crisis and Religious Revival in the Brahmo Samaj (1860-1884), Frans Damen, Orientalia Lovaniensa Analecta 1983

GENERAL

India in Britain, Kusoom Vadgama, Robert Royce 1974

India, British-Indian campaigns in Britain for Indian reforms, justice and freedom, Kusoom Vadgama 1997

Parsis in India and the Diaspora, John R Hinnells and Alan Williams, Routledge 2008

The Parsees in India, A Minority as Agent for Social Change, Eckerhard Kulke, Vikas Publishing House 1974

The Autobiography of an Unknown Indian, Nirad Chaudhuri 1951

Strangers in India, Penderel Moon, Reynal & Hitchcock 1945

Newcomers' Lives, the Story of Immigrants, edited by Peter Unwin, 2013

Ayahs, Lascars and Princes, Rozina Visram, Pluto Press 1986

The Structure of Hindu Society, Nirmal Kumar Bose, 1975

Index

C

Q

R